Collins

Breeze 5

Semester 2

Collins

Breeze 5

Semester 2

Sujata Aslam
Renu Vishwanath
K.G. Jeyalakshmi
Jyothsna Natraj

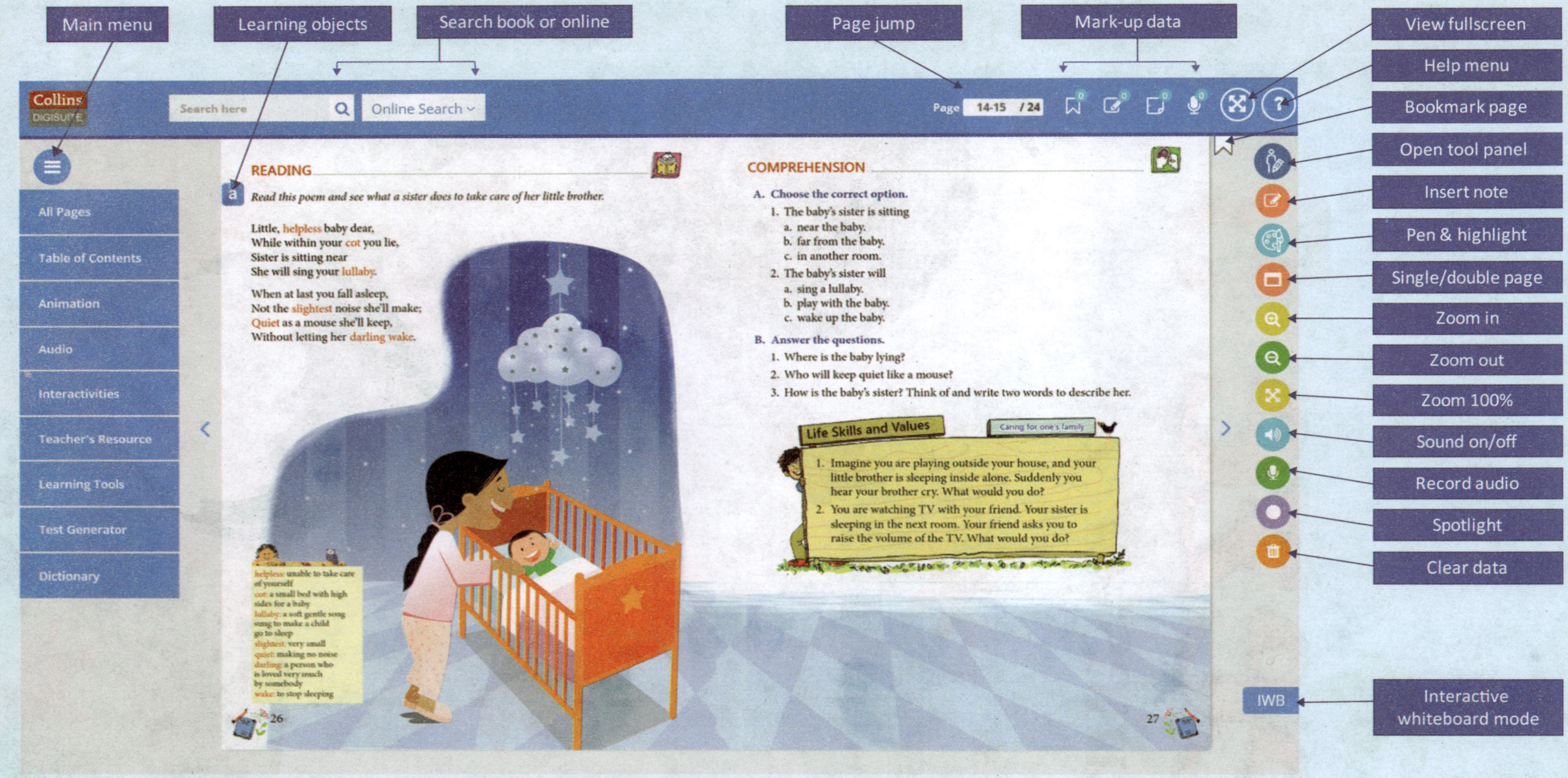

Student + Teacher			Teacher-only	
a animations	ia activities	g games	lp lesson plans	tn teacher's notes
ilt instructor-led tutorials	w worksheets	v videos	w worksheets	ak answer keys
	audio			

Preface

Breeze—an integrated semester course for classes 1 to 5 provides a comprehensive learning experience. This series of ten semester books teach lessons in an integrated manner, combining all the core subjects—English, Mathematics, Environmental Studies/Science, Social Studies and General Knowledge/Value Education. The lessons facilitate an interactive session in class for the learner's holistic development.

Breeze provides learning experiences with sufficient opportunity for exploration to young minds in their formative stage. The interactive approach of this series integrates multiple intelligences applied in every classroom across all levels.

Cross-curricular links have been created across the areas of learning for experiential and comprehensive development. The enquiry and skill based approach of the books contributes to the trans-disciplinary structure and comprehension. The books maintain a good balance between teacher-led and learner-initiated activities.

Breeze enables learners to understand the interdisciplinary nature of knowledge and apply this approach to problem solving. The well-graded course materials develop a link between natural, cultural and social environment. The course content across the subjects develop basic language skills through analysis, application and appreciation; develop critical and analytical thinking; enhance scientific temperament and create a strong sense of human values.

Some of the pedagogical elements integrated across all subjects include

- Learning Objectives
- Warm up
- New Words
- Do it Yourself
- Think and Answer
- Eco Zone
- Life Skills
- Value Zone
- Activity and Connect for cross-curricular links

Breeze series aims to develop 21st century skills including critical and creative thinking skills, effective communication skills, interpersonal and collaborative skills, and information and media skills in the young learners. This series is supported by comprehensive teacher's resources in the form of an interactive e-book with animations and interactivities, answer keys, lesson plans and a Test Generator for creation of quick test.

We value any feedback on this series. Please e-mail us at schoolmarketing.collins@harpercollins-india.com

Key Features

English

- **Warm-up:** A wide variety of activities at the beginning of chapters to ensure the learners' active engagement in the lesson
- **Reading:** A well-chosen selection of picture stories and comic strips from a wide range of literary genres
- **Comprehension:** Plenty of exercises including factual, inferential and extrapolative questions
- Cross-curricular boxes (*Science Scan, Maths Magic, Earth Speaks, Looking Back, and Fact File*) highlight topics interrelated with other subjects taught in the same grade
- **Glossary:** All new words in the text highlighted and their meanings provided along with a separate glossary for literary devices and literary terms
- **Life Skills and Values:** Separate thematic section on life skills and values
- **Vocabulary:** Boxed explanations of new vocabulary words and topics followed by a variety of exercises
- **Grammar:** Grade-appropriate grammar with detailed explanations and rules in simplelanguage
- **Listening and Speaking:** A wide variety of communicative activities and pronunciation covered in this section
- **Writing:** A well-graded section with a variety of creative-writing exercises including informal and formal letters, diary entries, flow charts, posters, stories, biographies, notices, reports, travelogues, character sketches, book reviews, recipes, acrostic poems, articles, and picture-based compositions
- **Activities:** A fun activity accompanying each poem
- **Projects:** Cross-curricular projects linked to topics taught in the particular grade in other subjects

Mathematics

Concepts explained in simple and easy-to-understand language

- **Exercises and Revision Exercise** within each chapter to recall and revise the concepts learnt
- **Mental Maths** to help practise calculation skills and deductive reasoning
- **Worksheets** to reinforce practice with fun exercises
- **Cross-curricular Links** to integrate knowledge across subjects
- **HOTS (Higher Order Thinking Skills)** and **Challenge** to sharpen the thinking skills beyond textual knowledge
- **Maths Lab Activity** to test skills for investigation, observation and analysis

Science

- **Revise and Recall, Think and Answer** test application of the concepts learned.
- **Science in Context** gives interesting extra information on the topic being discussed.
- **Summary** provides snapshot of the chapter content which helps students in quick revision.
- **Cross-curricular learning link** integrates knowledge across subjects.
- **Life Skills** test awareness, empathy and attitude towards self and others.
- Relevant **activities** hone experimental and deduction skills.
- **Project** questions link the concept learned to real-life applications.

Social Studies

- **Observe and Reflect** has pre-reading tasks that allow the learners to infer and relate to the topic.
- **Fact Zone** provides interesting titbits of information and **Find Out** tasks encourage referencing skills.
- **Do It Yourself** contains application-based activities for experiential learning.
- **Eco Zone** sensitizes learners towards conservation of environment.
- **Remember** and **Review Zone** at the end of the units facilitate understanding, recall and reinforcement, and assessment.
- **Think Zone** focuses on Higher Order Thinking Skills.
- **Life Skills Zone** equips learners with the basic skills they need to excel in life and **Value Zone** helps to build the right attitudes and values in learners.
- **Activity Zone** has varied creative tasks.

General Knowledge

- Each task comprises at least two kinds of inputs to help learners arrive at the answers and acquire knowledge at the same time.
- Special themes are an exciting mixed bag of environment education, life skills, values, India, sports, our world, science, language, art, personalities and entertainment to make learners become well-rounded individuals.
- **Activity pages**, aim to hone and cement specific verbal, visual and logical aptitudes through the common lens of general knowledge
- **Life skills**, draws attention to the science behind the safety measures we should take
- **Fact zone**, brings a good dose of fun to learning
- **India-specific content**

Value Education

- **Discuss** are warm up exercises, **Think and Say** are situations to test the application of the value taught and **Read Along** provides a story or poem related to the value being discussed in the chapter
- **Be smart** are exercises based on multiple intelligences
- **Remember** provides brief pointers that the learners can incorporate in their behaviour
- **Figure Out** are questions based on the story or poem taught and **Relate** are real life situations for problem solving
- **Create** provides creative tasks, **Enjoy** suggests media that communicates the value discussed, **Project** provides projects based on the values taught

Acknowledgements

English

The publishers wish to thank and acknowledge the following for granting us permission to use copyright material:

Chuskit Goes to School, written by Sujatha Padmanabhan, published by Pratham Books (© Pratham Books, 2007) on StoryWeaver. The story is a collaborative initiative of NIPWD (Namgyal Institute for People with Disabilities) and Pratham Books; Sigrun Srivastav for *Trapped; Underground* by James Reeves, © James Reeves from Complete Poems for Children (Faber Finds) Reprinted by permission of the James Reeves Estate; *Chipko Takes Root*, written by Jeyanthi Manokaran, published by Pratham Books (© Pratham Books, 2015) under a CC BY 4.0 license on StoryWeaver; Gareth Lancaster for *Sailing Out to Space*.

The publishers have applied for permission for an extract from The Wizard of Oz by L. Frank Baum. Acknowledgments for the passage will be made in the future editions of the book.

Every effort has been made to trace copyright holders and to obtain their permission for the use of copyright material. However, in some instances, we have been unable to trace the owners of the copyright pieces published here. The authors and publishers will gladly receive any information enabling them to rectify any error or omission in subsequent editions.

Images and Photographs

petovarga, blueringmedia, colematt; OnBlast.

Science

All illustrations AptaraCorp Ltd.

Images

Przemek Klos, Jerry Horbert, Martin Fowler, Ethan Daniels, Jeanette Dietl, chinahbzyg, Martin Fowler, MVPhoto; Oksana Alekseeva, aida ricciardiello; ChaiyonS021, David Lade; Jerry Horbert, Oksana Alekseeva, MVPhoto, chinahbzyg

Social Sciences

All illustrations Quadrum Solutions

Images

LongQuattro, jtairat; Jorgenmac, julichka; hocus-focus; RoyFWylam; samxmeg; chuntise; ttsz; chuntise; Petr Malyshev, AndrewJohnson; ajansen, rzdeb; estivillml, Photodynamic, Peter Mukherjee, TonyFeder; narvikk; Sylphe_7; Pamela Moore; naveen0301; dagsjo; fotoVoyager; skellos, Guenter Guni; omersukrugoksu; Mieszko9; Dirk Freder; JacobH; Robert_Ford; brytta, tomy2; wpohldesign; kgrahamjourneys; Kamchatka; brianeasley, Mlenny, tirc83; AlpamayoPhoto, Pgiam; rkfoote; RONSAN4D; Dmitry Chulov; Photodynamic, dagsjo, Guenter Guni; duncan1890; George Clerk; flyflyis, ttsz; frentusha, artisticco; druvo; Maps © Collins Bartholomew Ltd 2016

General Knowledge

All illustrations Henu Studio

Images

Don Bradman-GettyImages/Hulton Archive; Tiger Woods-GettyImages/Timothy Clary; Mohammad Ali-GettyImages-ULLSTEIN BILD; Michael Phelps-GettyImages/ULLSTEIN BILD; Nadia Comaneci-GettyImages/Daniel Zuchnik WireImage; Michael Jordan-GettyImages/Jason Merritt; Pele-GettyImages/Martin Bernetti; Jesse Owens-GettyImages/ULLSTEIN BILD; Dhyan Chand-static. sportskeeda.com; Martina Navratilova-GettyImages/ULLSTEIN BILD;Challenger Deep, Mariana Trench-corbisimages/NASA/Corbis; Caspian Sea Map-istock/200mm; Death Valley-istock/sphraner; Antarcticaistock/Marc-Andre_LeTourneux; Amazon River-istock/Phototreat; Northeast Greenland National Park-corbisimages/Radius Images/Corbis; Map of Antarctica-istock/duncan1890; Mawsynram-GettyImages/ROBERTO SCHMIDT; Angel Falls-istock/macbibi; Congo Riveristock/Guenter Guni; Dolphin-istock/beyhes; Hippopotamus-istock/Heatherfaye; Penguin-istock/AndreAnita; Jelly Fish-istock/cristianl; Seal-istock/Holger Mette; Star Fish-istock/Mutlu Kurtbas; Octopus-istock/Subaqueosshutterbug; Reindeer-istock/RolfAasa; Lizard Running on Water-GettyImages-Joe McDonald Visuals Unlimited; Playground-istock/Mark Bowden; Rising Sun-istock/Porntep-Kawjun; Tulips-istock/bluestocking; Sugar Bowl-istock/thumb; White Elephant-istock/davincidig; Thunderbolt-istock/Maxiphoto; Rainbow-istock/Preto_perola; Maple Leaf-istock/Marek Mnich; Long White Cloud-istock/gong hangxu; Gift-istock/ProjectB; Catamaran-istock/Gregi69; Submarine-istock/alxpin; Speedboat-istock/GavinD; Tugboat-istock/mdgmorris; Yacht-istock/Samo Trebizan; Parliament-GettyImages/Hindustan Times; Team-GettyImages/JOHN PRYKE AFP; Parcel-istock/wragg; Flight-istock/Nomadsoul1; Run-istock/GlobalStock; Raft-istock/Sportstock; Bouquet-istock/marilyna; Kettle-istock/worac; Building-istock/Deejpilot; Wrist Watch-istock/yogesh_more; Hedge-GettyImages/Benjamin Rondel Photonica; Cast-GettyImages/John O'Loughlin Moment.

Contents

English

1. Thunder and Anansi 9
2. The Wizard of Oz 21
3. Paper Boats 36
4. The Happy Prince 40
5. Dressing Up for Space 52
6. Sailing Out to Space 63
Project 2: Fascinating Moons 67

Mathematics

1. Measurement 69
2. Time 81
3. Average 92
4. Profit and Loss 97
5. Geometry 105
Assessment 1 116
6. Area and Perimeter 117
7. Volume and Nets 127
8. Data Handling 134
9. Symmetry 143
10. Mapping Skills 151
Assessment 2 158
Comprehensive Assessment 160
Answers 162

Science

1. Our Lifelines: Air and Water 168
2. Rocks and Minerals 180
3. Earth, Sun and Moon 189
4. Our Environment 199
5. Natural Disasters 208
6. Light and Shadow 218
7. Force and Energy 225
Looking Back 238

Social Studies

1. Environmental Pollution 241
2. Evolution of Transport 246
3. Evolution of Communication 252
4. British Period in India 257
5. Attaining Freedom 263
6. The Great Indians 269
7. Indian Government 275
8. United Nations 281
Assessment 287

GK

1. Let Us Compare 290
2. Great Sports People 291
3. Hill Stations of India 292
4. Road Signs 293
5. Earth Extremes 294
6. Animals Adapt 295
7. New Year in India 296
8. World Sobriquets 297
9. Natural Disasters 298
10. Northeast of India 299
11. Disposing Waste 300
12. Different Boats 301
13. Traditional Music Instruments 302
14. Word Search 303
15. Internet Country Codes 304
16. A Flock of Birds 305
Assessment 306

VALUE EDUCATION

1. It's Grandmother's Birthday! 307
2. Birthday Gift 312

ENGLISH

1.	Thunder and Anansi	**9**
2.	The Wizard of Oz	**21**
3.	Paper Boats	**36**
4.	The Happy Prince	**40**
5.	Dressing Up for Space	**52**
6.	Sailing Out to Space	**63**
	Project 2: Fascinating Moons	**67**

1 Thunder and Anansi

Myths in World Culture

OBJECTIVES

In this chapter, we will:

- *read an African folktale about a trickster.*
- *learn about synonyms and antonyms.*
- *learn the subject-verb-object structure and, the use of for and since.*
- *listen to a conversation and fill in the blanks.*
- *talk about reusing everyday items.*
- *learn to pronounce words with silent b, s, l, and r.*
- *learn to write a procedure.*

WARM-UP

A. What does the word *culture* refer to? Look at the organiser below and fill in the blank boxes with different aspects of culture.

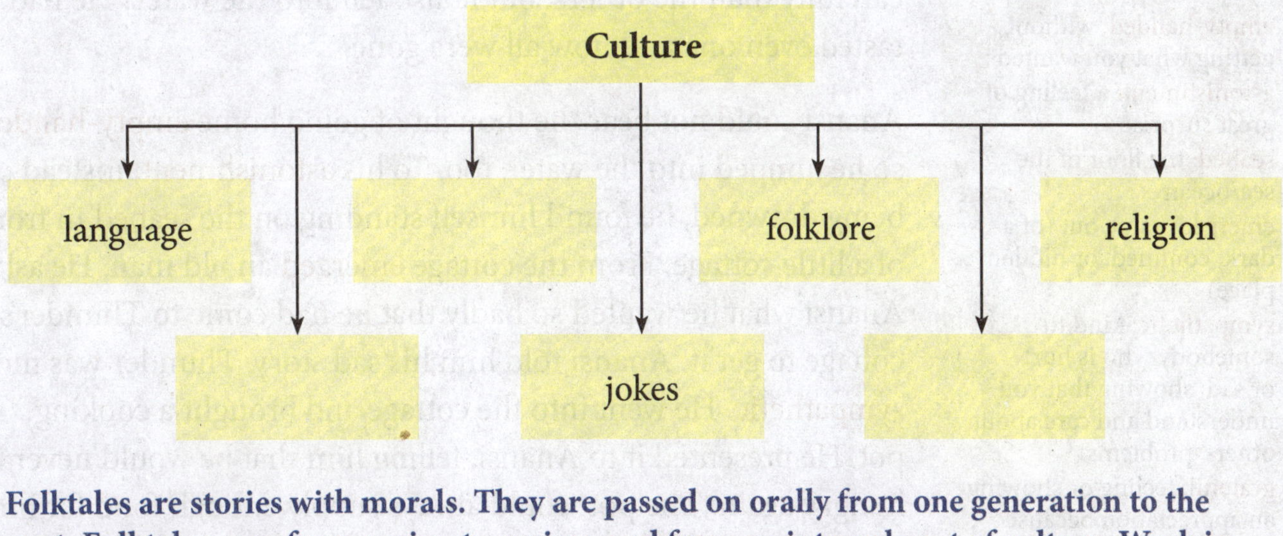

B. Folktales are stories with morals. They are passed on orally from one generation to the next. Folktales vary from region to region, and form an integral part of culture. Work in pairs and tell a folktale from your region.

Earth Speak

- Many countries around the world are hit by famines. A famine may be caused by drought, crop failure, overpopulation, etc.
- Famines result in widespread starvation, malnutrition, and even deaths.
- Palm trees grow in hot climates. There are over 2000 varieties of palm trees.
- The fruit of two palms, the date palm and the coconut palm, is consumed throughout the world.

trickster: a person who tricks or cheats people
famine: extreme scarcity of food
obtain: to get something by making an effort
island: a piece of land completely surrounded by water
empty-handed: without getting what you wanted
astonishment: a feeling of great surprise
seabed: the floor of the sea/ocean
emerged: came out (of a dark, confined, or hidden place)
sympathetic: kind to somebody who is hurt or sad; showing that you understand and care about others' problems
grateful: feeling or showing an appreciation because somebody has done something kind for you or has done as you asked

READING

Anansi is a popular character and a great trickster in several West African folktales. The word 'anansi' means 'spider' in Twi, the language of Ghana, a west-African country. This is because in some stories, Anansi can change himself into a spider. Read this story where he tries to trick his family, although without disguising as a spider.

There had been a long and severe famine in the land where Anansi lived. He had been unable to obtain food for his poor family. One day, gazing out to sea, he saw a tiny island with a tall palm tree on it. He determined to reach the tree and pluck nuts from it. But he did not know how to get there.

When Anansi reached the beach, he saw an old broken boat. It did not look very strong, but Anansi decided to try it. His first six attempts were unsuccessful. However, the seventh time, he was successful. He rowed the old boat to the island and reached the palm tree.

Having tied the boat to the trunk of the tree, he climbed towards the nuts. Plucking all he could reach, he dropped them down into the boat. Alas, every one missed the boat and fell into the water, until only the last one remained. This he aimed even more carefully than the others, but it also fell into the water! He had not tasted even one and now all were gone.

Anansi could not bear the thought of going home empty-handed, so he jumped into the water, too. To his astonishment, instead of being drowned, he found himself standing on the seabed in front of a little cottage. From the cottage emerged an old man. He asked Anansi what he wanted so badly that he had come to Thunder's cottage to get it. Anansi told him his sad story. Thunder was most sympathetic. He went into the cottage and brought a cooking pot. He presented it to Anansi, telling him that he would never be hungry again. The pot would always supply enough food for him and his family. Anansi was most grateful. He left Thunder with many thanks.

Anxious to test the pot, Anansi only waited till he was in the old boat again and said, 'Pot, pot, what you used to do for your master, do now for me.' Immediately, tasty food appeared in the pot! Anansi enjoyed a hearty meal.

When he reached land again, he wanted to run home and give all his family a good meal. But a selfish, greedy fear stopped him. *What if I should use up all the magic of the pot on them and have nothing more left for myself? I had better keep the pot a secret so that I can enjoy a meal whenever I want to.* So, he hid the pot.

Anansi reached home pretending to be tired and hungry. But there was not a grain of food in the house. His wife and poor children were very hungry, but selfish Anansi paid no attention to that. He congratulated himself at the thought of his magic pot, now safely hidden in his room. Whenever he felt hungry, he went to his room and enjoyed a good meal.

anxious: nervous about something which may or may not happen
hearty meal: a large meal making you feel full
pretending: behaving in a particular way to make others believe something that is not true

Anansi's family became weak and got thinner and thinner, but he grew plumper by the day. They began to suspect that Anansi was eating something nutritious secretly without sharing it with them. They decided to find it out.

Anansi's eldest son, Kweku Tsin, had the power of changing himself into any form he chose. He changed himself into a tiny fly and accompanied his father everywhere. One day, Anansi entered his room and closed the door. Kweku Tsin managed to slip inside. He saw Anansi take the pot and have a fine meal. Having placed the pot back in its hiding place after the meal, Anansi went out.

As soon as Anansi was out of sight, Kweku Tsin took out the pot, ordered it to prepare food, and called all his hungry family. They enjoyed a tasty, filling meal. When they had finished, Anansi's wife said that she would take the pot to the village and give everybody a meal.

This she did, but alas, in preparing so much food at one time, the pot grew too hot and melted away. What was to be done now? Anansi would be very angry. His wife forbade everyone to mention the pot.

Anansi returned home, and as usual went into his room. He searched for the pot but it was not there. *Someone must have discovered it*, he thought. He suspected his family to be the culprits and decided to punish them. But he said nothing to anyone about the matter and waited till morning.

As soon as it was morning, he started off for the shore, where the old boat lay. He got into the boat, which started of its own accord and took him to the palm tree. Anansi tied the boat to the tree and climbed the tree. This time when he aimed the nuts at the boat, they fell into it. He got down, threw the nuts into the water, and jumped after them.

Again, he found himself in front of Thunder's cottage. He told his story to Thunder, and Thunder seemed to show the same sympathy. This time he presented Anansi with a stick. Anansi was very eager to try the magic properties of his new gift, so he swam back to his boat very fast.

plumper: slightly fatter
suspect: to have an idea that something is probably true but without having definite proof
accompanied: went with
out of sight: not visible any more
forbade: ordered not to do something
culprits: persons who have done something wrong or against the law
of its own accord: without being asked, forced, or helped; by itself

'Stick, stick,' Anansi said, 'do for me what you used to do for your master.' As soon as Anansi said that, the stick began to beat him so severely that he had to jump into the water and swim ashore, leaving the boat and the stick to drift away. He returned home complaining about his bruises and wishing he had acted more wisely from the beginning.

ashore: towards or onto land, having come from an area of water such as the sea or a river
bruises: blue, brown or purple marks that appear on the skin after somebody has fallen or been hit

COMPREHENSION

A. Choose the correct option.

1. Anansi could not get food for his family because
   a. the market was very far off.
   b. he was too lazy to earn money.
   c. there was a famine in the land.
2. To feed his family, Anansi was determined to get
   a. a well-paying job.
   b. food from the market despite the difficulty.
   c. a few nuts from a palm tree, growing on an island.
3. Anansi was able to pluck a lot of nuts from the palm tree but
   a. they were all spoilt.
   b. they rolled far away.
   c. they fell into the sea.

4. Anansi learnt a lesson
   a. while enjoying a good meal.
   b. when the magic pot was stolen.
   c. when the magic stick beat him severely.

B. Read the sentences and number them in correct order.

1. The cooking pot was magical and produced tasty food. ☐
2. He did not drown; he reached an underwater cottage. ☐
3. After hearing Anansi's sad story, Thunder gave him a cooking pot. ☐
4. When all the nuts fell into the water, Anansi also jumped into the water. ☐
5. Anansi became plumper while his family grew thinner due to lack of food. ☐
6. The cottage belonged to Thunder, who asked Anansi what the matter was. ☐
7. His family began to wonder why Anansi was not growing thinner like them. ☐
8. Selfish and greedy Anansi did not show the pot to his family but hid it in his room. ☐

C. Answer the questions.

1. Why did Anansi travel in a broken boat?
2. Why did Anansi jump into the water after having failed to get the nuts in the boat?
3. Why did Anansi keep getting plumper?
4. When Anansi reached the palm tree the second time, the nuts he dropped fell into the boat. Instead of taking them back to his family, he threw the nuts into the water. Did he do the right thing? Justify your answer.
5. Why do you think Thunder gave a stick to Anansi the second time?
6. The character of Anansi changes as the story progresses. How?
7. Imagine you are Kweku Tsin. Explain how you felt when you found out the secret of your father getting plumper.
8. Imagine Thunder gave Anansi a robe that made him invisible, instead of the stick. Write a different ending for the story keeping that in mind.

Life Skills and Values — **Sharing/Creative thinking**

1. Anansi's wife decided to take the pot to the village and provide a meal to all the villagers. How else could she have used the pot?
2. Each one of us has a quality that we can use for the good of people around us. Think of ways in which you can do something to create a difference.

VOCABULARY

Synonyms and antonyms

- A **synonym** is a word which means the same or nearly the same as another word. For example:

  good – nice *right – correct*

- An **antonym** is a word which means the opposite of another word. For example:

  good – bad *right – wrong*

A. Fill in the crossword on synonyms and antonyms.

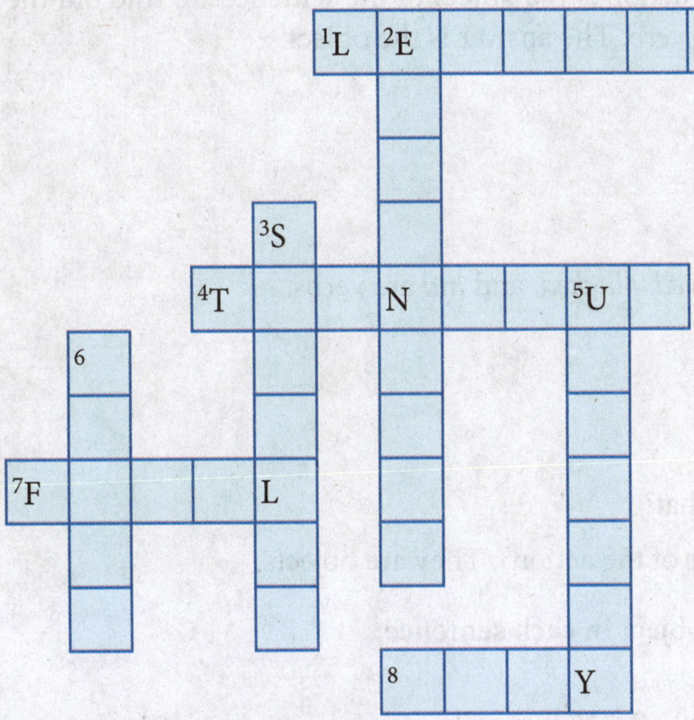

Across

1. synonym of *long*
4. synonym of *grateful*
7. synonym of *last*
8. antonym of *few*

Down

2. antonym of *cheap*
3. antonym of *deep*
5. synonym of *sad*
6. antonym of *noisy*

B. Fill in the blanks with the antonyms of the words given in the box.

big	*cheap*	*cloudy*	*far-off*	*few*	*hot*	*quiet*	*wet*

On a .... day, a little girl went to a park. There were .... people in the park and it was .... She sat on the .... grass and took out a .... bottle of water from her basket. She drank the water and put the bottle back. She saw a woman with a .... can of juice in her hands. She also wanted to have juice and went to the .... stall. The juice was ...., so she didn't buy it.

GRAMMAR

Subject-verb-object structure

- A **sentence** is a group of words that contains a subject and a verb. It expresses a complete idea.
- The most basic sentence structure in the English language is:

  subject + verb + object
- The *action* word is the verb.
- Whoever/Whatever performs an action is the **subject** of a sentence. To find out the subject of the sentence, put 'who' or 'what' before the verb. The answer is the subject.
- Whoever/Whatever receives the action is the **object** of the sentence. To find out the object of the sentence, put 'what' after the verb. The answer is the object.

Read the sentences.

Anansi rowed the boat.
Anansi plucked the nuts.
Anansi hid the cooking pot.

In the three sentences above, *rowed, plucked,* and *hid* are verbs.

Who rowed/plucked/hid?

Anansi (doer of the action)

So *Anansi* is the subject.

Anansi rowed/plucked/hid what?

Boat/nut/cooking pot (receiver of the action). They are objects.

A. Identify the subject, verb, and object in each sentence.

1. I read a story last night.
   a. Subject: .... b. Verb: .... c. Object: ....
2. The young boy played the piano.
   a. Subject: .... b. Verb: .... c. Object: ....
3. My mother baked a cake yesterday.
   a. Subject: .... b. Verb: .... c. Object: ....
4. Sameer likes history very much.
   a. Subject: .... b. Verb: .... c. Object: ....
5. She designs clothes beautifully.
   a. Subject: .... b. Verb: .... c. Object: ....
6. I accidentally tore my T-shirt.
   a. Subject: .... b. Verb: .... c. Object: ....

B. Use the words in the table to make as many sentences as possible. Underline the subjects, verbs, and objects separately in your sentences. Write S, V, and O under them respectively. One has been done for you.

We ate pizza.
S V O

We		ate	a car
They	is/ are	built	pizza
Varun	was/ were	forgot	cricket
The dog		played	waffles
The children		riding	the wall
My neighbours		studying	the books
My sister and I		guarding	the house

for and *since*

- We use *for* and *since* to talk about time.
- We use *for* when we talk about a period of time—how long an activity lasts.

  The school will be shut for two months.

  They have been living in the hills for three years.
- We use *since* when we talk about the starting time of an action or event—when something began.

  The children have been shouting slogans since 9 a.m.

  The water in the river has been rising since March.

***for* + a period of time**	***since* + a point in time (till now)**
when we measure how long something lasts	when we know when something started in the past
The action/event has a start point and an end point.	The action/event has a start point and continues in the present.

C. Complete the phrases with *for* or *since*.

1. .... July
2. .... ten years
3. .... the last month
4. .... we moved here
5. .... the day I left Delhi

D. Fill in the blanks with *for* or *since*.

1. He has been planting trees .... January 2017.
2. The boys have been watching the film...................... 2 p.m.
3. He worked on the project to save water .... three years.
4. Tara has been studying .... 9 o' clock.
5. Gauri, the village council leader, spoke to the villagers .... an hour.

LISTENING AND SPEAKING

Listening

A. Listen to the conversation between the children and fill in the blanks.

1. Anansi is an .... character from the country of ....
2. The .... people were the first to start telling stories about Anansi.
3. Anansi is a .... cum ....
4. Anansi is also known as ...., ..., and ....
5. In the US, he is known as ....
6. All his stories have a .... ; they teach a lesson.
7. According to one story, Anansi filled a .... with wisdom and tried to hide it in a ....
8. However, the .... dropped and all the wisdom fell out.
9. It was carried to all parts of the .... by the wind and the ....
10. ...., ..., and .... games have been made on Anansi stories.

Speaking

B. Work in pairs. Identify an item of everyday use, such as a newspaper. Think of at least four different ways in which the item may be reused. Share your ways with the class. You may follow the examples given below.

Newspaper

- Place crumpled newspaper in wet shoes to dry them off.
- Use newspapers to clean glass tabletops, mirrors, and crockery.
- Cover unripe fruit with newspaper for a couple of days to ripen it.

Pronunciation

Silent letters *b*, *s*, *l*, and *r*

- A silent letter in a word is a letter that is not pronounced.
- About sixty per cent of English words have silent letters.
- The letter **b** is silent when it comes
  - after *m* at the end of a word. For example:

    lamb *limb*
  - before *t* at the end of a word. For example:

    debt
- The letter **l** is usually silent when it comes just before *m* and *k*. For example:

  calm *folk*
- The letter **r** is silent when it comes before a consonant or at the end of a word. For example:

  garden *hear*
- The letter **s** is sometimes silent when it comes before *l*. For example:

  island *aisle*

C. Write the silent letter in the box.

1. butter ☐
2. chalk ☐
3. doubt ☐
4. dumb ☐
5. half ☐
6. isle ☐
7. Norway ☐
8. plumber ☐
9. purple ☐
10. walk ☐

D. Choose the correct option.

1. The letter **b** is silent in
   a. comb. b. bat. c. business.
2. The letter **l** is silent in
   a. tall. b. slim. c. calf.
3. The letter **r** is silent in
   a. storm. b. great. c. wearing.
4. The letter **s** is silent in
   a. psychologist. b. moist. c. aisle.

WRITING

Describing a procedure

Anansi did not need to cook. All he had to do was to order the magic pot to cook! But in real life, we must follow a procedure or a recipe to prepare a dish. Describe the procedure/recipe for making a sandwich with your favourite filling.

You may begin like this:

- Take four slices of bread.
- Spread butter...

2 The Wizard of Oz

Travel and Adventure

OBJECTIVES

In this chapter, we will:

- *read a play based on the popular American novel The Wizard of Oz.*
- *learn some French words used in English.*
- *learn the use of direct and reported speech, reporting verbs, and inverted commas.*
- *listen to character description from a play.*
- *talk about reducing the impact of natural disasters; learn the three different pronunciations of ch in words.*
- *practise writing a speech.*

WARM-UP

The word *travel* comes from the old French word *travaillier*. Find the following travel-related words in the word grid.

cruise	*expedition*
excursion	*light*
globetrotting	*journey*
pilgrimage	*trek*
tour	*voyage*

a	x	t	i	v	b	r	k	m	o
o	j	o	u	r	n	e	y	h	b
t	b	u	r	d	g	s	z	f	p
x	p	r	e	q	f	t	i	g	k
m	b	i	z	c	l	v	k	l	o
e	x	p	e	d	i	t	i	o	n
k	l	t	x	c	g	g	f	b	b
t	y	v	c	s	h	j	g	e	f
r	g	m	u	o	t	u	k	t	w
e	w	c	r	u	i	s	e	r	t
k	j	z	s	l	w	j	q	o	i
a	s	p	i	x	h	s	a	t	u
g	y	v	o	y	a	g	e	t	o
d	v	k	n	s	e	i	g	i	w
l	o	w	h	k	u	t	v	n	m
p	i	l	g	r	i	m	a	g	e

READING

A little girl, Dorothy, gets lost in a strange land. Let's read how she faces unfamiliar and difficult situations there.

Characters

Narrator	Dorothy, a little girl
Toto, Dorothy's dog	Good Witch of the North
Scarecrow	Tin Man
Lion	Wizard of Oz
Wicked Witch of the West	Winged Monkeys
Good Witch of the South	

Narrator: Dorothy lived with her Uncle and Aunt in the Kansas prairies. One day Dorothy and her dog, Toto, were playing inside the house when a large tornado appeared. It picked the house right up off its foundation with Dorothy and Toto still inside! It carried them high into the sky. After several miles, the house landed with a crash.

SCENE 1

Narrator: After the crash, Dorothy walks to the door and finds herself in a strange land. Standing before her is a crowd of tiny people, called the Munchkins. The Munchkins seem very happy to see Dorothy.

Dorothy: Who are you?

Good Witch of the North: I'm the Witch of the North. We'd like to thank you for killing the Wicked Witch of the East.

Dorothy: What do you mean? I haven't killed anyone.

Earth Speak

- Kansas is a state in the United States of America. It is covered by prairies.
- Prairies are vast stretches of grasslands. They are suitable for agriculture.
- A tornado is a violent storm with strong circular winds. It can be very dangerous as it can break apart buildings, knock down trees, and even toss cars into the air.
- Tornadoes look like funnels or wedges.

Good Witch of the North: (*pointing to the corner of the house*) Look there! Can you see those two feet in silver shoes sticking out? Your house landed on top of the Wicked Witch of the East. We had been the Witch's slaves for years. Today, you have rid us of the Witch and we are free!

(*handing over the silver shoes*) Here, take these silver shoes of the Wicked Witch of the East. They are yours now; they're magical.

Dorothy: Oh, thank you so much! The shoes fit me perfectly. (*after a pause*) Does anyone know how I can get back to Kansas?

(*Everyone shakes their head.*)

Good Witch of the North: We haven't heard of Kansas. But, maybe, the Wizard of Oz can help you. He lives in the Emerald City.

Dorothy: How can I reach the Emerald City?

Good Witch of the North: Follow, follow, follow the Yellow Brick Road.

Narrator: The little Munchkins lead Dorothy to the Yellow Brick Road. She waves good-bye and skips down the road with Toto.

SCENE 2

Narrator: After a while, Dorothy reaches a cornfield and stops to rest. Close by on a pole is a scarecrow put there to frighten away the birds.

Scarecrow: Hello!

Dorothy: (*surprised*) Did you speak?

Scarecrow: Yes, how do you do? And who are you?

Dorothy: I am Dorothy, and this is my dog, Toto. We are from Kansas. We are going to meet the Wizard of Oz.

Scarecrow: I am a scarecrow. I have been stuffed with straw and have no brains. I do wish I had some.

emerald: a bright green precious stone ; here used as a proper noun, as the name of a city

scarecrow: a figure made to look like a person, that is dressed in old clothes and put in a field to frighten birds away

Dorothy: Would you like to come with us?

Scarecrow: Yes. *(Dorothy helps him climb down the pole.)* Let's go.

Narrator: The Scarecrow comes down and they go off together.

SCENE 3

Narrator: Soon Dorothy and the Scarecrow come to a patch of trees where they hear a noise. In the middle of the trees is a man made of tin. He stands motionless with an axe in his hand.

Dorothy: Did you say something?

Tin Man: Yes. Please bring me some oil!

Narrator: Dorothy finds some oil and oils the Tin Man from head to toe.

Tin Man: Thank you. I had been out chopping down trees some time ago when it suddenly started to rain. Before I could get out of the rain, I was rusted badly and could barely move. I'd have stayed here forever if you hadn't come along. Say, why are you here?

Dorothy: We are going to meet the Wizard of Oz.

Tin Man: (*looking curious*) Do you think the Wizard could give me a heart?

Scarecrow: Maybe, he can. Would you like to join us?

Tin Man: Yes, I will come with you.

Narrator: Dorothy, the Scarecrow, and the Tin Man set off together and travel for many miles.

motionless: not moving; still
chopping: cutting into pieces
rusted: covered in a reddish-brown substance called rust

SCENE 4

Narrator: The travellers now reach a thick forest. Suddenly, a fierce lion leaps onto the path with a loud roar. He pushes the Scarecrow and then jumps on the Tin Man. As the beast opens his mouth, Dorothy rushes forward and punches the lion on the nose!

Dorothy: You big beast, you ought to be ashamed of yourself. You're nothing but a big coward.

Lion: (*rubbing his nose and almost crying*) I know I'm a coward, but I can't help it.

Dorothy: Oh, I am sorry! Please don't cry. I just can't understand how a lion like you is a coward.

Lion: I was born that way; I wish to have courage so I could be the King of Beasts.

Dorothy: Come with us to the Wizard of Oz. I'm sure the Wizard will give you courage.

Dorothy, the Scarecrow, the Tin Man, and the Lion: Oh, we're off to see the Wizard, the Wonderful Wizard of Oz.

SCENE 5

Narrator: At long last, the travellers come to the Emerald City. It is the most beautiful place that any of them has ever seen. Dorothy and her friends come to the palace of the great Wizard of Oz. They walk up to the guard at the door and ask for the Wizard. The guard leads them to a large room. The Wizard is dressed in a long green robe and is seated on a marble throne.

palace: the official home of a king, queen or ruler
robe: a long loose outer piece of clothing, especially one worn as a sign of rank at a special ceremony
throne: a special chair used by a king or queen to sit on during ceremonies

Wizard of Oz: I am Oz, the Great Wizard. Welcome! What brings you here?

Dorothy: I want to go back home to Kansas.

The Scarecrow: I'd like some brains.

The Tin Man: I need a heart.

The Lion: I want courage.

Wizard of Oz: (*with a serious face*) I can help you only if you bring me the broomstick of the Wicked Witch of the West.

Dorothy: Oh! So we will have to travel once again! (*to the others*) Let's go!

Narrator: The Guard gives the travellers directions to find the Wicked Witch of the West. They run as fast as they can.

SCENE 6

Narrator: After some time, Dorothy, the Lion, and Toto feel very tired and decide to rest. They lie down on the soft grass and, in no time at all, fall fast asleep while the Tin Man and the Scarecrow stand guard. The Wicked Witch of the West spots them from afar with her magical powers.

Wicked Witch of the West: Who's that girl with silver shoes? She has four friends with her. I have only one eye but it's as powerful as a telescope! Let me use my magical Golden Cap and summon my slaves, the Winged Monkeys.

(*to the Winged Monkeys*) Go and get that girl with the silver shoes! And capture her friends too!

Narrator: The Winged Monkeys capture Dorothy and her friends and bring them to the Wicked Witch of the West.

Wicked Witch of the West: (*to Dorothy*) Give me those shoes!

Dorothy: No! They're mine! The Good Witch of the North gave me these shoes!

Narrator: The Wicked Witch of the West tries to get the shoes off but she can't. They are magic shoes and can only be removed if Dorothy wishes so.

broomstick: a broom with a long handle and small thin sticks at the end, or the handle of a broom
spots: sees or notices, especially suddenly or when it is not easy to do so
from afar: from a distance
summon: to order someone to come to you
capture: to catch somebody and keep him/her as a prisoner

Wicked Witch of the West: If you don't give me your shoes, I'll kill your dog.

Narrator: The Witch reaches for Toto, who bites her hand.

Wicked Witch of the West: Ouch! You'll pay for this, you bad dog!

Narrator: Dorothy sees a pail of water nearby, grabs it, and throws the water on the Wicked Witch of the West. Instantly, the Wicked Witch gives a loud cry and begins to melt. Soon she disappears. The Winkies, the creatures of the land, are happy because they are free from the Wicked Witch's spell.

Dorothy: Look! The Wicked Witch's broom is on the floor! Let's take it to the Wizard!

Narrator: Dorothy takes the Golden Cap and orders the Winged Monkeys to take them back to the Wizard of Oz.

SCENE 7

Narrator: Dorothy and her friends return to the Wizard.

Wizard: I'm happy to see you. Do you have the Witch's broom?

Dorothy: Yes, great Wizard. Not only do we have the broom, we've also killed the Wicked Witch.

Narrator: The news of the Wicked Witch's death spreads throughout the Emerald City and there is great rejoicing.

Dorothy: (*to the Wizard*) Now, will you help us, please?

Wizard of Oz: I am sorry but I am not a wizard. I am just an ordinary old man. But wait, I can do something. Scarecrow, I am filling your head with pins and needles. This will make you sharp. Tin Man, I am placing this heart-shaped clock inside you. Now, you have a heart. Lion, take this saucer and drink the foul-tasting green liquid in it. You are brave to drink that. It's what I call real courage. Dorothy, I can't help you. Why don't you go to the Good Witch of the South. She may be able to help you get back to Kansas.

Narrator: Dorothy and her friends set out once again to meet the Good Witch of the South.

rejoicing: expressing great happiness about something
foul-tasting: having a very unpleasant taste
set out: to start (a journey)
castle: a large strong building with thick high walls and towers, built in the past by kings or queens to defend themselves against attack

SCENE 8

Narrator: The travellers reach the beautiful castle of the Good Witch of the South.

Good Witch of the South: How can I help you?

Dorothy: I want to go back home, to Kansas.

Good Witch of the South: You could have gone back home a long time ago if you knew you had magic with you.

Dorothy: What do you mean?

Good Witch of the South: The silver shoes will take you home. All you need to do is click your heels together three times.

Dotothy: Really? I am so happy! I can finally go back home. (*to the Good Witch of the South*) Take this Golden Cap, and thank you for your help!

Come, Toto. (*clicking the heels of her shoes together three times*) Take me back to Kansas!

Good Witch of the South: Goodbye! Scarecrow, you will now rule over the Emerald City. Tin Man, you will rule over the Winkies. Lion, you will rule over the beasts in the forest.

Narrator: Soon, Dorothy is back home. She is happy to be back with her uncle and aunt but knows that she would never forget her wonderful adventures in the land of Oz.

COMPREHENSION

A. Mark the sentences as true (T) or false (F).

1. Dorothy lived in Kansas with her parents.
2. Toto was Dorothy's pet monkey.
3. Dorothy's house was swept away in a flash flood.
4. Dorothy's house finally settled in the Land of the Munchkins.
5. The house landed on the Wicked Witch of the East and killed her.

B. Read the sentences and number them in correct order.

1. Nobody knew where Kansas was.
2. She presented Dorothy with the silver shoes of the witch.
3. The Good Witch of the North welcomed Dorothy to her land.
4. She asked the people how she could go back to her home in Kansas.
5. She was advised to go to the Wizard of Oz in the Emerald City for help.
6. On the way, she met the Scarecrow, the Tin Man, and the Lion, who also went with her.
7. She was also advised that she could reach the Emerald City by following the Yellow Brick Road.
8. When they met the Wizard, he asked them to bring the broom of the Wicked Witch of the West.

C. Choose the correct option.

1. The Scarecrow wanted the Wizard
   a. to give him brains.
   b. to give him a heart.
   c. to give him a longer tail.
2. The Tin Man had rusted because
   a. he had fallen in a puddle.
   b. he had got wet in the rain.
   c. he had gone swimming in a river.

3. The Lion was
   a. a coward and wanted courage.
   b. very brave and wanted some weapons.
   c. very strong and wanted to learn martial arts.

D. Answer the questions.

1. What did the Wicked Witch of the West want Dorothy to give her?
2. What did the Wizard give to the Scarecrow, the Tin Man, and the Lion? Did he really help them? Explain.
3. *You could have gone back home a long time ago if you knew you had magic with you.* Who is speaking to whom here? What magic is being referred to?
4. The Scarecrow wanted brains, the Tin Man wanted a heart, and the Lion wanted courage. If you were given a choice, what would you ask for? Give reasons for your choice.
5. How do you think Dorothy felt when she reached home?

Life Skills and Values

Cultivating patience/ Adventure travel

1. Dorothy is a girl of patience. Do you agree? Why/Why not?
2. Travel adventures are life lessons and make us wiser. Do you agree? Why/Why not?

VOCABULARY

French words in English

- There are many words used in English that originated in other languages but are now considered a part of English vocabulary. For example:

  café is originally a French word

- Here are a few more French words and their meanings.

  adieu: goodbye
  bon voyage: happy journey
  boutique: a small shop that sells fashionable clothes or expensive gifts
  chic: stylish
  crèche: a place where young children are cared for while their parents are working, shopping, studying, etc.
  décor: the style in which the inside of a building is decorated
  restaurant: a place where you can buy and eat a meal

Write meaningful sentences using any of the above three words of French origin.

1. ....

2. ....

3. ....

GRAMMAR

Direct Speech and Reported Speech

- We can report the words of a speaker in two ways.
- They are direct speech and reported speech.

Direct speech

- Reporting the exact words of a speaker as spoken by the speaker is called **direct speech**.
- The exact words of the speaker are put within inverted commas ('...').

Dorothy said to the Good Witch, *'I haven't killed anyone.'*
'Your house landed on top of the Wicked Witch,' replied the Good Witch.

Reported speech

- Reporting what somebody said in our own words, without using the speaker's exact words is called **reported speech** or **indirect speech**.

Dorothy told the Good Witch *that she hadn't killed anyone.*
The Good Witch replied *that her house had landed on top of the Wicked Witch.*

Rules for changing direct speech into reported speech

- We make the following changes when we change direct speech into reported speech:
- The inverted commas are removed.
- Changes are made in the pronouns.
- A reporting verb, such as *said, told, asked*, is used.
- Changes are made in the tense of the verb if the reporting verb is in the past tense.

A. Identify whether the sentences are in direct speech (D) or reported speech (R).

1. The Good Witch of the North told Dorothy that the silver shoes were magical. ☐
2. Dorothy asked the Scarecrow, 'Did you speak?' ☐
3. The Scarecrow said, 'I have been stuffed with straw and have no brains.' ☐
4. The Tin Man said, 'Please bring me some oil.' ☐
5. Dorothy exclaimed that it was a beautiful road. ☐

B. Change the sentences into reported speech.

1. The Lion said, 'I want courage.'

   ....

2. The Good Witch said, 'The Wizard of Oz can help you.'

   ....

3. The Good Witch of the South said to Dorothy, 'The silver shoes will take you home.'

   ....

4. The Wizard said to the Lion, 'You were brave to drink that.'

   ....

Reporting verbs

- When we report something in reported speech, we use a reporting verb.

  Dorothy told the Good Witch that she hadn't killed anyone.

  In the sentence above, *told* is a reporting verb.

- The use of a reporting verb depends on the meaning of the sentence. Some more examples of reporting verbs are *said, requested, replied, advised, asked*, and *enquired.*

  'Please give me a glass of milk,' said Dorothy to a Munchkin.

  Dorothy requested a Munchkin to give her a glass of milk.

  The Wizard said to Dorothy, 'You should fly back to Kansas.'

  The Wizard advised Dorothy to fly back to Kansas.

C. Choose the reporting verb to report each statement.

1. 'I'll send you a letter every day from Kansas.'

   a. insisted b. promised

2. 'If I were you, I'd go to the Wizard of Oz.'

   a. asked b. suggested

3. 'I'll guard you while you sleep, Dorothy.'

   a. offered b. requested

4. 'You should've told me about the shoes earlier.'

   a. announced b. complained

5. 'Welcome to our city, young girl.'

   a. greeted b. announced

Inverted commas

- Inverted commas ('...') are punctuation marks used to mark the beginning and end of direct speech.
- In direct speech, full stops/question marks/exclamation marks are put inside the inverted commas. For example:

  Dorothy said to the Scarecrow, 'Come with me to the Wizard.'
- They are also used to mark a word or a phrase being discussed or to show that it is being quoted from somewhere. In this case, the full stops/question marks/exclamation marks are put outside the inverted commas. For example:

  The professor spoke on 'The Impact of Cyclones'.

  In her own words, it is her 'most favourite book'.
- Names of articles, short stories, or poems are also put in inverted commas. For example:

  I loved the story, 'Kabuliwallah'.
- Remember that American English usually uses double inverted commas ("...").

D. Insert inverted commas in the sentences, wherever necessary.

1. Sandra said, Have you seen the movie The Wizard of Oz?
2. Kanta said, It's raining outside. Shall we play carrom indoors?
3. Madhu said, What a beautiful rainbow!
4. I don't agree with you, said Kamal, I think my pen is better.
5. I have to write an essay on Means of Transport.
6. The board displayed the quote, A room without books is like a garden without flowers.

LISTENING AND SPEAKING

Listening

A. Listen to the description of a character in a play and fill in the blanks.

1. *The Tempest* is a play written by .... Shakespeare.
2. Prospero is the the .... character in the story.
3. He is a .... duke.
4. He is engrossed in learning ....
5. He uses magic to .... others, create storms and provide entertainment to others.
6. He is a .... personality.

Speaking

B. Every year, thousands of lives are lost in natural disasters such as earthquakes, famines, cyclones, and landslides. Form groups and discuss how we can reduce their impact on the lives of the affected. Use the following points:

1. What is a natural disaster?
2. How does a natural disaster affect human life and the environment?
3. Are natural disasters caused by nature alone, or do human activities also trigger natural disasters?
4. What can we do to reduce the impact of a natural disaster?

Pronunciation

Pronunciation of *ch*

- The letter combination ch is pronounced in three different ways.
- In most words, ch has the /ch/ sound. For example:

  chase, chicken, choose, church, much, rich
- In words borrowed from French, ch has the /sh/ sound. For example:

  chauffeur, chef, machine, moustache
- In words borrowed from Greek, ch has the /k/ sound. For example:

  ache, character, chemist, choir, school

C. Identify the sound of *ch* in the following words and place them in the correct boxes.

anchor architect brochure chair charade chocolate chop chord Christmas crochet parachute

/ch/ sound	/sh/ sound	/k/ sound
1.	1.	1. ....
2.	2.	2. ....
3.	3.	3. ....
4.	4.	4. ....

WRITING

Writing a speech

To write a speech, follow these steps.

- Think about the topic and make an outline of your thoughts.
- Write as if you were speaking. Use short and simple sentences.
- Identify your audience—fellow students, teachers, parents, etc.
- Begin your speech by greeting your audience: *Good morning/Good afternoon, Dear…*
- Then introduce your topic. You can also begin with a famous person's quote about the subject or a well-known adage.
- Present your ideas and illustrate them with examples.
- Summarise your points in the end and thank the audience.

Write a short speech on any one of the following topics.

1. I learn when I travel
2. Education and travel
3. How school trips benefit us

3 Paper Boats

Travel and Adventure

OBJECTIVES

In this chapter, we will:

- *read and understand a beautiful poem celebrating a child's love for travel.*
- *understand and appreciate metaphor.*
- *learn to make dolls from different countries.*

WARM-UP

Make origami paper boats in different colours. Write the names of different places you wish to visit on the boats. Hang the paper boats on a hanger or a stick with strings of different lengths. Hang the mobile hanging in the classroom.

READING

Floating a paper boat is one of the most favourite activities of children. Read this beautiful poem by Rabindranath Tagore to find out what goes on in the mind of a little child who floats his paper boats in a stream.

Day by day I float my paper boats one by one
down the running stream.
In big black letters I write my name on them
and the name of the village where I live.
I hope that someone in some strange land will
find them and know who I am.
I load my little boats with *shiuli* flower from
our garden, and
hope that these blooms of the dawn will be
carried safely to land in the night.
I launch my paper boats and look up into the
sky and see
the little clouds setting their white bulging
sails.
I know not what playmate of mine in the sky
sends them down

the air to race with my boats!
When night comes, I bury my face in
my arms and dream that my
paper boats float on and on under the
midnight stars.
The fairies of sleep are sailing in them,
and the lading is their baskets full of
dreams.

Science Scan

- An object sinks or floats in water depending on how much water it displaces.
- When an object enters water, two forces act upon it. There is a downward force (gravity) and an upward force (buoyancy). Buoyancy is determined by how much water is displaced by the object.
- An object will float if buoyancy is more than gravity. All boats, from the heaviest to the lightest, float on this principle.

running: flowing; moving
stream: a small narrow river
***shiuli*:** white flowers with bright orange stems that blossom in autumn; the official flower of the state of West Bengal
blooms of the dawn: flowers of early morning. (*Shiuli* flowers bloom at night and fall to the ground early in morning)
launch: to put (a boat or ship) into the water
bulging: sticking out in a round shape
lading: goods that are loaded on a ship, boat, etc.

COMPREHENSION

A. Mark the sentences as true (T) or false (F).

1. The poet floats his paper boats in a small puddle. ☐
2. He writes his name and address on the paper boats. ☐
3. He puts red roses in the boats. ☐
4. He thinks that sleep fairies sail in his boats at night. ☐
5. The travellers do not carry anything with them in the paper boats. ☐

B. Read the lines from the poem and answer the questions.

1. *I know not what playmate of mine in the sky*
   sends them down the air to race with my boats!
   a. What does the word *them* refer to here?
   b. Where, according to the poet, is his playmate?
   c. Why does the poet's playmate send them down the air?
2. *The fairies of sleep are sailing in them,*
   and the lading is their baskets full of dreams.
   a. What is meant by the word *lading*?
   b. Who does the poet say is sailing in his paper boats?
   c. What are the travellers carrying with them in the paper boats?

C. Answer the questions.

1. Does the poet write anything on his paper boats? If yes, what and why?
2. Why does the poet put flowers in the paper boats? What is the significance of taking flowers from his own garden?
3. What have the clouds been compared to in the poem?
4. What does the poet do when it is night?

Life Skills and Values

Safety during travel

1. What things should we keep in mind to stay safe while travelling to a new place?
2. Is it preferable to visit a new place during the daytime or at night? Why?

5. The poet creates vivid images in our minds through his words. For example, in the first stanza, we can *see* a little boy floating paper boats in a stream. Describe in your own words an image you like from the poem.
6. If you were in place of the poet, what would you load in the paper boats and why?

VOCABULARY

Metaphor

- A **metaphor** is a figure of speech in which something is referred to as something else to show a similarity.
- The poet calls parts of clouds *bulging sails*. This is a metaphor.
- The clouds have been compared to sails.
- Another example of metaphor is 'The baby is a delicate flower,' which means the baby is delicate like a flower.

The sentences use metaphors. Underline the two nouns in each sentence that have been compared.

1. Life is a journey to an unknown place.
2. My neighbour thinks life is a fashion show.
3. Shakespeare rightly said that the world is a stage.
4. His mother's soothing words were a balm for him.
5. Our body is a machine that works round the clock.

ACTIVITY

Dolls from different countries

Follow the instructions and make dolls representing different countries of the world.

- Take a strip of slightly stiff paper and fold it in the shape of an accordion.
- Draw the template of the paper doll on the top fold.
- Now cut the doll according to the template through all the folds.
- Open the paper cut-out. You will get a chain of dolls appearing to be holding hands.
- Colour the dolls in the colours of the flags of different countries.
- You will get a chain of dolls representing different countries. Put up the doll chain in your classroom.

4 The Happy Prince

Courage in Compassion

OBJECTIVES

In this chapter, we will:

- *read the story of a prince and a swallow.*
- *learn the correct use of expressions with do and make.*
- *learn about the active and passive voice.*
- *learn the difference between whose and which.*
- *listen to a passage and extract information.*
- *interview a character from the story.*
- *learn about silent letters k, g, n, and w.*
- *learn to write a travelogue.*

WARM-UP

Some people devote their entire life for the welfare of others. Match the names of some such courageous and kind people with their descriptions.

Name	Description
1. Mahatma Gandhi	a. A Nobel Peace Prize winner and South Africa's first non-White President, he fought for equal rights for the Black community in his country. He was imprisoned for almost three decades for this reason.
2. Martin Luther King Jr	b. A social activist and a leader of the Indian Independence Movement, he preached non-violence, peaceful disobedience, and equality among people of all castes and religions.
3. Nelson Mandela	c. A leader of the Civil Rights Movement in the United States of America, he fought for equality and justice for Americans of all races.

READING

A statue of a prince observes that some people of his country are suffering. Is he able to help them? Read this adaptation of a story by Oscar Wilde to find out.

High on a column stood the statue of the Happy Prince, gilded with gold, two bright sapphires for eyes and a large red ruby on his sword hilt.

He was much admired. 'Why can't you be like the Happy Prince?' asked a mother of her little boy who was crying.

'He looks like an angel,' said the Charity Children.

One night a little Swallow flew over the city. His friends had gone away to Egypt for winter. But he had stayed behind, for he was in love with a Reed. 'It is ridiculous,' twittered the other Swallows, and flew away.

After they had gone he felt lonely. 'Will you come away with me?' he said to the Reed, but the Reed refused. 'I am off to the Pyramids,' the swallow cried.

All day long he flew, and then he arrived in the city. 'Where shall I put up?'

Then he saw the statue of the Happy Prince. 'I will put up there,' he cried.

He alighted between the feet of the Happy Prince and found a golden bedroom. Just as he was going to sleep, a drop of water fell on him. 'How curious!' he cried. 'There isn't a single cloud in the sky, yet it is raining.'

Looking Back

- The pyramids of Egypt were built by ancient Egyptians around 4000 years ago as burial places to honour their pharaohs. A pharaoh was a political and religious leader of Egyptians.
- There are around 138 Egyptian pyramids. They are all built to the west of the River Nile. The largest is the Great Pyramid of Giza, which is one of the Seven Wonders of the Ancient World.

gilded: covered with a thin layer of gold or gold paint
sapphires: clear, bright blue precious stones
ruby: a dark red precious stone
hilt: the handle (of a sword)
reed: a plant that grows in shallow water
twittered: talked, making short high sounds
pyramids: large buildings with a square or triangular base and sloping sides that meet in a point at the top
alighted: landed after flying
curious: strange and unusual

Another drop fell. He looked up—the Happy Prince was crying.

'Who are you?' the Swallow said.

'I am the Happy Prince.'

'Why are you weeping then?' asked the Swallow.

'When I was alive,' answered the statue, 'I did not cry. My courtiers called me the Happy Prince. So I lived, and so I died. Now that I am dead, they have set me up where I can see all the misery of my city. Though my heart is made of lead, yet I weep.'

'Far away,' continued the statue, 'there is a poor house. I can see a seamstress. Her face is thin and worn. She is making a gown for the Queen's maids-of-honour. Her boy has fever, and wants oranges. She has only water. Swallow, will you take her my ruby?'

'I'd rather not,' answered the Swallow. But the Happy Prince looked so sad that the Swallow agreed. 'It is very cold here,' he said, 'but I will stay for one night.'

courtiers: persons who are part of the court of a king or queen
lead: a heavy, soft grey metal
poor house: (in former times) an institution in which poor people could live. It was paid for by the public.
seamstress: a woman who sews and makes clothes

The Swallow plucked the ruby, and flew away with it. At last he came to the poor house. The boy was tossing on his bed, and the mother was asleep. He laid the great ruby on the table and flew back.

'It is curious,' he remarked, 'but I feel quite warm now, although it is so cold.'

'That is because you have done a good deed,' said the Prince.

When day broke, he flew to the river and had a bath.

'To-night I go to Egypt,' said the Swallow.

'Swallow,' said the Prince, 'will you stay one night longer?'

'I am waited for in Egypt,' answered the Swallow.

'I can see a young man,' said the Prince. 'He is trying to finish a play for the Director of the Theatre, but he is too cold and hungry to write. My eyes are made of sapphires. Pluck out one of them and take it to him.'

'Dear Prince,' said the Swallow, 'I cannot do that,' and began to weep.

'Little Swallow,' said the Prince, 'do as I say.'

The Swallow plucked out the Prince's eye. He went and put the sapphire on the table without the student seeing him. When the student looked up, he found the sapphire. 'This is from some great admirer,' he cried. 'Now I can finish my play.'

'I come to say good-bye,' said the Swallow the next day.

'Swallow,' said the Prince, 'will you stay one night longer?'

'It is winter,' answered the Swallow.

'In the square below,' said the Happy Prince, 'there stands a little match-girl. Her matches have got spoiled. Her father will beat her if she does not bring some money. Give her my other eye.'

'I will stay with you,' said the Swallow, 'but I cannot pluck out your eye.'

Science Scan

- The seasonal movement of a group of animals from one region to another is called migration.
- Some birds migrate over thousands of kilometres for food or more comfortable weather.
- The Arctic tern has the longest migration of any bird in the world.
- British swallows spend their winters in South Africa.

square: an open area in a town, usually with four sides, surrounded by buildings

'Do as I say,' said the Prince.

The Swallow plucked out the Prince's other eye. He swooped past the match-girl, and slipped the jewel into her hand. 'What a lovely bit of glass!' cried the girl. She ran home, laughing.

'You are blind now,' the Swallow said, 'I will stay with you always.'

'No, little Swallow,' said the Prince, 'you must go to Egypt.'

'I will stay with you,' said the Swallow. All the next day he sat on the Prince's shoulder, and told him stories.

'Swallow,' said the Prince, 'you tell me wonderful stories, but I want to know of the suffering of men. Fly over my city, and tell me what you see.'

swooped: flew downwards, quickly and suddenly
making merry: enjoying oneself
starving: suffering or dying because of a lack of food to eat
leaf: (here) a very thin sheet of metal

The Swallow flew over the city, and saw the rich making merry, while the beggars were sitting in the cold. He saw the white faces of starving children. Under a bridge, two little boys were lying in one another's arms to keep themselves warm. He flew back and told the Prince what he had seen.

'I am covered with gold. You must take it off, and give it to my poor.'

The Swallow picked off the gold, leaf by leaf, till the Happy Prince looked dull and grey.

Then the snow came. The poor Swallow grew colder, but he would not go. He tried to keep himself warm by flapping his wings.

But at last he knew that he was going to die. He flew to the Prince's shoulder. 'Good-bye, dear Prince!' he murmured.

'I am glad that you are going to Egypt,' said the Prince.

'It is not to Egypt that I am going,' said the Swallow. 'I am going to the House of Death.'

He kissed the Happy Prince, and fell dead. A loud crack sounded inside the statue, as if something had broken. The leaden heart had snapped into two.

The next morning the Mayor was walking by. As he passed, he looked up: 'How shabby the Happy Prince looks!' he said. 'And there's a dead bird at his feet!'

'He is no longer beautiful or useful,' said the Art Professor. So, they pulled down the statue and melted it.

'How strange!' said the overseer. 'This broken lead heart will not melt. We must throw it away.' They threw it on a dustheap where the dead Swallow was lying.

'Bring me the two most precious things in the city,' said God to His Angel; the Angel brought Him the leaden heart and the dead bird.

'You have rightly chosen,' said God, 'for in my garden of Paradise, this little bird shall sing for evermore, and in my city of gold the Happy Prince shall praise me.'

snapped: broke suddenly with a sharp noise
Mayor: the head of the government of a town or city, elected by the public
shabby: (looking) old and in bad condition
dustheap: a pile of waste or discarded material
precious: rare and worth a lot of money
Paradise: a perfect place where people are said to go when they die

COMPREHENSION

A. Fill in the blanks to complete the sentences.

1. The statue of the Happy Prince was covered with ....
2. It had two bright .... for eyes and a large red ....on his sword hilt.
3. The Swallow's friends had gone to .... for winter.
4. The little Swallow stayed back as he was in love with a ....
5. The little Swallow decided to stay at the feet of the .... when he reached the city.

B. Choose the correct option.

1. Though it was winter, the Swallow felt quite warm as
   - a. the weather had changed.
   - b. he lay at the feet of the Happy Prince.
   - c. the good deed he had done gave him a warm feeling.
2. The Swallow decided to stay with the Happy Prince as
   - a. it had become warm in Egypt.
   - b. he began to like the city very much.
   - c. he wanted to help the Happy Prince who had become blind.
3. When the Swallow flew over the city, he saw that
   - a. the city had many beautiful skyscrapers.
   - b. there was no poverty and suffering in the city.
   - c. the poor suffered terribly while the rich enjoyed themselves.

C. Read the sentences from the story and answer the questions.

1. '*Why are you weeping then?*'
   - a. Who asks this question and to whom?
   - b. Why is the speaker surprised?
2. *A loud crack sounded inside the statue, as if something had broken.*
   - a. What had broken inside the statue?
   - b. Why had it broken?
3. '*Bring me the two most precious things in the city.*'
   - a. Who said this and to whom?
   - b. What were the two most precious things brought?

D. Answer the questions.

1. Why was the Happy Prince crying?
2. Why did the Happy Prince want to give the ruby to the seamstress?
3. To whom did the Happy Prince send a sapphire from his eye? Why?
4. What impression do you form of the Happy Prince?
5. Do you think that the Swallow was a true friend? Give two reasons to support your answer.
6. If you were the little match-girl, how would you have felt on receiving 'a lovely bit of glass'? How do you think her father would have reacted?

Life Skills and Values

Compassion and patriotism

1. The Happy Prince and the little Swallow display both courage and compassion. Do you agree with this? Why/Why not?
2. What qualities should a leader of a country possess? Is it his/her duty to do something for the people of his/her country? Explain.

VOCABULARY

Expressions with *do* and *make*

- *Do* is used to
  - talk about work or tasks.

    I have done the household chores.
  - talk about activities in general.

    Please let me know if I can do something for you.
- *Make* is used to
  - create or build something new.

    He made a cup of tea for his grandmother.
  - indicate the materials that have been used to make something.

    My earrings are made of silver.

A. Underline the correct verb in each sentence.

1. They have all gone to *make/do* shopping.
2. A famous sculptor *made/did* the statue of the Prince.
3. The Prince *did/made* his best to help the poor people in the city.
4. The seamstress had to *make/do* a dress for the queen's maids-of-honour.
5. The Swallow felt warm because he had *made/done* a good deed.

B. Match the sentence parts in the two columns in a meaningful way.

Column A	Column B
1. We all should do	a. which woke me up.
2. The bird made a loud sound	b. our duty sincerely.
3. The art professor made a point	c. for the statue to be removed.
4. The mayor made arrangements	d. which made him sleepy in the day.
5. The playwright did his work at night	e. when he said that the statue was no longer beautiful.

GRAMMAR

Active and passive voice

- When the subject of a sentence performs the action, the sentence is said to be in the **active voice**. For example:

  The Swallow plucked the ruby.

In the sentence above, *the Swallow* is the subject and *plucked* is the verb. The subject performed the action of plucking.

- When the subject of a sentence receives the action, the sentence is said to be in the **passive voice**. For example:

  The ruby was plucked by the Swallow.

  The ruby is the subject and it was plucked. The subject receives the action here, so the sentence is in the passive voice.

- In the simple tenses, the form of the verb in the passive voice is:

  the correct form of the verb **be** (*am/is/are/was/were/will be*) + the **past participle of the verb**. For example:

  The student found the sapphire. (active voice)

  The sapphire was found by the student. (passive voice)

  They will write letters. (active voice)

  Letters will be written by them. (passive voice)

A. Read the sentences. Write *A* if the sentence is in the active voice and *P* if it is in the passive voice.

1. The match-girl was scolded by her father. ☐
2. My courtiers called me the Happy Prince. ☐
3. The Swallow laid the great ruby on the table. ☐
4. The little bird sang a sweet song in praise of God. ☐
5. The leaden heart was thrown away by the workers. ☐

Whose and which

- *Whose* and *which* can both be used to ask questions.
- They can be used as both pronouns and adjectives.
- *Whose* is used to ask questions about someone or something that belongs to someone else. *Whose* is the possessive form of *who*. For example:

  Whose is this umbrella? (used as a pronoun)

  Whose umbrella is this? (used as an adjective)

- *Which* is used to ask questions when there are two or more possible answers or alternatives. For example:

  Which is your cabin? (used as a pronoun)

  Which month has 28 days? (used as an adjective)

B. Fill in each blank with *whose* or *which*.

1. .... birthday is it today?
2. .... is this bicycle?

3. .... house is yours?
4. .... younger brother is he?
5. .... is your favourite season?
6. .... author's book sold a million copies?
7. .... country was hit by an earthquake yesterday?
8. Look at these paintings made by my brother. .... painting do you like the most?

LISTENING AND SPEAKING

Listening

A. Listen to the descriptions of four animals. Make notes while you listen. Then complete the table.

Name	Species	Habitat	Diet category	Fearless trait
Hummingbird		The Americas		
	The rat family			
			Omnivores	
				Can attack large animals like bears and wolves.

Speaking

B. Work in pairs. Imagine you are a television/newspaper reporter who has been asked to interview any one of the characters in the story 'The Happy Prince'. Ask your partner relevant questions. Next, reverse the roles and continue the interview.

Here are some examples of questions to ask:

- What role does your character play in the story?
- Why did your character behave in the way it did?
- Could you have acted differently in the situation?

Remember to be polite while asking questions.

Pronunciation

Silent letters *g*, *k*, *n*, and *w*

- There are many silent letters in English, which makes the pronunciation of words quite difficult.
- The letter **g** is often silent when it comes before *n* at the beginning or end of a word. For example: *foreign gnome reign sign*
- The letter **k** is silent when it comes before *n* at the beginning of a word. For example: *knife know knowledge*
- The letter **n** is silent when it comes after *m* at the end of a word. For example: *column hymn solemn*
- The letter **w** is usually silent when it comes before *r* at the beginning of a word. For example: *write wrap wrestle*

C. Read the clues to identify words with a silent letter. Circle the silent letters in the words. One is done for you.

1. It can be difficult to untie. ....knot..........
2. This is the opposite of *right*. ....
3. You cut vegetables with it. ....
4. This is another word for *pattern*. ....
5. It's a country other than your own. ....
6. This season comes just before winter. ....
7. The meaning of this word is *to leave one's job*. ....
8. This part of the body comes between the hand and the arm. ....

WRITING

Writing a travelogue

- A travelogue is a piece of writing about travels or places visited.
- It gives us detailed information about the attractions of a place.
- To write a travelogue, you must first organise your ideas on the following lines:
  - Location of the place and how it is to be reached
  - Description of the place
  - Cultural or historical background
  - Tourist attractions there
  - Some dos and don'ts to be followed
  - Your own experiences

Recall your most recent trip to a place and write a travelogue in about three paragraphs. Follow the guidelines given.

5 Dressing Up for Space

Space

OBJECTIVES

In this chapter, we will:
- *read and comprehend an article on spacesuits.*
- *learn about the etymology of words.*
- *learn about the kinds and transformation of sentences.*
- *learn about if clauses.*
- *listen to a space story and order sentences.*
- *enact a short skit on a UFO, or describe a lunar eclipse.*
- *write a short story based on pictures.*

WARM-UP

Have you ever seen the night sky? It is filled with many celestial bodies such as stars, moons, and planets. How many celestial bodies do you know about? Work in pairs and match the name of each celestial body with its description.

Celestial body	Description
1. asteroid	a. a piece of rock or metal from outer space that has fallen to the earth's surface
2. comet	b. a celestial object made up of ice and dust that moves around the sun and looks like a bright star with a tail
3. meteor	c. an artificial body placed in orbit around the earth or moon or another planet to collect information or for communication
4. meteorite	d. a small rocky body orbiting the sun; large numbers of these, ranging enormously in size, are found between the orbits of Mars and Jupiter
5. satellite	e. a small body of matter from outer space that burns up when entering the earth's atmosphere and appears as a streak of light in the night sky

READING

Outer space has very harsh conditions. Let's find out what astronauts wear to keep themselves safe in outer space.

Space is, no doubt, a difficult place to travel to and even more difficult to live in. First, there is no air in space. Then it is very cold, unless the sun is shining directly at you. And since there is no air to protect you, the rays of the sun can burn you!

To survive in space, a special spacesuit is needed to protect your body from the effects of the extreme heat and cold, and to provide you with air so that you can breathe. Spacesuits are full of air to provide the pressure that your body is used to on earth. So, they look bloated. Spacesuits also protect you from space dust which travels faster than a bullet!

Its special gold-lined visors protect your eyes from bright sunlight. A spacesuit is a complete astronaut protection unit, a very intricate and well-designed machine. It has a heating and cooling system and arrangements for air and water to drink on the go. It even allows the astronaut to relieve himself while in the suit!

spacesuit: a special suit worn by astronauts in space
bloated: full of liquid or gas and larger than normal
visors: a pair of transparent, movable shields attached to a helmet to protect the eyes or face
intricate: detailed and complicated
relieve oneself: to urinate or pass stool
bulky: large and heavy

The invention of the first spacesuits

Spacesuits were first invented around the 1930s. As one goes higher up in the atmosphere, the air becomes thinner and pilots need air to breathe. In the beginning, the suits were somewhat clumsy as they were quite stiff, bulky, and difficult to move around in.

The earliest astronauts stayed inside their spacecraft but scientists soon realised that the astronauts would also be working in space and so they started working on better spacesuits for these missions.

The first spacesuits were silver in colour because scientists at that time felt that this would reflect the sunrays. They had pipes in them that supplied air and water to keep the astronauts cool.

Newer spacesuits for EVA

Soon space missions required extravehicular activity (EVA) on the part of the astronauts. That means the astronauts had to move out of the spacecraft to walk on the moon and, later, to repair the space shuttles while they are in orbit around the earth. The suits had to be changed. They were attached to the spacecraft by a thick tube that carried air and water, and stopped them from floating away.

During Apollo missions, the spacesuits were modified further. They were big backpacks with air, water, and batteries so that the astronauts could do a moonwalk for about eight hours. The thick tubes were removed. The astronauts had more freedom to move around.

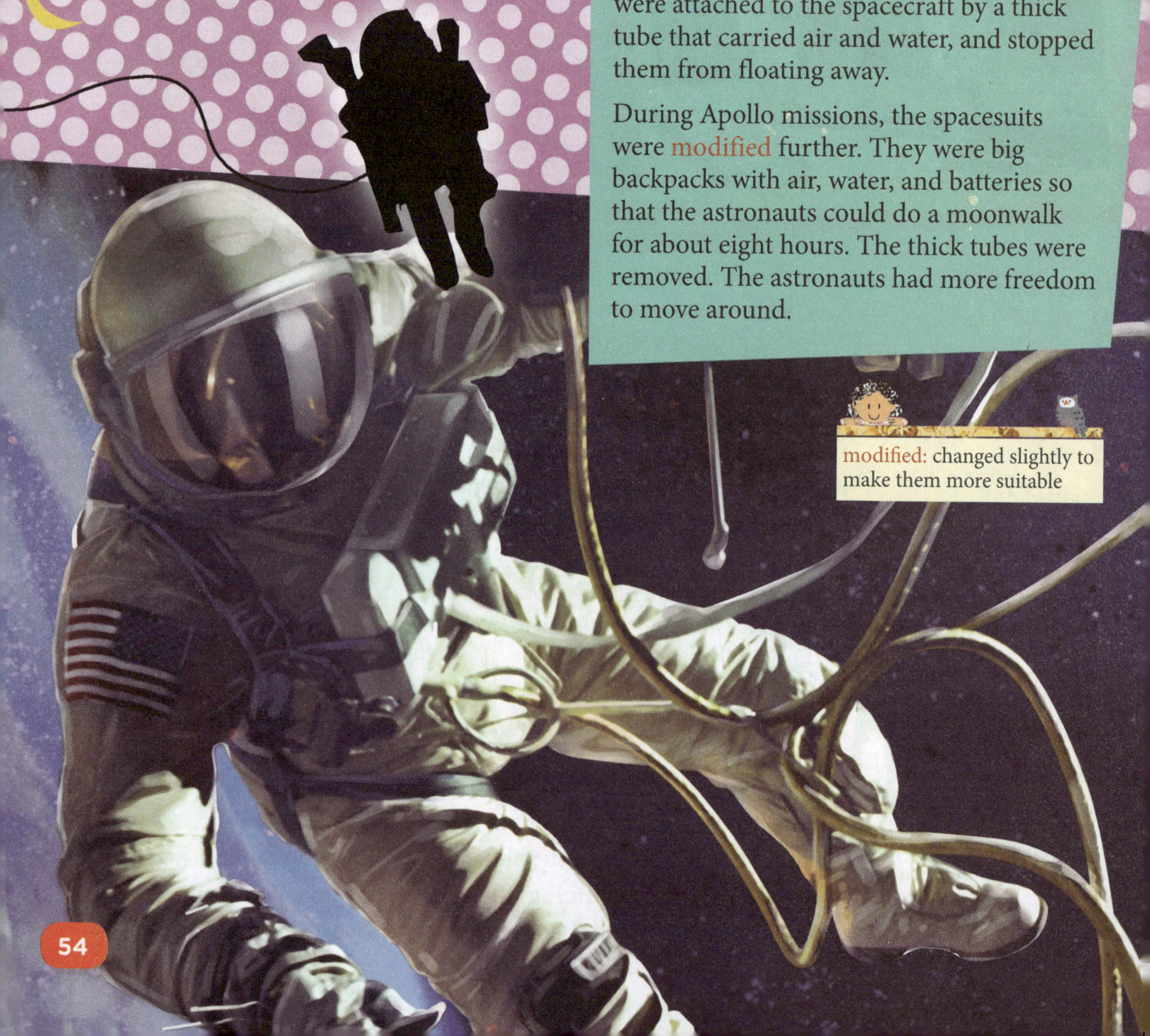

modified: changed slightly to make them more suitable

Flying in SPACE

A spacesuit attached to a rocket-powered backpack is called a manned maneuvering unit (MMU). It has rocket motors to help the astronaut to 'fly' around in space. There is a camera in the astronaut's helmet, so the other crew members and scientists on earth can monitor what the astronaut is doing.

Modern-day spacesuits

Modern day astronauts don't need to wear spacesuits at all, most of the time. When they are inside a spacecraft, they wear overalls, or even their own clothes. They wear special white spacesuits only when they need to go out into space to do repair work or perform experiments.

The most commonly used spacesuit these days is the orange spacesuit. It is worn only during launch and re-entry. The suit has a parachute and other survival items. It is orange to make it easier to spot the crew.

Interesting facts

Initially, spacesuits were made to fit each astronaut but now they are off the rack—readymade! They are made up of different parts in many sizes that can be attached and will fit astronauts of different sizes. Astronauts can select a suit, pack their bags, and go!

overalls: a loose piece of clothing made of heavy cloth and worn over other clothes
off the rack: made to a standard average size and not made especially to fit you

Future spacesuits

In the future, you might be able to go into space for a holiday! Scientists are researching to design spacesuits that will be smaller, lighter, and more comfortable. These suits will be better fitted and made of fabric, with less metal and rubber. Movement in the spacecraft will be easier.

Spacesuits have eleven layers. The layers are sewn and cemented together. They are about four inches thick. It takes almost two-and-a-half years to produce a suit and it costs around two million dollars.

The spacesuit is too heavy for training on earth. The astronauts use special lightweight parts on earth and they do a lot of training in water. In the pool, they do all the things they will do on their mission.

A spacesuit is not easy to put on. It takes an astronaut over an hour to wear a spacesuit, with the help of an assistant.

Under their helmets, astronauts wear a hat called a Snoopy cap. It has a microphone and speakers, so astronauts can talk to each other. Under the spacesuit, astronauts wear another light suit. It covers their entire body except their head, hands, and feet. There are water tubes in this layer to keep the astronaut cool.

Fact File

- National Aeronautics and Space Administration (NASA) is an American agency that works on space research projects.
- Apollo 11 was NASA's first space mission to land on the moon, and astronaut Neil Armstrong was the first human to step on the moon. On landing on the moon, Armstrong said: 'That's one small step for (a) man, one giant leap for mankind.'
- Indian Space Research Organisation (ISRO), headquartered in Bengaluru, is the Indian agency that works on space exploration projects.
- Other than successfully launching satellites into orbits, ISRO has also launched *Mangalyaan* and *Chandrayaan* missions to Mars and the moon, respectively.

Science Scan

- We cannot hear in space because there is no medium there for sound waves to travel.
- It takes an average of eight minutes and twenty seconds for the light of the sun to reach Earth.

fabric: material made by weaving wool, cotton, etc, used for making clothes

COMPREHENSION

A. Fill in the blanks with words from the article.

1. A spacesuit is a complete ....
2. Spacesuits were invented around the ....
3. Spacesuits are filled with air, so they look ....
4. There is no .... to protect you from the sun in space.
5. Spacesuits protect the astronauts from both .... and cold.

B. Choose the correct option.

1. The first spacesuits were silver in colour because
   a. silver shines in the dark.
   b. scientists liked this colour.
   c. scientists thought this colour would reflect the burning hot sunrays.
2. Earlier spacesuits had long pipes attached to them which
   a. supplied air to breathe.
   b. supplied cool water to the suits.
   c. stopped the astronauts from floating away in space.
3. Nowadays, when the astronauts are travelling in a spacecraft,
   a. they wear metal suits.
   b. they wear rubber suits.
   c. they wear overalls or their own clothes.

C. Match the sentence parts in the two columns in a meaningful way.

Column A	Column B
1. The orange spacesuit is worn	a. by training in a big pool.
2. The Snoopy cap worn under the helmet	b. only during launch and re-entry.
3. Astronauts take over an hour to put on a spacesuit,	c. is called a manned maneuvering unit.
4. A spacesuit attached to a rocket-powered backpack	d. and they need a helper to put on all the different parts.
5. Astronauts learn how to move around in space in their spacesuits	e. has a radio microphone and speakers so that astronauts can talk to each other.

D. Answer the questions.

1. Describe the earliest spacesuits.
2. What does EVA mean?

3. Why did spacesuits need to be modified during Apollo missions?
4. How do modern spacesuits fit everybody?
5. Why are spacesuits bright orange in colour?
6. How much time and money are needed to make a spacesuit?
7. Do you think in the future everyone will be able to travel to space for a holiday? Give reasons to support your answer.

Life Skills and Values

Imagination

1. Albert Einstein said, 'Imagination is more important than knowledge.' What would happen if we did not have the power of imagination? Would our lives be the same?
2. If you were an astronaut, which planets or celestial objects would you like to explore in space?

VOCABULARY

Etymology

- **Etymology** is the study of the origin of words and their development over the years.
- Many words of the English language come from other languages such as Greek, French, Spanish, and Hindi.
- They are sometimes known as loan words.
- Several of these words are now so common in English that they are considered an essential part of English vocabulary. For example:

Word	Origin
sepoy	Hindi
school	Greek
perfume	French
tomato	Spanish

- Some dictionaries mention the origin of a word that has been borrowed from another language.

Write the name of the language (Greek, Hindi, French, Spanish) from which the following words have been borrowed. You can use the Internet for help.

1. alligator	....	2. ballet	....
3. charpoy	....	4. coat	....
5. croissant	....	6. guru	....
7. mania	....	8. plaza	....
9. shampoo	....	10. war	....

GRAMMAR

Kinds of sentences

There are four kinds of sentences.

- A **declarative sentence** makes a statement of fact. A full stop is put at the end of a declarative sentence. For example:

  Space is a very difficult place to explore.

- An **interrogative sentence** asks a question. A question mark is put at the end of an interrogative sentence. For example:

  Is space a difficult place to explore?

- An **imperative sentence** makes a request or an order. A full stop is put at the end of an imperative sentence. For example:

  Please come with me.

- An **exclamatory sentence** expresses a sudden and strong feeling. An exclamation mark is put at the end of an exclamatory sentence. For example:

  What a difficult place is space to explore!

A. Read these sentences and write *D* for declarative, *In* for interrogative, *Im* for imperative and *E* for exclamatory sentences.

1. Do you wish you could travel in space? ☐
2. A spacesuit weighs approximately 280 pounds. ☐
3. Please take me with you when you go on a holiday. ☐
4. India is making great progress in space technology. ☐
5. How exciting it must have been for Neil Armstrong to be the first man on the moon! ☐

Transformation of sentences

- Read the example sentences above and notice the changes made when sentences are transformed from one kind to another.
- Note that:
  - a declarative sentence starts with the subject.
  - an interrogative sentence starts with a question word like *what, who*, etc. or with a helping verb like *does, is*, etc.
  - an imperative sentence starts with the base form of a verb or with *please*, etc. followed by the base form of the verb.

B. Change the following sentences as directed. One is done for you.

1. She is fascinated by space and galaxies.
   (*Change into an interrogative sentence.*)
   Is she fascinated by space and galaxies?
2. Apollo 11 was the first manned spacecraft to land on the moon.
   (*Change into an interrogative sentence.*)
   ....
3. Would you like to have lunch with an astronaut?
   (*Change into a declarative sentence.*)
   ....
4. What an unusual place the moon is!
   (*Change into a declarative sentence.*)
   ....
5. Man has landed on the moon.
   (*Change into an interrogative sentence.*)
   ....

If clauses

- An **if clause** is a clause that expresses a condition.
- It is part of a longer sentence. For example:

  If an astronaut wears a spacesuit, the rays of the sun will not burn him.

The first part of the sentence is an *if* clause.

It uses *If + the simple present tense.*

The second part of the sentence uses the future tense.

So, wearing a spacesuit will make sure that the astronaut is protected from the heat.

- We use sentences with an *if* clause and the simple future to show that the action in the 'if' part of the sentence will result in the action in the other part of the sentence. For example:

  If I meet an astronaut from NASA, I will take his autograph.
  If I work hard, I will be able to fulfil my dream of becoming an astronaut.

- *If clauses* are also called conditional clauses.
- They specify a condition on which the action of the other clause is dependent.

C. Put the verbs in brackets in the correct tense.

1. If I .... (go) for a walk, I .... (take) you along.
2. If I .... (see) him, I .... (give) him your number.
3. If he .... (come) back early, he .... (cook) for himself.
4. If he .... (want) to become an astronaut, he .... (study) science.

D. Match the sentence parts in the two columns.

Column A	Column B
1. If I visit NASA,	a. I will visit Mars.
2. If I send an email,	b. I shall write an email to NASA.
3. If I enroll to be an astronaut,	c. I may be invited to visit NASA.
4. If I learn to use the computer,	d. I shall enroll to be an astronaut.

LISTENING AND SPEAKING

Listening

A. Listen to the story *My Space Adventure*. Then, read the sentences and number them in order.

1. I ate cookies and pizza. ☐
2. I got inside a rocket and pressed a button. ☐
3. I landed on the moon after I saw a large asteroid. ☐
4. I saw something frightening. It was an alien's spaceship. ☐
5. One of them got out and I asked him: 'What is your name, my alien friend?' ☐
6. Soon, I heard something: 'Sweetheart, it's time to have breakfast!' called mom. ☐
7. I found my tri-coloured flag. I gave it to him and he went back in his spaceship. ☐
8. He didn't answer; instead he gave me a gift. When I opened it, I saw it was a tiny camera. ☐
9. 'Oh! it was only a dream,' I thought. Even though it was only a dream, it was a great adventure. ☐
10. I put on a spacesuit and a helmet with earphones and speakers, and slept in a sleeping bag with straps. ☐

Speaking

B. Work in groups and prepare a short skit on the topic *'The day I saw a UFO'. Enact the skit in the class.* Or Find out what a lunar eclipse is and how it happens. Describe it to your class.

WRITING

Writing a short story based on pictures

Look at the pictures and write a short story based on them. No picture has been given for the end of the story; end it in your own way. Give your story a suitable title.

6 Sailing Out to Space

Space/Imagination

OBJECTIVES

In this chapter, we will:

- *read and comprehend a poem that will take us on a virtual ride to space.*
- *learn about the rhyme scheme of a poem.*
- *make a chart or scrapbook on a human colony on Mars.*

WARM-UP

Read some fascinating facts about space and space travel.

- The word *astronaut* comes from the Greek words *astron*, which means *star*, and *nautes*, which means *sailor*.
- A space shuttle must start its journey at a minimum speed of nearly 29,000 km per hour, almost nine times faster than a rifle bullet!
- Astronauts report that space smells like hot metal. Some astronauts feel that it smells like a raspberry!
- Astronauts eat dried, frozen food in space. It includes frozen vegetables and desserts, refrigerated food, fruit, etc.
- If one cries in space, the tears don't fall but form bubbles around the eyes because of weightlessness in space.
- We can now use phones and the Internet even in space!

READING

Have you ever dreamt of travelling to space? What would you do in space? Read this poem by Gareth Lancaster to find out what the poet wants to do there.

I dream of sailing out to space[1],
Upon a yacht of stars.
With port holes all along the sides,
I'd gaze amazed at Mars.

With mast made strong with spider[2] webs,
And sail of fluffy cloud,
I'd watch the Earth go sweeping past,
As out to space I ploughed.

With stars in front and stars behind,
And planets far and near,
I'd sail my yacht around the rings,
Of Saturn with a cheer.

Science Scan

- Saturn is the second-largest planet in the solar system, but it is very light for its size.
- Saturn has beautiful rings around it, made of billions of tiny chips of ice and dust.

Literary Device

- The consonant s has been repeated in *strong with spider web* and *sailing out to space*. Such a repetition of a sound is called **alliteration**.

yacht (pronounced *yawt*): a large sailing boat, often with an engine and a place to sleep on, used for pleasure trips and racing
port holes: small, circular windows on the outside of a ship
amazed: very surprised
made strong: (here) tied together
fluffy: soft and light
ploughed: moved through something
cheer: happiness

Science Scan

- Jupiter, the largest planet in our solar system, is a very stormy planet. One storm, called the Great Red Spot, has lasted over 300 years. This storm is also called the *eye of Jupiter*.
- Jupiter has many moons.

And onwards passing Jupiter,
To watch the big, red storm.
Then far around its outer moons,
And through an asteroid swarm.

I dream of sailing out to space[3],
To catch a star or two.
Exploring through the universe,
And just take in the view.

asteroid: any one of the many small planets that go around the sun
swarm: a large group
exploring: travelling around in order to learn about the place
universe: the whole of space and everything in it, including the earth, the planets and the stars

Literary Device

3. The line *I dream of sailing out to space* has been repeated for making a better impact. This is called repetition.

COMPREHENSION

A. Read the lines from the poem and answer the questions.

1. *I'd sail my yacht around the rings...*
   a. Which place is the speaker talking about?
      i. A lake ii. Space iii. The sea
   b. What rings does he refer to?
      i. Boxing rings ii. Rings around Saturn
      iii. Rings worn by a lady on her fingers
2. *I dream of sailing out to space,*
   To catch a star or two.
   a. What is the speaker's dream?
      i. To go on a cruise ii. To travel to space iii. To travel around the world
   b. What does he wish to do while fulfilling his dream?
      i. To catch stars ii. To see wild animals iii. To visit famous places

B. Answer the questions.

1. What is the yacht in the poet's dream made of?
2. How are the masts fixed to the yacht?
3. What is used to make sails for the yacht?
4. Write a brief description of the yacht as described by the poet.
5. Draw your own spaceship in which you would travel and describe it. How far would you go in your spaceship?

Life Skills and Values

Imagination

1. Imagination is the basis of all discoveries and inventions. Do you agree? Give reasons to support your answer.
2. Long, long ago, before spaceships were invented, scientists only imagined what travelling in space would feel like. How did their imagination help them invent and discover new things?

VOCABULARY

Rhyme scheme

- The rhyme scheme is the pattern in which the ends of lines in a poem rhyme.
- To write the rhyme scheme of a poem, we use letters in alphabetical order to show which lines rhyme with each other.
- The end of the first line is marked **a**.
- If the next line rhymes with the line marked **a**, it will also be marked **a**. Otherwise, it will be marked **b**.
- All the rhyming lines are marked with the same letter. For example:

I dream of sailing out to space, **a**
Upon a yacht of stars. **b**
With port holes all along the sides, **c**
I'd gaze amazed at Mars. **b**

The words *stars* (second line) and *Mars* (fourth line) rhyme with each other. The rhyme scheme of this stanza is **abcb**.

A. Read the poem and write its rhyme scheme.

Twinkle, twinkle, little star,
How I wonder what you are.
Up above the world so high,
Like a diamond in the sky.
Twinkle, twinkle, little star,
How I wonder what you are!

B. Now write a stanza (four lines) on any topic with the rhyme scheme *abab*.

ACTIVITY

A colony on Mars

Space scientists have been studying the planet Mars for a long time. They are studying the possibility of human beings living on Mars.

Make a chart or a scrapbook titled *Living as Martians*. Include the following information in it with relevant illustrations:

- How far is Mars from Earth?
- Why do scientists think that living on Mars may be possible?
- What problems do you think we may face on Mars?

Draw what you think a human colony on Mars will look like.

PROJECT 2

FASCINATING MOONS

The moon is the brightest object in the night sky. It is also the Earth's only natural satellite. A satellite is an object moving around a planet.

Do you know some planets in our solar system have several moons, while two of them don't have any moons at all?

Find out the following information using the Internet, books, newspapers, etc. and make a chart.

1. What are the names of the planets in the solar system?
2. How many moons does each planet have?
3. Which is the biggest moon in the solar system?
4. Which is the smallest moon in the solar system?
5. Who were the first people to land on our moon?
6. When did they land there?

MATHEMATICS

1. Measurement 69

2. Time 81

3. Average 92

4. Profit and Loss 97

5. Geometry 105

Assessment 1 116

6. Area and Perimeter 117

7. Volume and Nets 127

8. Data Handling 134

9. Symmetry 143

10. Mapping Skills 151

Assessment 2 158

Comprehensive Assessment 160

Answers 162

1 Measurement

Learning Objectives

- To relate different units of measurements
- To express length in mm, cm, m, km and other higher units
- To express mass in mg, g, kg and other higher units
- To express capacity in mℓ, ℓ and other higher units
- To carry out the basic operations on measurement and solve word problems
- To learn how to estimate measures

RELATING DIFFERENT UNITS OF MEASUREMENTS

Given below are tables showing the place value system for different units of length, mass and capacity.

In addition to the basic units such as metre for length, gram for mass and litre for capacity, there are other units that help to convert units from smaller to bigger units and vice versa.

Units of length		
Milli (m)	Millimetre (mm)	$\frac{1}{1000}$ of a metre
Centi (c)	Centimetre (cm)	$\frac{1}{100}$ of a metre
Deci (d)	Decimetre (dm)	$\frac{1}{10}$ of a metre
Basic unit		Metre (m)
Deca (da)	Decametre (dam)	10 metres
Hecto (h)	Hectometre (hm)	100 metres
Kilo (k)	Kilometre (km)	1000 metres

Units of mass		
Milli (m)	Milligram (mg)	$\frac{1}{1000}$ of a gram
Centi (c)	Centigram (cg)	$\frac{1}{100}$ of a gram
Deci (d)	Decigram (dg)	$\frac{1}{10}$ of a gram
Basic unit		Gram (g)
Deca (da)	Decagram (dag)	10 grams
Hecto (h)	Hectogram (hg)	100 grams
Kilo (k)	Kilogram (kg)	1000 grams

Units of capacity		
Milli (m)	Millilitre (mℓ)	$\frac{1}{1000}$ of a litre
Centi (c)	Centilitre (cℓ)	$\frac{1}{100}$ of a litre
Deci (d)	Decilitre (dℓ)	$\frac{1}{10}$ of a litre
Basic unit		Litre (ℓ)
Deca (da)	Decalitre (daℓ)	10 litres
Hecto (h)	Hectolitre (hℓ)	100 litres
Kilo (k)	Kilolitre (kℓ)	1000 litres

MEASUREMENT OF LENGTH, MASS AND CAPACITY

Converting from Higher Units to Lower Units

× 10   × 10   × 10   × 10   × 10   × 10

Thousands	Hundreds	Tens	Ones	Tenths	Hundredths	Thousandths
kilo (km, kg, kℓ)	hecto (hm, hg, hℓ)	deca (dam, dag, daℓ)	metre gram litre (m,g,ℓ)	deci (dm, dg, dℓ)	centi (cm, cg, cℓ)	milli (mm, mg, mℓ)

To convert higher units to lower units, multiply by 10, 100, 1000, etc.

Examples

(a) 67 km 50 cm = __________ cm

1 km = 1,00,000 cm (5 jumps of 10 each make it 1,00,000)

67 km = 67 × 1,00,000 = 67,00,000 cm

Now, on adding the centimetre, you get:

67 km 50 cm = 67,00,000 + 50 = 67,00,050 cm

(b) 4 g 3 dg 2 cg = __________ mg

1 g = 1000 mg (3 jumps of 10 each make it 1000)

1 dg = 100 mg (2 jumps of 10 each make it 100)

1 cg = 10 mg (1 jump of 10 makes it 10)

So, 4 g = 4 × 1000 mg = 4000 mg

3 dg = 3 × 100 mg = 300 mg

2 cg = 2 × 10 mg = 20 mg

On adding them all, you get:

4 g 3 dg 2 cg = 4000 + 300 + 20 = 4320 mg

(c) 2 kℓ 5 hℓ = __________ ℓ

1 kℓ = 1000 ℓ (3 jumps of 10 each make it 1000)

2 kℓ = 2 × 1000 = 2000 ℓ

1 hℓ = 100 ℓ (2 jumps of 10 each make it 100)

5 hℓ = 5 × 100 = 500 ℓ

On adding the two, you get:

2 kℓ 5 hℓ = 2000 ℓ + 500 ℓ = 2500 ℓ

Converting from Lower Units to Higher Units

To convert lower units to higher units divide by 10, 100, 1000, etc.

(a) 45 cm = __________ km

1,00,000 cm = 1 km

45 cm = 45 ÷ 1,00,000

= 0.00045 km

(b) 15 cg 212 mg = __________ g

100 cg = 1 g; 1,000 mg = 1 g

15 cg = $\frac{15}{100}$ g; 212 mg = $\frac{212}{1000}$ g

15 cg 212 mg = 0.15 g + 0.212 g = 0.150 + 0.212 = 0.362 g

Thus, 15 cg 212 mg = 0.362 g

(c) 5 dℓ 4 cℓ = __________ ℓ

10 dℓ = 1 ℓ and 100 cℓ = 1 ℓ

Therefore, 5 dℓ = $\frac{5}{10}$ ℓ = 0.5 ℓ and 4 cℓ = $\frac{4}{100}$ ℓ = 0.04 ℓ

On adding the two, you get:

= 0.50 ℓ + 0.04 ℓ (converting into like decimals)

= 0.54 ℓ

5 dℓ 4 cℓ = 0.54 ℓ

Exercise 1.1

1 Fill in the blanks.

(a) Height of a postbox = 165 cm = __________ mm

(b) Width of a river = 1.2 km = __________ m

(c) Length of an umbrella = 75 cm = __________ m

(d) Length of a book rack = 245 cm = __________ m

2 Convert the following.

(a) 3000 mm to cm (b) 8 km 16 cm to cm (c) 879 dm to hm

(d) 27 dag to mg (e) 924 mg to kg (f) 394 dg to dag

(g) 12 daℓ to mℓ (h) 7 kℓ to dℓ (i) 2 dℓ 7 cℓ to ℓ

3 Write the weight of each of the following objects as directed.

(a) 

0.045 kg in g

(b) 

0.7 kg in g

(c) 

150 g in kg

(d) 

715 g in kg

4 Write the capacity of each of the following as directed.

(a) 

0.22 ℓ in mℓ

(b) 

5.25 ℓ in mℓ

(c) 

325 mℓ in ℓ

(d) 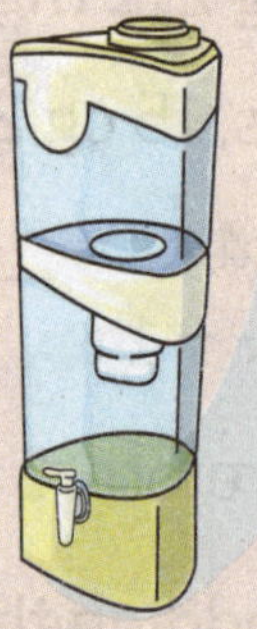

5,250 mℓ in ℓ

ADDITION AND SUBTRACTION

To add or subtract the measurements first convert all the measurements into the same unit and then add or subtract.

1. Add the following.

(a) 54 m + 25 m 7 cm

	m	cm
	54	0
+	25	7
	79	7

Therefore, 54 m + 25 m 7 cm = 79 m 7 cm

(b) 3 kg 425 g + 35 kg 5 g + 192 kg + 23 kg 55 g (Express your answer in kg.)

3 kg 425 g = 3.425 kg

35 kg 5 g = 35.005 kg

192 kg = 192.000 kg

23 kg 55 g = 23.055 kg

$$\begin{array}{r} 3.425 \\ +\ 35.005 \\ +\ 192.000 \\ +\ 23.055 \\ \hline 253.485 \\ \hline \end{array}$$

3 kg 425 g + 35 kg 5 g + 192 kg + 23 kg 55 g = 253.485 kg

(c) 9 ℓ 650 mℓ + 15 ℓ 375 mℓ

	ℓ	mℓ
	9	650
+	15	375
	25	025

Therefore, 9 ℓ 650 mℓ + 15 ℓ 375 mℓ = 25 ℓ 25 mℓ

2. Subtract the following.

(a) 76 m – 45 m 75 cm

$$\begin{array}{rrrr} \text{m} & & \text{cm} & \\ & & 9 & \\ & 5 & \cancel{10} & 10 \\ 7 & \cancel{6} & \cancel{0} & \cancel{0} \\ -4 & 5 & 7 & 5 \\ \hline 3 & 0 & 2 & 5 \\ \hline \end{array}$$

Therefore, 76 m – 45 m 75 cm = 30 m 25 cm

(b) 17 g 56 mg from 25 g 4 mg
(Express your answer in mg.)

17 g 56 mg = 17,056 mg

25 g 4 mg = 25,004 mg

Write the smaller number below the bigger number and then subtract.

$$\begin{array}{rrrrr} & \cancel{14} & 9 & 9 & \\ 1 & \cancel{4} & \cancel{10} & \cancel{10} & 14 \\ \cancel{2} & \cancel{5} & \cancel{0} & \cancel{0} & \cancel{4} \\ -1 & 7 & 0 & 5 & 6 \\ \hline 0 & 7 & 9 & 4 & 8 \\ \hline \end{array}$$

Therefore, 25,004 mg – 17,056 mg = 7948 mg

(c) 8 ℓ 750 mℓ − 3 ℓ 300 mℓ

8 ℓ 750 mℓ − 3 ℓ 300 mℓ = 5 ℓ 450 mℓ

	ℓ	mℓ
	8	750
−	3	300
	5	450

MULTIPLICATION AND DIVISION

1. Multiply the following.

(a) 4 hm 2 dam 3 dm × 6 (Express your answer in hm.)

4 hm 2 dam 3 dm = 4000 dm + 200 dm + 3 dm = 4203 dm

1000 dm = 1 hm

Therefore, 4203 dm = 4203 ÷ 1000 = 4.203 hm

4.203 hm × 6 = 25.218 hm

$$\begin{array}{r} 4.203 \\ \times\quad 6 \\ \hline 25.218 \\ \hline \end{array}$$

(b) 32 g 340 mg × 4 (Express your answer in g.)

32 g 340 mg = 32,000 mg + 340 mg = 32340 mg

1000 mg = 1 g

Therefore, 32,340 mg = 32,340 ÷ 1000 = 32.34 g

32.34 g × 4 = 129.36 g

$$\begin{array}{r} 32.34 \\ \times\quad 4 \\ \hline 129.36 \\ \hline \end{array}$$

(c) 46 ℓ 400 mℓ × 5 (Express your answer in ℓ.)

46 ℓ 400 mℓ = 46,000 mℓ + 400 mℓ = 46,400 mℓ

1000 mℓ = 1 ℓ

Therefore, 46,400 ÷ 1000 = 46.4 ℓ

46.4 ℓ × 5 = 232 ℓ

$$\begin{array}{r} 46.4 \\ \times\quad 5 \\ \hline 232.0 \\ \hline \end{array}$$

(d) 8996 mℓ ÷ 4 (Express your answer in ℓ.)

1000 mℓ = 1 ℓ

Therefore, 8996 mℓ = 8996 ÷ 1000

= 8.996 ℓ

8.996 ℓ ÷ 4 = 2.249 ℓ

$$\begin{array}{r} 2.249 \\ 4\overline{)8.996} \\ 8 \\ \hline 9 \\ 8 \\ \hline 19 \\ 16 \\ \hline 36 \\ 36 \\ \hline 00 \end{array}$$

Exercise 1.2

1 **Add the following.**

(a) 23 m + 10 m 3 cm
(b) 4 kg 250 g + 3 kg 950 g
(c) 1 ℓ 300 mℓ + 850 mℓ
(d) 9 cm 4 mm + 2 cm 7 mm
(e) 1 kg 450 g + 1 kg 650 g
(f) 3 ℓ 500 mℓ + 5 ℓ 700 mℓ

2 **Subtract the following.**

(a) 15 m – 7 m 40 cm
(b) 3 kg 350 g – 1 kg 450 g
(c) 5 ℓ 400 mℓ – 3 ℓ 250 mℓ
(d) 6 cm 4 mm – 4 cm 8 mm
(e) 6 kg – 2 kg 750 g
(f) 10 ℓ 500 mℓ – 2 ℓ 750 mℓ

3 **Multiply the following.**

(a) 3 hm 3 dam 5 dm × 7 (Express your answer in hm.)
(b) 76 g 250 mg × 3 (Express your answer in g.)
(c) 45 km 37 m × 13 (Express your answer in m.)
(d) 5678 mm × 45 (express in m)
(e) 3987 g × 18 (to dag)
(f) 12.34 hℓ × 56 (in hℓ)

4 **Divide the following.**

(a) 4773 mℓ ÷ 3
(b) 10800 kg ÷ 12
(c) 954 g ÷ 9
(d) 12 km 300 m ÷ 5 (Express your answer in m.)
(e) 76125 m by 25 (Express in km)
(f) 52344 mg by 18 (in gm)

Basic Operations

(a) A victory stand in a school measures as shown in the figure below. What is the height of the stand in millimetres and the length of the base in centimetres?

The height of the stand = 1.15 m + 1.15 m = 2.30 m

1 m = 1000 mm

2.30 m = 2.30 × 1000 = 2300 mm

So, the height of the stand is 2300 mm

The length of the base = 1.45 m + 1.45 m + 1.45 m = 4.35 m

4.35 m = 4.35 × 100 cm =4.35 cm

So, the length of the base of the stand is 435 cm.

Winners of a karate competition

(b) A mouse weighs 3.485 kg lesser than a cat. If the cat weighs 4.5 kg, what is the weight of the mouse in grams?

The weight of the mouse = 4.5 kg − 3.485 kg

$$\begin{array}{r} 4.\overset{4}{\cancel{5}}\overset{\overset{9}{\cancel{10}}}{\cancel{0}}\overset{10}{\cancel{0}} \\ -\,3.4\,8\,5 \\ \hline 1.0\,1\,5 \\ \hline \end{array}$$

The weight of the mouse in kilograms = 1.015 kg

1 kg = 1000 g

Therefore, 1.015 kg = 1.015 × 1000 g = 1015 g

So, the weight of mouse in grams is 1015 g.

(c) If each pearl in this bangle is 3 mm long and there are 38 pearls in it, then what is the length of the bangle? Express in centimetres.

The length of each pearl = 3 mm

The length of the bangle in millimetres = 38 × 3 = 114 mm

10 mm = 1 cm

114 mm = 114 ÷ 10 = 11.4 cm

Therefore, the bangle is 11.4 cm long.

(d) How many mugs of capacity 75 mℓ can be used to fill a flask of 3.75 ℓ?

The capacity of the flask = 3.75 ℓ

1 ℓ = 1000 mℓ

3.75 ℓ = 3.75 × 1000 mℓ = 3750 mℓ

The capacity of the coffee mug = 75 mℓ

Divide 3750 mℓ by 75 mℓ to find how many coffee mugs can fill the jug.

3750 ÷ 75 = 50

Therefore, 50 coffee cups will fill the jug.

Exercise 1.3

1. A circular athletic track measures 525 m. How many kilometres will the athletes run if they were to run 4 rounds of the track?

2. A tortoise moved 250 m in 1 hour, 265 m in the second hour and 245 m in the third hour. How many kilometres did it move in 3 hours?

3. A kangaroo hops to a height of 1 m 8 cm and moves a distance of 2 m 50 cm in one hop. What is the difference between the height and the distance it covers?

4. A sweet box has 3 kg sweets in it. If each piece of sweet weighs 50 g, how many sweets are there in the box?

5. A box made of iron weighs 70 kg. A suitcase of clothes is 2500 g lighter than the box. What is the weight of the suitcase in grams?

6. A pair of shoes weighs 1250 g. A shoe rack can hold a weight of 10 kg in it. How many pairs of shoes of 1250 g can be kept in the rack?

7. 2 kg of potatoes were brought for the potato-picking race. If each potato weighs 25 g, how many potatoes are there in 2 kg?

8. A bucket holds 15 litres of water. If a family uses 5 buckets a day, how many millilitres of water do they use?

9. Pammi is making soup. She took 15 glasses of water. If the capacity of one glass is 150 mℓ, how many litres of water did she use? Will a 3 ℓ pan be enough to make the soup?

10. A camel can drink 120 ℓ of water at one time. How many buckets of water will be needed to satisfy its thirst if each bucket can hold 10 ℓ of water?

ESTIMATING MEASURES

In real life, measures are usually estimated. To estimate measures, we must know the real measures of objects in our surroundings.

To estimate any measure, compare it with a known measure.

Look at the following examples.

The thickness of a pencil lead: about 1 mm

The length of an ant: about 1 cm

The weight of a feather: about 1 mg

The weight of a cake: about 1 kg

Exercise 1.4

Circle the most appropriate options for the objects shown below.

1	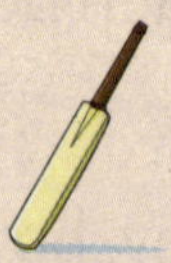 The length of a cricket bat	90 mm	90 cm	9 m
2	 The length of a fire engine	80 cm	8 m	80 mm
3	 The weight of a pair of spectacles	150 g	150 kg	15 g
4	 The weight of a key	30 g	300 g	2 kg
5	 The capacity of an earthen lamp	1 mℓ	10 mℓ	1 ℓ
6	 The capacity of an ice cream cup	250 mℓ	2 ℓ	20 mℓ

Revision Exercise

1 Choose the correct option for each of the following.

(a) 1 km 25 m = __________

(i) 1250 m (ii) 1250 cm (iii) 1250 mm (iv) 1025 m

(b) 6.5 cm = __________

(i) 65 km (ii) 65 mm (iii) 6.5 mm (iv) 6.5 m

(c) 2250 mℓ = __________

(i) 2.250 ℓ (ii) 22 ℓ 50 mℓ (iii) 2.25 kℓ (iv) 225 ℓ

(d) 6.002 kg = __________

(i) 6 kg 200 g (ii) 620 g (iii) 6 kg 20 g (iv) 6 kg 2 g

(e) 8750 g = __________

(i) 8.750 kg (ii) 87.50 kg (iii) 87 kg 50 g (iv) 8 kg 75 g

2 Lionel is 74 cm tall. His mother is 103 cm taller than him but 12 cm shorter than Lionel's father. How tall is Lionel's father?

3 Mrs Sharma has 3 ropes of different colours. The red rope is 2 m shorter than the black rope and the green rope is 150 cm longer than the black rope. The length of the black rope is 2 times of 4 m. Find the total length of all the ropes both in metres and centimetres.

4 The table given below shows distances travelled by 4 boys on their bicycles.

Name of the Boys	Distance Travelled
Ali	1 km 5 m
Benny	1 km 50 m
Cheng Yi	1500 m
Deepak	1005 m

(a) Who rode the longest distance? (b) Who rode the least distance?

5 **The weights of different balls are given in the table below.**

Football	Baseball	Golf ball	Tennis ball	Basketball
0.426 kg	0.142 kg	0.045 kg	0.057 kg	0.6 kg

(a) What is the weight of all the balls together?

(b) Convert all the kilogram weights into grams.

(c) Which ball is the heaviest?

(d) Which ball is the lightest?

(e) What is the difference in the weights of the football and the tennis ball?

6 Mr Hari's family requires 125 litres of water in a day. The capacity of the overhead tank in his house is 1000 litres. If he fills the tank once in a week, can the family use it for the whole week?

7 **Circle the correct unit.**

(a) A tetra packet of drink contains 500 — ℓ mℓ g

(b) A laptop weighs about 4 — kg m g

(c) The width of a forefinger is about 3 — cm mm m

(d) A tea kettle holds about 2 — mℓ m ℓ

(e) A basket of flowers weighs about 500 — kg ℓ g

HOTS (Higher Order Thinking Skills)

There are 10 bags full of coins. Each bag contains 1000 coins. But there is one bag that has forged coins. Each real coin weighs 1 g and each forged coin weighs 1.1 g. How will you find the bag of forged coins? You are allowed to weigh only once.

(***Hint:*** Take 1 coin from Bag 1, 2 coins from Bag 2, 3 coins from Bag 3 and so on.)

2 Time

Learning Objectives

- To convert one unit of time into another
- To learn addition and subtraction of time
- To find the time duration

Let's Get Started

The outline map of India is given below. The time taken to reach Chennai from New Delhi, Mumbai and Bengaluru in a train and in an aeroplane are indicated.

(a) How much time (in days and hours) does it take to reach Chennai from New Delhi by train?

(b) If Santosh flies from Mumbai on Monday at 10:30 a.m., when will he reach Chennai? Write the time using a.m. or p.m.

(c) Nupur took a flight from Bengaluru at 5:00 p.m. When did she reach Chennai? Write the time using 24-hour clock.

(d) John flew from New Delhi and reached Chennai at 3:40 p.m. When did the flight take off from New Delhi?

(e) If the train from Bengaluru starts at 6:00 a.m., at what time will it reach Chennai?

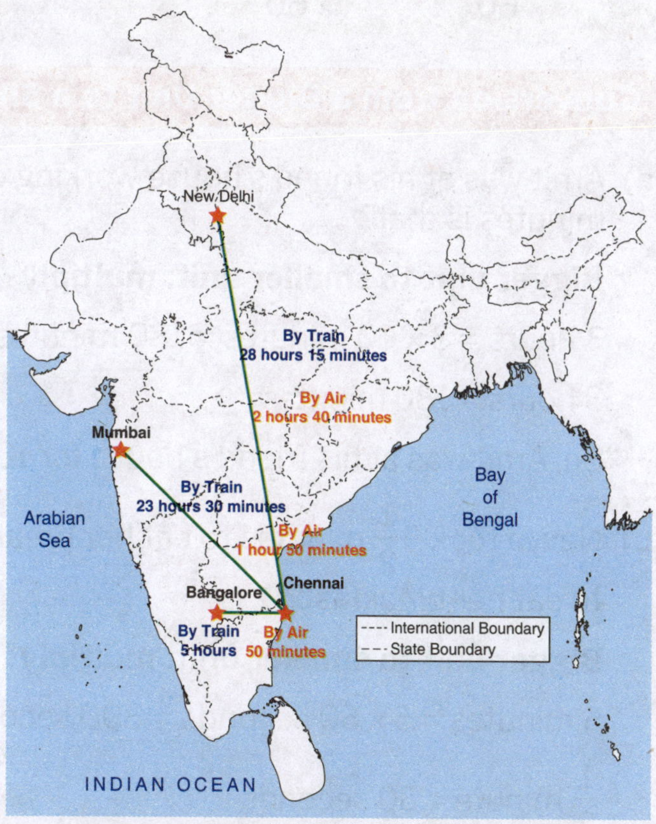

To Chennai	From Delhi	From Mumbai	From Bengaluru
By train			
By air			

TIME

You may have seen some clocks with three hands. The third hand is the second hand, the others being the minute hand and the hour hand.

When the second hand goes around the clock once, 1 minute passes by.

Different units of time can also be converted into one another just like the units of measurement.

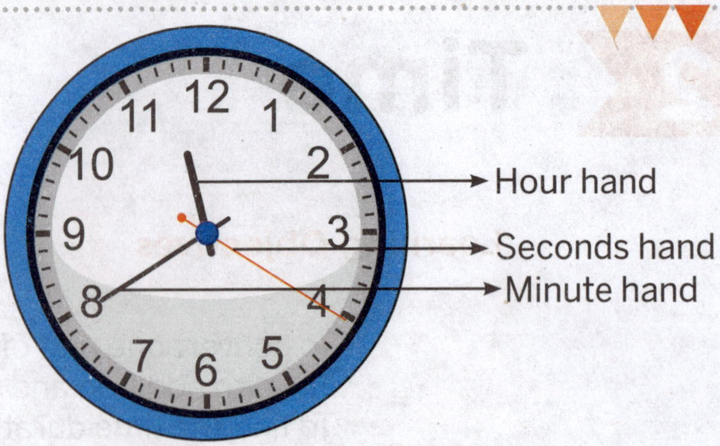

1 hour = 60 minutes   1 minute = 60 seconds

Bigger unit to smaller unit – multiply

Hours → Minutes → Seconds

$\times 60$ $\times 60$

Smaller unit to bigger unit – divide

Seconds → Minutes → Hours

$\div 60$ $\div 60$

Conversion from a Bigger Unit to a Smaller Unit

(a) Amit was at his friend's house working on a project for 3 hours. How many minutes is that?

Bigger unit to smaller unit: multiply

3 hours = 3×60 minutes = 180 minutes

3 hours = 180 minutes

So, Amit was at his friend's house for 180 minutes.

(b) Navya took $5\frac{1}{2}$ minutes to eat her breakfast. How many seconds did she take to eat her breakfast?

Bigger unit to smaller unit: multiply

5 minutes = 5×60 seconds = 300 seconds

$\frac{1}{2}$ minute = 30 seconds

$5\frac{1}{2}$ minutes = 300 + 30 = 330

$5\frac{1}{2}$ minutes = 330 seconds

Navya ate her breakfast in 330 seconds.

Conversion from a Smaller Unit to a Bigger Unit

(a) Shuka was painting for 120 minutes. How many hours is that?

Smaller unit to bigger unit: divide

120 minutes = (120 ÷ 60) hours = 2 hours

120 minutes = 2 hours

So, Shuka was painting for 2 hours.

$$\begin{array}{r|l} & 2 \rightarrow \text{hours} \\ 60 & 120 \\ & \underline{12} \\ & 000 \end{array}$$

(b) Hema blew 10 balloons in 600 seconds. How many minutes is that?

Smaller unit to bigger unit: divide

600 seconds = (600 ÷ 60) minutes = ________

600 seconds = ________ minutes

Hema blew 10 balloons in ________ minutes.

$$\begin{array}{r|l} & 10 \rightarrow \text{minutes} \\ 60 & 600 \\ & \underline{60} \\ & 000 \end{array}$$

Remember: 12 noon or 12 midnight is also written as 12'o clock.

Exercise 2.1

1 **Choose the correct unit of time (hours/minutes/seconds). One has been done for you.**

(a) Making instant noodles = <u>2 minutes</u>

(b) Taking one breath = 2 ________

(c) Climbing 20 stairs = 5 ________

(d) Eating dinner with family = 30 ________

(e) Writing an exam = 2 ________

2 **Convert the following into minutes.**

(a) 6 hours (b) 8 hours 15 minutes (c) 9 hours

(d) 4 hours 34 minutes (e) 10 hours (f) $7\frac{3}{4}$ hours

3 **Convert the following into hours and minutes.**

(a) 300 minutes (b) 348 minutes (c) 280 minutes

(d) 100 minutes (e) 540 minutes (f) 210 minutes

4 **Convert the following into seconds.**

(a) 25 minutes (b) 50 minutes (c) $15\frac{1}{4}$ minutes

(d) $12\frac{3}{4}$ minutes (e) 11 minutes (f) 33 minutes

5 **Convert the following into minutes and seconds.**

(a) 500 seconds (b) 420 seconds (c) 234 seconds

(d) 158 seconds (e) 760 seconds

ADDITION AND SUBTRACTION OF TIME

Addition

Sheeja took 1 h 30 min to cook the food and 45 min to clean the kitchen. What is the total time taken by Sheeja to finish cooking and cleaning?

Time taken for cooking = 1 h 30 min

Time taken for cleaning = 45 min

Total time taken = 1 h 30 min + 45 min = 1 h 75 min

75 min = 60 min + 15 min = 1 h 15 min

∴ 1 h 75 min = 1 h + 1 h 15 min = 2 h 15 min

h	min
1	30
− 0	45
1	75

75 min → 15 min, 60 min → 1 h

60 min = 1 h

Therefore, Sheeja took 2 h 15 min to finish cooking and cleaning.

Examples: Add the following.

(a) 20 min 15 s + 12 min 50 s

min	s
20	15
− 12	50
32	65

60 s = 1 min

∴ 20 min 15 s + 12 min 50 s = 32 min 65 s = 33 min 5 s

(b) 15 years 9 months + 12 years 7 months

Years	Months
15	9
− 12	7
27	16

12 months = 1 year

∴ 15 years 9 months + 12 years 7 months = 27 years 16 months = 28 years 4 months

Subtraction

Examples: Subtract the following.

(a) 20 min – 15 min 15 s

	min	s
	19 / ~~20~~	60 / ~~00~~
–	15	15
	04	45

∴ 20 min – 15 min 15 s = 4 min 45 s

(b) 12 years 5 months – 7 years 7 months

	Years	Months
	11 / ~~20~~	17 / ~~5~~
–	7	7
	04	10

∴ 12 years 5 months – 7 years 7 months = 4 years 10 months

Exercise 2.2

1 Add the following.

(a) 3 min 20 s + 2 min 30 s

(b) 2 h 45 min + 1 h 35 min

(c) 9 years 5 months + 7 years 10 months

(d) 4 min 30 s + 4 min 30 s

(e) 5 h 20 min + 55 min

(f) 4 years 11 months + 10 months

2 Subtract the following.

(a) 10 min – 8 min 23 s

(b) 6 h 45 min – 5 h 55 min

(c) 11 years 7 months – 3 years 4 months

(d) 10 years 2 months – 5 years 8 months

STARTING TIME AND FINISHING TIME

Finding the Finishing Time

- Rajan started writing a story at 7:20 p.m. He finished it after 2 hours 15 minutes. What was the time when he finished his story?

  Starting time + Time period = Finishing time

  The time spent on an activity or an event is called its duration or time period.

  To find the finishing time, count forward from the start time.

  7:20 p.m. + 2 hours 15 minutes

Break up the time period to make it easier to add.

7:20 p.m. + 2 hours = 9:20 p.m.

9:20 p.m. + 15 minutes = 9:35 p.m.

So, Rajan finished his story at 9:35 p.m.

Finding the Starting Time

- Asif is drawing pictures for Rajan's story. He took 4 hours 10 minutes to draw the pictures. If he finished drawing at 2:40 p.m., at what time did he start?

  Finishing time – Time period = Starting time

  You are given the time period and the finishing time. To find the start time, count backwards from the finishing time.

  2:40 p.m. – 4 hours 10 minutes = ________________

  Break up the time period to make it easier to subtract.

  2:40 p.m. – 2 hours = 12:40 p.m.

  12:40 p.m. – 2 hours = 10:40 a.m.

  10:40 a.m. – 10 minutes = 10:30 a.m.

  So, Asif sarted drawing at 10:30 a.m.

FINDING THE NUMBER OF DAYS

Some events or activities last longer than 24 hours. Then you have to find the number of days the event or the activity lasted.

Finding the Finishing Date

- The London 2012 Summer Olympics started on 27th July and went on for 17 days. When did it get over?

  Starting date + Time period = Finishing date

  To find the finishing date, count forward from the start date.

  Starting with 27th July, calculate 17 days.

  Break up the number of days to make it easier to add.

  27th July to 31st July = 5 days (You have to include 27th July when you count because the games began on that day. So, counting from 27th to 31st you get 5 days.)

  1st August to 12th August = 12 days

  The London 2012 Summer Olympics got over on 12th August.

Finding the Starting Date

- The Rio de Janeiro 2016 Olympics ended on 21st August. It lasted for 17 days. On what date did it begin?

  Finishing date – Time period = Starting date

  To find the finishing date, count backward from the start date.

  21st August – 17 days

  Break up the number of days to make it easier to subtract.

  21st August to 12th August = 10 days

  11th August to 5th August = 7 days

  The Rio de Janeiro 2016 Olympics started on 5th August 2016.

Exercise 2.3

1 Write the finishing time using a.m. or p.m.

(a) 2 hours after 1:20 a.m.
(b) 45 min after 5:45 p.m.
(c) 4 hours 35 min after 7:05 a.m.
(d) 1 hour 10 min after 12 noon
(e) 5 hours 20 min after 6:40 p.m.
(f) 2 hours 50 min after 10:50 p.m.

2 Write the starting time using a.m. or p.m.

(a) 25 min before 3:05 p.m.
(b) 6 hours 30 min before 9:20 p.m.
(c) 5 hours 15 min before 12 midnight
(d) 3 hours 10 min before 4:20 a.m.
(e) 7 hours 40 min before 11:10 a.m.
(f) 6 hours 9 min before 3:12 a.m.

REAL-LIFE APPLICATIONS

Festival Shopping

Karan, Kirti and their sister Neha are going for shopping with their parents for the coming festival. They left home at 10:15 a.m. and drove to the biggest mall in the city. They reached the mall at 11:00 a.m. They went into a clothing store and bought clothes for all. When they finished shopping, it was 12:25 p.m. They window shopped at the mall for some more time and then went to the top floor for juice and cold drinks. They spent half an hour there. When they left the mall, it was 1:45 p.m. As they were hungry, they drove to a restaurant for lunch. From the restaurant, they left for the footwear shop and reached there at 3:10 p.m. The parents bought footwear for all three children and headed home. They reached home at 5:15 p.m.

(a) How much time did they spend from the time they left home and finished shopping for clothes?

Time taken to reach the mall = 45 minutes (From 10:15 a.m. to 11:00 a.m.)

Time spent in shopping for clothes = 1 hour 25 minutes

(From 11:00 a.m. to 12:25 p.m.)

Total time spent = 45 min + 1 h 25 min

(45 min + 25 min = 70 min = 60 min + 10 min = 1 h 10 min)

= 1 h + 1 h 10 min = 2 h 10 min

They spent 2 hours 10 minutes.

(b) After how many hours of leaving the mall did they reach the footwear shop?

Time when they left the mall = 1:45 p.m.

Time when they reached the footwear shop = 3:10 p.m.

Time interval between 1:45 p.m. and 3:10 p.m. = 3:10 p.m. – 1:45 p.m.

(Since the number of minutes is not enough in 3:10, borrow from the hour. Borrowing an hour (60 minutes) from 3 we get 2 hours 70 minutes.)

2 h 70 min – 1 h 45 min = (2 h – 1 h) + (70 min –45 min) = 1 h 25 min

So, the time taken between leaving the mall and reaching the footwear shop is 1 h 25 min.

(c) Karan and Kirti, the twins, are 11 years and 1 month old. Their sister Neha is 5 years and 7 months old. What is the difference between their ages?

Difference between their ages = 11 years 1 month – 5 years 7 months

It is easier to subtract years and months separately. Since the number of months is not enough in 11 years 1 month, borrow 1 year from the year. Borrowing a year (12 months) from 11 years you get 10 years 13 months.

= 10 years 13 months – 5 years 7 months
= (10 years – 5 years) + (13 months – 7 months) = 5 years 6 months

So, the difference between Neha's age and the twins' age is 5 years and 6 months.

Exercise 2.4

Solve the following word problems.

1. Sandhya attended a party which lasted for 4 hours. How many minutes did Sandhya spend at the party?

2. Rupa lit 15 candles in $2\frac{1}{4}$ minutes. How many seconds did she take? How many candles can she light in $4\frac{1}{2}$ minutes?

Park

3. Mr Singh's family went to a beach on Sunday. After spending 4 hour 45 minutes in the beach, they visited a park. If they spent 1 hour 45 minutes there, how many hours did they spend outside their home on Sunday?

4. Christine was the winner of the reading competition. If the runner-up took 2 minutes 24 seconds to read the passage and Christine beat her by 20 seconds, how much time did Christine take?

5. The surgery that started at 6:20 a.m. went on for 3 hours 20 minutes. At what time did it get over?

6. Mithun dropped a seed into an empty pot on 3rd May. After 17 days, he saw a sapling growing in the pot. On what date did he see the sapling?

7. Summer season in the Antarctic is from October through February and winter is from March through September. How many months of summer and winter does the Antarctic have?

8. The fire-fighters arrived at a burning building and got the fire under control in 45 minutes. If the fire was doused by 12:10 p.m., when did the fire-fighters arrive?

9. A potter took 3 hours 20 minutes to make the earthen pots. If he started at 6 a.m., when did he finish?

10. The young girl at the beach worked on the sand for 5 hours and 50 minutes and created a beautiful castle. If she finished by 1:10 p.m., at what time did she start?

Revision Exercise

1 State whether the following statements are true (T) or false (F).

(a) To convert a smaller unit of time to a bigger unit of time, you should divide. ☐

(b) The second hand is the slowest moving hand on the clock. ☐

(c) When the second hand moves around the clock once, five minutes have passed. ☐

(d) 1 hour has 3600 seconds. ☐

(e) 48 hours make two days. ☐

2 Match the following.

(a) 5:20 a.m.	(i) 1956 hours
(b) 11:15 p.m.	(ii) 0830 hours
(c) 7:56 p.m.	(iii) 1417 hours
(d) 8:30 a.m.	(iv) 0520 hours
(e) 2:17 p.m.	(v) 2315 hours

3 Complete the tables.

(a)

Hours	Minutes	Seconds
$2\frac{1}{4}$		8100
	105	
		7200

(b)

Starting Time	Duration	Finishing Time
11:15 a.m.	1 h 40 min	
	4 h 20 min	3:35 p.m.
12:05 p.m.		5:45 p.m.

(c)

Starting Date	Duration	Finishing Date
23rd January		25th March
15th December	30 days	
	50 days	5th July

4 Choose the correct answers.

(a) Which month is 3 months after March?

(i) July (ii) December (iii) June (iv) May

(b) What time is 4 hours after 2200 hours?

(i) 2:00 a.m. (ii) 2:00 p.m. (iii) 12 noon (iv) 12 midnight

(c) What time is 6 hours before 1:00 p.m.?

(i) 1900 hours (ii) 0800 hours (iii) 2000 hours (iv) 0700 hours

(d) How much time has passed from 2:25 p.m. to 5:15 p.m.?

(i) 2 hours 35 min (ii) 1 hour 50 min (iii) 2 hours 15 min (iv) 2 hours 50 min

(e) How many months and days are there from 17th June to 11th October?

(i) 3 months 23 days (ii) 4 months

(iii) 3 months 25 days (iv) 4 months 11 days

5 Listed below are some of the deadliest volcanoes that have erupted.

Name of the Volcano	Year of Eruption	Death Toll
Mount Etna, Italy	1669	20,000
Krakatoa, Indonesia	1883	36,417
Mount Pele, Martinique, Caribbean Island	1902	29,025
Mount St. Helens, USA	1980	57
Nevada de Ruiz Volcano, Columbia	1985	23,000
Mount Merapi, Indonesia	2010	353

(a) After how many years of Mount Etna eruption did the Krakatoa eruption take place?

(b) How many years before the Mount St. Helens eruption did the Mount Pele eruption take place?

(c) What is the difference in number of years between the Nevada de Ruiz Volcano eruption and Mount Merapi eruption?

3 Average

Learning Objectives

- To understand the basic concept of average
- To compute the average of fractions
- To solve word problems on average

Let's Get Started

Study the following information.

The average age of the students in Class 5 is 10 years.

The average height of the students in Class 5 is 120 cm.

Based on the given information, can we say that the age of each student in Class 5 is 10 years? Can we say that the height of each student in Class 5 is 120 cm? Obviously, no. Some of the students may be 9 years old, while some others may be 11 years old. A similar situation holds true for the students with respect to their heights.

However, the average age of 10 years gives us an idea about the age of students in this particular class. It is the representative value of the age of each student. The same can be said about the heights.

AVERAGE

Average is the value that is evenly distributed among a given number of quantities. Average is also called **arithmetic mean** or **mean**.

Average can be calculated using the relation:

$$\text{Average} = \frac{\text{Sum of the quantities}}{\text{Number of quantities}}$$

That means, if there are 2 quantities say *a* and *b*, then

$$\text{Average} = \frac{a+b}{2}$$

Before calculating an average, make sure that all the measurements are in the same unit.

Example 1: Find the average of 5 and 7.

$$\text{Average} = \frac{5+7}{2} = \frac{12}{2} = 6$$

Therefore, the average of 5 and 7 is 6.

Note that 6 lies in between 5 and 7.

Example 2: Find the average of 12 kg, 11 kg and 13 kg

$$\text{Average} = \frac{12+11+13}{3} = \frac{36}{3} = 12 \text{ kg}$$

Therefore, the average of 12 kg, 11 kg and 13 kg is 12 kg.

AVERAGE OF FRACTIONS

We can find the average of fractions using the same relation.

Example 1: Find the average of $\frac{1}{2}, \frac{1}{3}$ and $\frac{1}{6}$

$$\text{Average} = \frac{\frac{1}{2}+\frac{1}{3}+\frac{1}{6}}{3} = \frac{\frac{3+2+1}{6}}{3} = \frac{\frac{6}{6}}{3} = \frac{1}{3}$$

Therefore, the average of $\frac{1}{2}, \frac{1}{3}$ and $\frac{1}{6}$ is $\frac{1}{3}$.

Example 2: Find the average of $\frac{1}{2}, \frac{2}{6}, \frac{1}{4}$ and $\frac{3}{12}$

$$\text{Average} = \frac{\frac{1}{2}+\frac{2}{6}+\frac{1}{4}+\frac{3}{12}}{4} = \frac{\frac{6+4+3+3}{12}}{4} = \frac{\frac{16}{12}}{4} = \frac{\frac{4}{3}}{4} = \frac{4}{3\times4} = \frac{1}{3}$$

Therefore, the average of $\frac{1}{2}, \frac{2}{6}, \frac{1}{4}$ and $\frac{3}{12}$ is $\frac{1}{3}$.

Exercise 3.1

Find the average of the following.

1. 3, 5 and 7
2. 2.4, 3.1, 1.2 and 1.3
3. 10 g, 20 g, 30 g, 40 g and 50 g
4. 3 cm, 2.5 cm, 1.5 cm and 5 cm
5. $\frac{1}{4}$, $\frac{2}{4}$ and $\frac{1}{4}$
6. $\frac{1}{15}$, $\frac{1}{2}$ and $\frac{1}{3}$
7. $\frac{2}{5}$ and $\frac{3}{10}$
8. $\frac{1}{5}$, $\frac{1}{15}$ and $\frac{1}{10}$
9. 2, 4, 6, 8, 10 and 12
10. 1.4 kg, 2.3 kg, 3.5 kg and 4.8 kg

Word Problems on Average

Example 1: The earnings of a vendor in a week are ₹150, ₹200, ₹250, ₹185, ₹205, ₹245 and ₹235. Find his average earning per day.

To find the average earning per day, we have to find the sum of the earnings during the week and divide the sum by 7 as there are 7 days in a week.

$$\text{Average} = \frac{\text{Sum of the quantities}}{\text{Number of quantities}}$$

$$\text{Average} = \frac{150+200+250+185+205+245+235}{7} = \frac{1470}{7}$$

$$= ₹210$$

Therefore, the average earning of a vegetable vender is ₹210 per day.

Example 2: The weight of Sneha is 25 kg. The weight of Raju is 11 kg more than that of Sneha, whereas the weight of Ritha is 5 kg less than that of Sneha. Find the average weight of the three friends.

Weight of Sneha = 25 kg

Weight of Raju = 25 kg + 11 kg = 36 kg

Weight of Ritha = 25 kg − 5 kg = 20 kg

$$\text{Average} = \frac{\text{Sum of the quantities}}{\text{Number of quantities}}$$

$$\text{Average} = \frac{25+36+20}{3} = \frac{81}{3} = 27 \text{ kg}$$

Therefore, the average weight of the three friends is 27 kg.

Example 3: The average weight of Kamala and Vimala is 27 kg. If Kamala's weight is 24 kg, find the weight of Vimala.

Average weight = 27 kg

Total weight = Kamala's weight + Vimala's weight

= 27 × 2 = 54 kg

Given Kamala's weight is 24 kg

Therefore, Vimala's weight = Total weight – Kamala's weight

= 54 kg – 24 kg = 30 kg

Exercise 3.2

1. The maximum temperatures in a city from Monday to Sunday are 34.4°C, 33.2°C, 34.3°C, 35.3°C, 34.5°C, 37°C and 29.3°C respectively. What is the average temperature of the particular week?
2. The lengths of three threads are 0.5 m, 35 cm and 0.35 m. Find the average length of the threads in cm.
3. The average height of A, B and C is 120 cm. A's height is 115 cm and B's height is 125 cm. Find the height of C.
4. What is average of the first 5 odd numbers?
5. John completes $\frac{1}{5}$ parts of the whole work in a day, while Khan completes $\frac{2}{4}$ parts of whole work in a day. Find the average of the work done by John and Khan in a day.
6. Given below are the timings of the study hours of Santhu for a week.

Day	Mon	Tue	Wed	Thu	Fri	Sat	Sun
Minutes	45	50	60	55	30	35	40

   Find the average time spent by Santhu studying during that week.
7. Heera spent ₹25, ₹20, ₹15 and ₹40 from Monday to Thursday respectively. Find the average money spent by her.
8. The runs scored by a batsman in five matches are 45, 38, 75, 52 and 40. Find the average runs scored by him.

Revision Exercise

1 Find the average of the following.

(a) 12 cm and 10 cm (b) 250 ml and 1.5 *l*

(c) 100 g and 0.5 kg (d) 150 cm and 10 m

2 Match the following numbers with their averages.

(a) $\frac{1}{2}$ and $\frac{1}{5}$ (i) 13

(b) 7 and 13 (ii) 6

(c) 10, 13 and 16 (iii) $\frac{7}{20}$

(d) 4 and 8 (iv) 10

3 The marks obtained by Subhash in English, Maths and Science are 16, 26 and 24 respectively. Find the average marks scored by him.

4 Find the average of all the even numbers between 30 and 40.

5 Cross the watermelon whose weight is equal to the average weight of the five watermelons given below.

1.05 kg 1.05 kg 0.95 kg 0.95 kg 1.00 kg

HOTS (Higher Order Thinking Skills)

1. The average of three numbers is 7. The average of two among them is 6. Find the third number.

2. If the average of four fractions is $\frac{25}{48}$, then find the missing fraction.

$$\frac{1}{1}+\frac{1}{2}+(?)+\frac{1}{4}=\frac{25}{48}\times 4$$

4 Profit and Loss

Learning Objectives

- To find cost price, selling price and profit or loss
- To find the profit or loss percentage
- To learn about application of overhead expenses

PROFIT AND LOSS

Kumar is a potter. He sells designer pottery in his shop. He spends money to buy things such as clay, colour, moulds, etc. that are required in pottery. The cost of making something is called its **cost price (C.P.)**.

Kumar sells his pottery for a price that is more than the cost of making the pots. The price at which something is sold is called its **selling price (S.P.)**.

1

Cost Price = ₹275
Selling Price = ₹299

2

Cost Price = ₹435
Selling Price = ₹480

3

Cost Price = ₹573
Selling Price = ₹610

4

Cost Price = ₹580
Selling Price = ₹625

5

Cost Price = ₹647
Selling Price = ₹699

6

Cost Price = ₹163
Selling Price = ₹185

7

Cost Price = ₹251
Selling Price = ₹270

The potter was making these items and then selling them. In some cases, the shopkeeper may buy something from outside and then resell them. The price at which the item was bought is then its cost price. The price at which he sells is the item's selling price.

The cost price (C.P.) of Pot 1 is ₹275 and its selling price (S.P.) is ₹299.

Selling price (S.P.) =	₹299
Cost price (C.P.) =	– ₹275
	₹ 24 → Profit

Kumar earns ₹24 on this pot.

Here, the selling price (S.P.) is more than the cost price (C.P.), so the difference is the **profit**. The profit is also referred to as **gain**.

The lid of Pot 3 fell down and broke. Kumar had to sell it without the lid. So, he reduced its cost and sold it for ₹550 instead of selling it for ₹610.

Cost price (C.P.) =	₹573
Selling price (S.P.) =	– ₹550
	₹ 23 → Loss

Kumar lost ₹23 on this pot.

Here, the cost price (C.P.) is more than the selling price (S.P.), so the difference is the **loss**.

If S.P. > C.P., then Profit = S.P. – C.P.

If C.P. > S.P., then Loss = C.P. – S.P.

To Find the Cost Price

(a) Bindu sells handmade jewellery. If she sold one set of jewellery for ₹447 at a loss of ₹52, what was the cost of the jewellery?

Selling price (S.P.) = ₹447

Loss = ₹52

Cost price (C.P.) = Selling price (S.P.) + Loss

= ₹447 + ₹52

= ₹499

Therefore, the cost price of the jewellery was ₹499.

If Loss then, C.P. = S.P. + Loss.

If Profit then, C.P. = S.P. – Profit.

(b) Raju sold a study table for ₹2035 and made a profit of ₹350. What was its cost price?

Selling price (S.P.) = ₹2035

Profit = ₹350

Cost price (C.P.) = Selling price (S.P.) – Profit

= ₹2035 – ₹350

= ₹1685

Therefore, the cost price of the study table was ₹1685

To Find the Selling Price

(a) Altaf bought a wooden cabinet of the Mughal period for ₹31,560 and sold it for a profit of ₹2250. What was the selling price of the wooden cabinet?

Cost price (C.P.) = ₹31,560
Profit = ₹2250
Selling price (S.P.) = Cost price + Profit
= ₹31,560 + ₹2250
= ₹33,810

Therefore, Altaf sold the wooden table for ₹33,810.

(b) Casper bought a bicycle for ₹19,260 and after some years sold it for a loss of ₹4260. What was the selling price of the bicycle?

Cost price (C.P.) = ₹19,260
Loss = ₹4260
Selling price (S.P.) = Cost price (C.P.) – Loss
= ₹19,260 – ₹4260
= ₹15,000

Therefore, Casper sold the bicycle for ₹15,000.

If Profit then, S.P. = C.P. + Profit.

If Loss then, S.P. = C.P. – Loss.

Exercise 4.1

1 Complete the following tables. The first rows have been done for you.

(a)

Sl. No.	C.P.	S.P.	Profit/Loss	Profit/Loss Amount
(i)	₹5630	₹5580	S.P. < C.P. = Loss	₹50
(ii)	₹10,475	₹10,754		
(iii)	₹22,958	₹22,589		
(iv)	₹3650	₹3565		

(b)

Sl. No.	S.P.	Profit	Loss	C.P.
(i)	₹1542	—	₹200	S.P. + Loss = ₹1542 + ₹200 = ₹1742
(ii)	₹55,761	₹1700	—	
(iii)	₹4500	₹344	—	
(iv)	₹13,763	—	₹525	

(c)

Sl. No.	C.P.	Profit	Loss	S.P.
(i)	₹8642	₹200	—	C.P. + Profit = ₹8642 + ₹200 = ₹8842
(ii)	₹4050	—	₹300	
(iii)	₹1033	₹215	—	
(iv)	₹12,377	—	₹650	

2 Find the profit or loss on an item that was bought for ₹536 and sold for ₹563.

3 Ritika sold a Christmas tree for ₹4675 and made a profit of ₹500. What was the cost price of the Christmas tree?

4 If some fruits were bought for ₹320 and sold for a profit of ₹78, then what was the selling price of the fruits?

5 A glass painting was bought for ₹2270 and sold for a loss of ₹350. What was the selling price of the painting?

PERCENTAGE OF PROFIT OR LOSS

We often come across newspaper clippings where profit or loss is mentioned in the percentage form.

XYZ Ltd. earns 30% profit for the year 2015 – 2016

5% off on purchase of ₹1000 and above

Remember: The profit% or loss% is always calculated on the cost price (C.P.).

To calculate Profit% or Loss%, we use the following relations:

$$\textbf{Profit}\% = \left(\frac{\textbf{Profit}}{\textbf{C.P.}} \times 100\right)\% \qquad \textbf{Loss}\% = \left(\frac{\textbf{Loss}}{\textbf{C.P.}} \times 100\right)\%$$

Example 1: A shopkeeper bought rice at the rate of ₹25 per kg from the wholesaler. He sold the rice at the rate of ₹30 per kg. What will be his profit percentage?

C.P. of rice = ₹25

S.P. of rice = ₹30

Since S.P. > C.P., there is profit.

Profit = S.P. – C.P.

= ₹30 – ₹25 = ₹5

Therefore, Profit = ₹5.

$$\text{Profit\%} = \left(\frac{\text{Profit}}{\text{C.P.}} \times 100\right)\%$$

$$\text{Profit\%} = \left(\frac{5}{25} \times 100\right)\%$$
$$= 20\%$$

Therefore, profit = ₹5 and profit percentage = 20%.

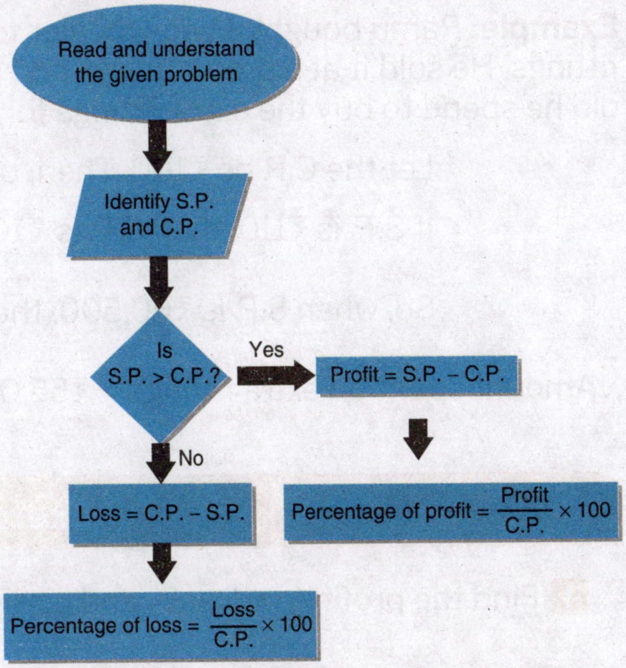

Example 2: A cooker was bought for ₹1000 and sold for ₹800. Find the loss/profit and loss/profit percentage.

C.P. of cooker = ₹1000; S.P. of cooker = ₹800

Since C.P. > S.P., there is loss.

Loss = C.P. – S.P. = ₹1000 – ₹800 = ₹200

Therefore, Loss = ₹200.

$$\text{Loss\%} = \left(\frac{\text{Loss}}{\text{C.P.}} \times 100\right)\% \Rightarrow \text{Loss\%} = \left(\frac{200}{1000} \times 100\right)\% = 20\%$$

Therefore, loss = ₹200 and loss percentage = 20%.

Application of Overhead Expenses

Renu went with her father to purchase a washing machine. They bought it for ₹14,000. The shop was not near their home. So, they had to arrange a vehicle to take the washing machine to their home. They paid conveyance charge (transportation charge) of ₹1000. Hence, the C.P. of the washing machine is not only ₹14,000 but it also includes the conveyance charges. Here, ₹1000, which was paid as the conveyance charge, is known as **overhead expenses**.

Now, C.P. of the washing machine = Original cost + Conveyance charge

= ₹14,000 + ₹1000 = ₹15,000

The expenses referred to as overhead expenses include expenses like amount spent on repairs, labour charges, transportation, etc. These are included in the cost price.

Example: Ramu bought a two-wheeler for ₹50,000 and then bought some extra fittings. He sold it at a profit of 10% and got a selling price of ₹60,500. How much did he spend to buy the extra fittings for the vehicle?

Let the C.P. be ₹100. Then, profit = 10%, S.P. = ₹110.

If S.P. is ₹110, then C.P. is ₹100.

So, when S.P. is ₹60,500, then C.P. = $\frac{60500 \times 100}{110}$ = ₹55,000

∴ Amount spent on extra fittings = ₹55,000 – ₹50,000 = ₹5000.

Exercise 4.2

1. Find the profit% or loss% and complete the table.

	Cost Price (₹)	Selling Price (₹)	Profit%	Loss%
(a)	100	150		
(b)	1000	900		
(c)	1500	1050		
(d)	3000	2400		
(e)	1800	2160		

2. Karan purchased a toy car for ₹1000 and sold it for ₹1250. Find his profit %/loss%.
3. Rita purchased a bag for ₹500 and sold it for ₹450. Find the profit or loss incurred by Rita. What is the percentage of profit or loss?
4. By selling a bag for ₹735, Reena made a profit of ₹35. Find the profit%.
5. Find the loss% when an article costing ₹5000 is sold for ₹4000.
6. Ravi brought a bicycle for ₹2000 and spent ₹500 on extra fittings. He then sold it for ₹3000. Find the overall profit or loss percentage.
7. A shopkeeper purchased an article for ₹10,000 and spent ₹1000 on transportation. He sold the article for ₹8800. Find the amount of loss incurred and loss%.

8 The cost of a toy is ₹400. Nagu sold it for a profit of ₹80. Find the selling price of the toy and also the profit%.

9 An article was sold for ₹2550 with a loss of 15%. Find the cost of the article.

10 A gift item was sold for ₹525 at a profit of 5%. Find the cost price of the gift item.

Revision Exercise

1 **Fill in the blanks.**

(a) When the cost price is more than the selling price, then it is a __________ .

(b) When the selling price is more than the cost price, then it is a __________ .

(c) If there is a profit, then selling price = ______________________________ .

(d) If there is a loss, then cost price = ________________________________ .

2 **State whether the following statements are true (T) or false (F).**

(a) If the selling price is more than the cost price, the seller makes a profit.

(b) If the selling price is more than the cost price, then the seller incurs a loss.

(c) If the cost price is more than the selling price, the seller makes a profit.

(d) If the cost price is lesser than the selling price, then the buyer earns a profit.

3 **Prakash bought 25 kg beans, 20 kg carrots, 15 kg onions, 15 kg papayas and 20 kg oranges for ₹2700 from the market. He sold them to his customers at the following prices.**

(a) 22 kg beans at ₹30 per kg and rest at ₹25 per kg

(b) Carrots at ₹28 per kg

(c) 12 kg onions for ₹46 per kg and 3 kg onions at ₹40 per kg

(d) 13 kg papaya at ₹14 per kg and the rest were rotten, so he could not sell them

(e) 8 kg oranges at ₹43 per kg; he kept 1 kg for himself and sold the rest at ₹39 per kg

Find his overall profit or loss.

4 **Complete the following table.**

Cost Price (C.P.) in ₹	Selling Price (S.P.) in ₹	Profit (₹)	Loss (₹)	Profit%	Loss%
100	110				
5000	4500				
800		160			

5 Suri buys a calculator for ₹700 and sells it for a loss of ₹42. What is the percentage of loss incurred?

6 Joy bought a DVD player for ₹1750 and sold it for ₹1925. Find Joy's profit%.

HOTS (Higher Order Thinking Skills)

1. The cost price of 12 fans is equal to the selling price of 8 fans. Find the profit/loss per cent.
2. Match each of the following statements with the correct question and the correct operation required to answer the question.

Statement	Question	Operation
I bought a chocolate, a biscuit packet and a 150 ml fruit juice pack.	What amount should each pay me?	Addition
I bought 100 books, each of the same cost.	How much should I get back?	Multiplication
I paid some amount to the shopkeeper and waited for the change.	How much did I pay for all?	Division
I bought the entrance tickets for all of my friends at the zoo.	How much did I pay for all?	Subtraction

5 Geometry

Learning Objectives

- To learn about what is a ray
- To learn about angles and identify the parts of an angle
- To identify different types of angles
- To measure the given angles using a protractor
- To learn about applications of angles in real life
- To learn about circles and identify different parts of a circle

Let's Get Started

A **point** determines an exact location. It is shown by a capital letter.

Example: Point K is denoted as •K

A **line segment** connects two end points.

Example: Line segment $\overline{AB}$ 

A **line** extends on both sides endlessly.

Example: Line $\overleftrightarrow{LM}$ 

RAY

Have you ever watched the beautiful sunrays falling on you during sunrise or sunset? What do you mean by a ray?

In geometry, a **ray is a part of a line**. It has an end point on one side and extends indefinitely on the other side. It is denoted by the end point and any another point on the ray. The symbol used for the ray is ⟶.

Example: 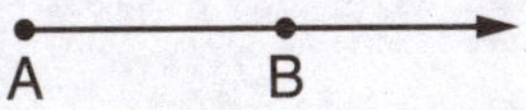

Ray AB is written as $\overrightarrow{AB}$.

ANGLES

In the previous classes, you might have learned about corners and sides. What do you mean by corners? A corner is a place where two or more sides meet.

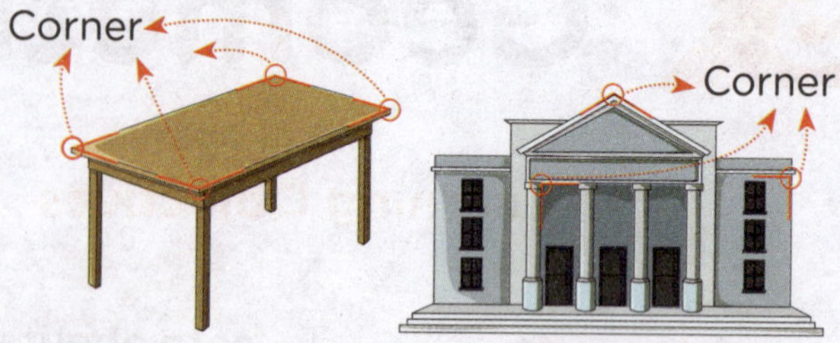

The two sides which meet at a corner form an **angle**. In geometry, when two rays meet at a point, they form an angle.

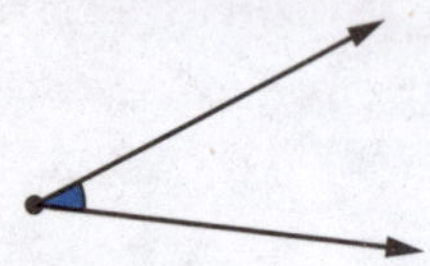

We can see angles all around us in our everyday life.

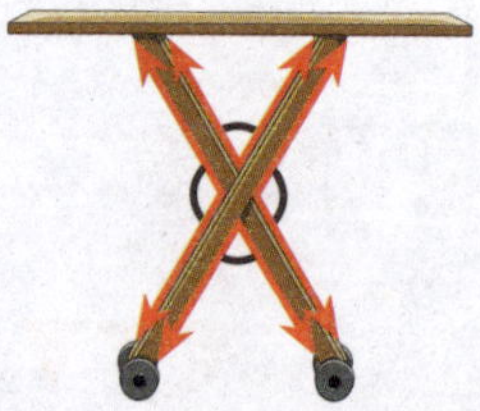

PARTS OF AN ANGLE

- Consider the rays **OA** and **OB**. They are meeting at
  a point **O** and forming an angle.
- The point where two rays meet is called the **vertex** of the angle. Here, **O** is the vertex.
- The rays which form the angle are called the **arms** of the angle. Here, **OA** and **OB** are the arms.

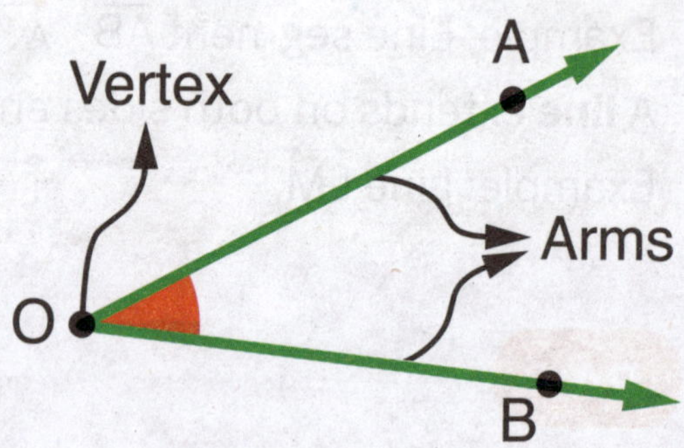

- This angle is named as **angle AOB** or **angle BOA**. The symbol ∠ is used to write the word 'angle'. Angle AOB is written as **∠AOB** and angle BOA is written as **∠BOA**.
- The middle letter denotes the angle to which we are referring. It is always the **vertex** of the angle.

Exercise 5.1

1 Name the following figures as point, line, line segment or ray.

(a) 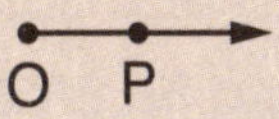

(b) 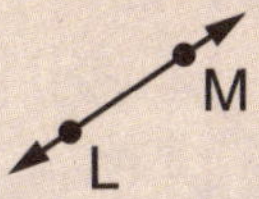

(c) 

(d) •C

(e) 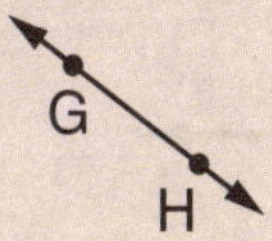

2 Name the rays and lines in the following figure.

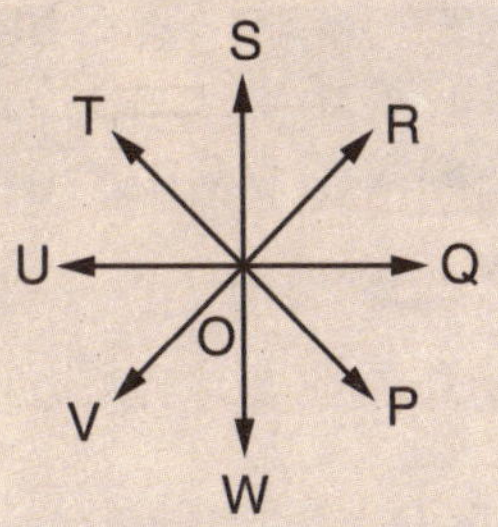

Rays	**Lines**
$\overrightarrow{OS}$	$\overleftrightarrow{TP}$

3 Identify and mark different angles in the following figures.

(a) 

(b) 

(c) 

(d) 

4 Mark the angles in the following figures. Write the names of the angles, their vertices and their arms. One has been done for you.

(a) 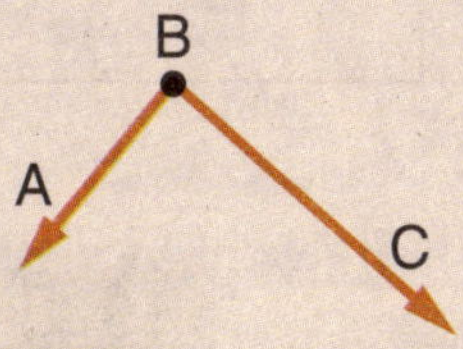

Angle:
Vertex:
Arms:

(b) 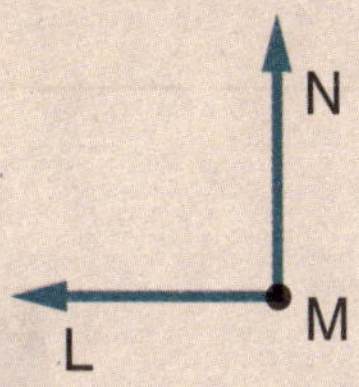

Angle:
Vertex:
Arms:

(c) 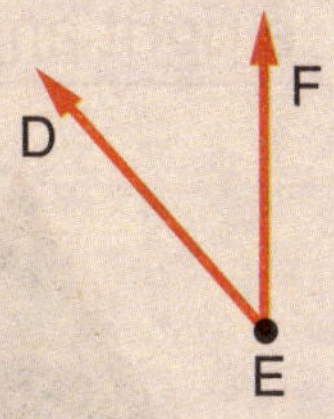

Angle:
Vertex:
Arms:

TYPES OF ANGLES

Right Angles

Look at the angles in the following figures. Which shape do they remind you of? The 'L' shape. The angles which are in the L shape are known as **right angles**.

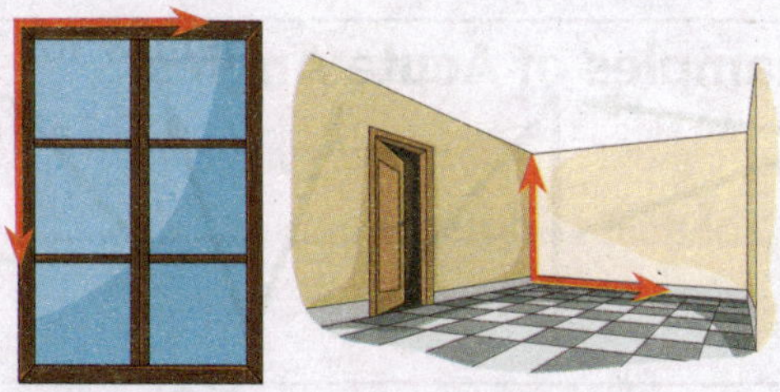

Here are a few examples of right angles.

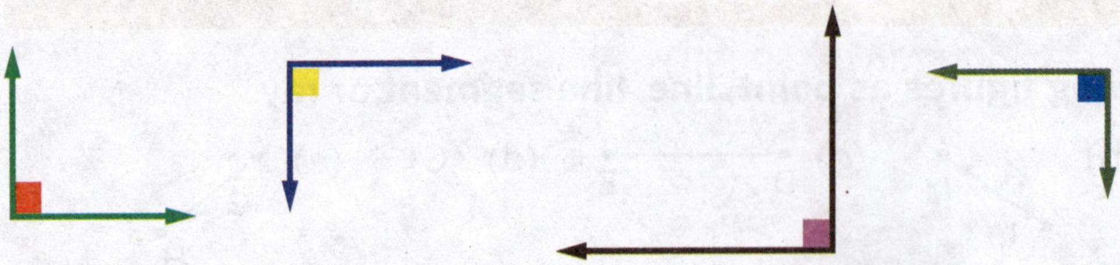

You can make a right angle tester using paper. Cut a circle from a sheet of paper.

Fold it into half. Again fold it into half.

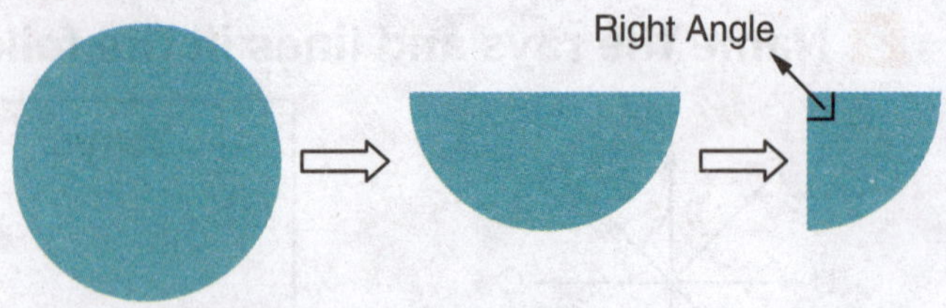

Acute and Obtuse Angles

Look at the angles in the following figures. Use your right angle tester and write whether each angle is more than a right angle or less than a right angle.

More than a right angle

Less than a right angle

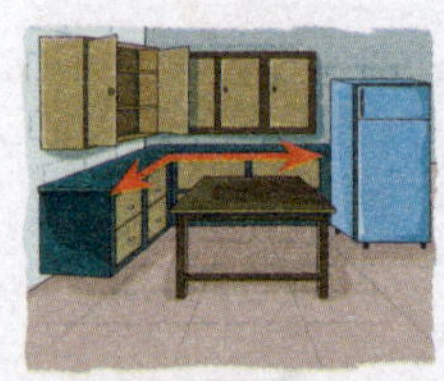

The angles that are less than right angles are called **acute angles**.

The angles that are more than right angles are called **obtuse angles**.

Examples of Acute Angles:

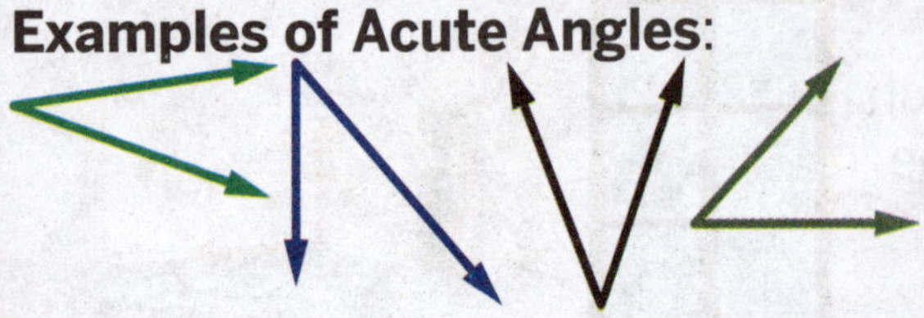

Examples of Obtuse Angles:

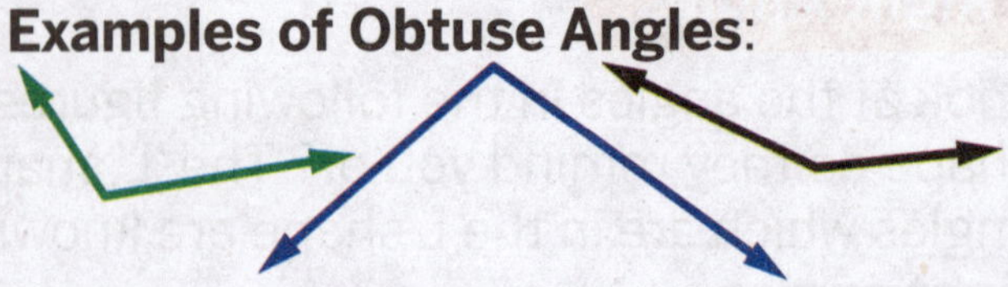

Straight Angles

Angles whose arms lie in the opposite directions from the vertex and form a straight line are known as **straight angles**. When two right angles are placed next to one another, we get a straight angle.

Examples of straight angles

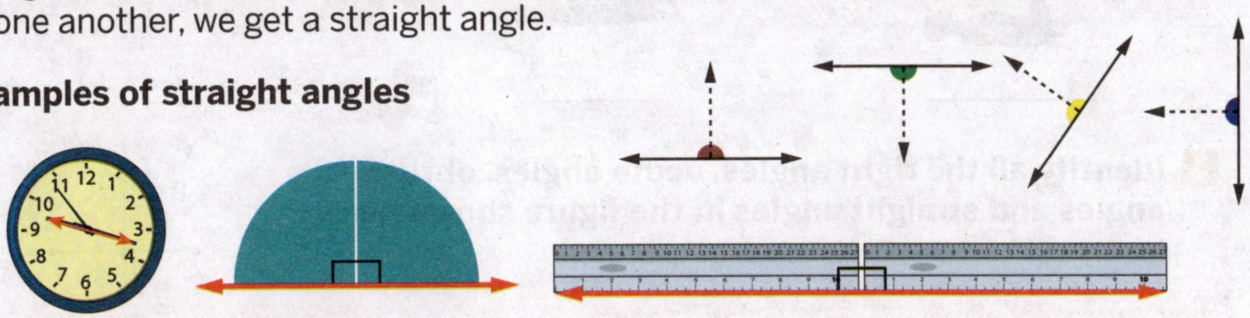

Exercise 5.2

1 **Identify whether the angles marked in the following figures are acute (A), obtuse (O), right (R) or straight (S) angles.**

(a) 

A

(b) 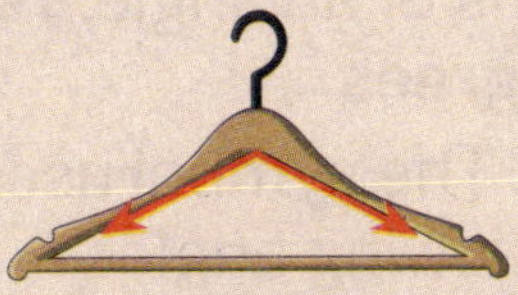

(c) 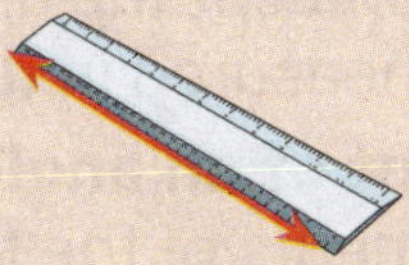

(d) 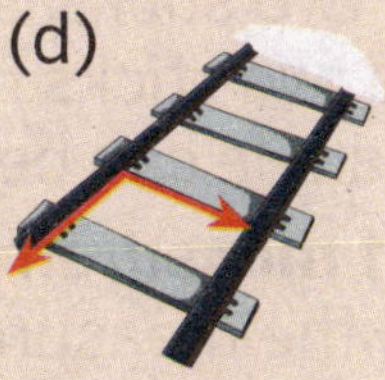

(e) 

(f) 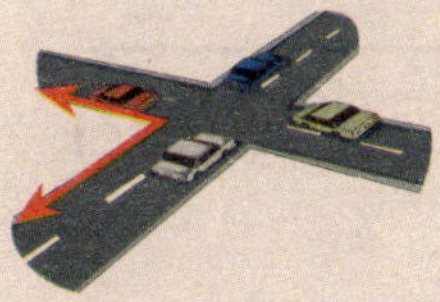

(g) 

(h) 

(i) 

2 **The following are different postures in yoga. Write the type of angle formed in each posture.**

(a) 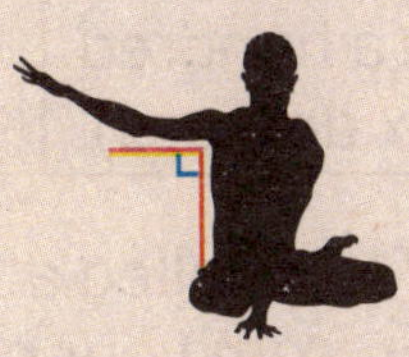

____

(b) 

____

(c) 

____

(d)

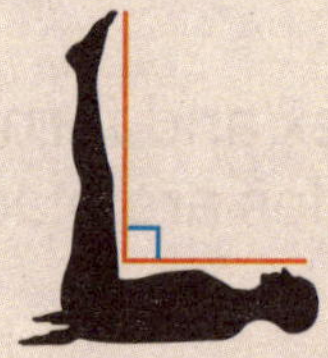

____

(e)

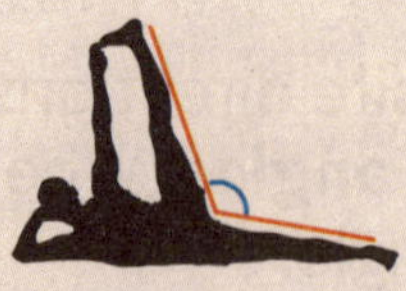

____

(f)

____

3 **Identify all the right angles, acute angles, obtuse angles and straight angles in the figure shown here.**

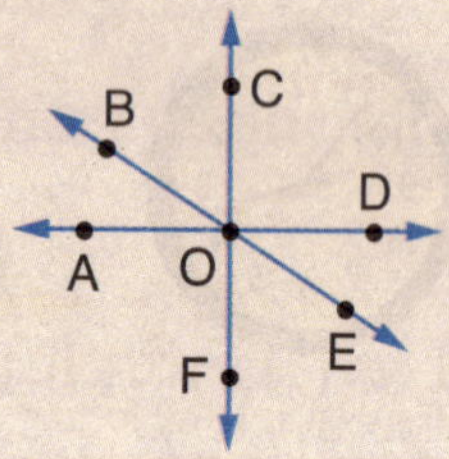

Measurement of Angles

Take two sticks and form different angles keeping one stick constant and moving the other slowly without changing the meeting point of the two sticks. Observe that the gap between the two sticks is increasing. Can we measure the gap between the two sticks? Here, the two sticks represent the arms of an angle. The gap between the two arms of any angle can be measured in **degrees**.

A degree is a unit of measurement of an angle. The symbol used for representing degrees is °. Observe the measurements of the following angles.

$\angle QPR = 1°$ (one degree)

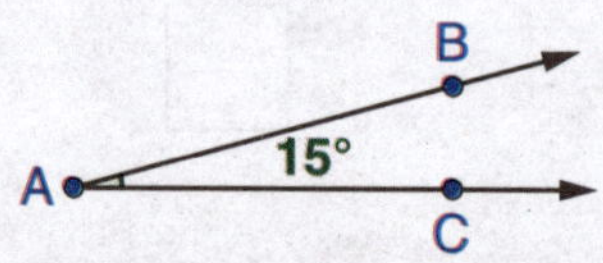

$\angle BAC = 15°$ (fifteen degrees)

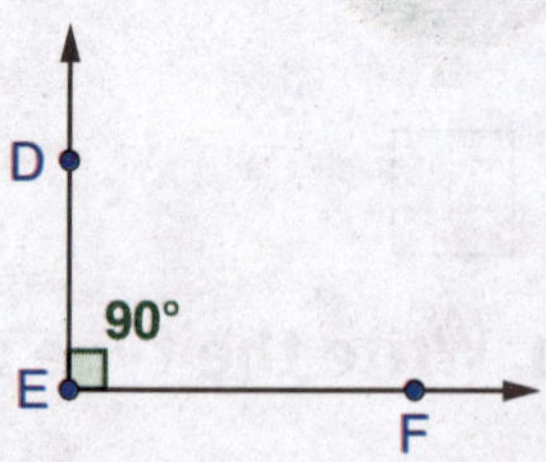

$\angle DEF = 90°$ (ninety degrees)

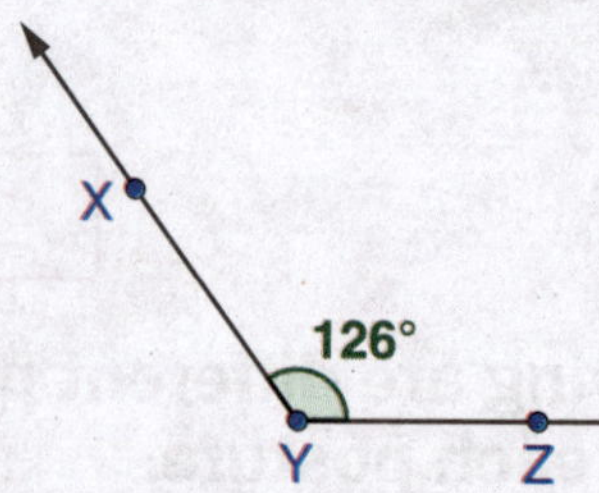

$\angle XYZ = 126°$ (a hundred and twenty-six degrees)

Have you seen a D-shaped instrument in your geometry box? It is called a **protractor** and is used to measure angles. Take the protractor from your geometry box and observe it carefully. You can see that there are two rows of measurements from 0° to 180° going in opposite directions. They are called **scales**. One is the

inner scale and the other is the **outer scale**. There are 180 divisions between 0 and 180. Each division represents **one degree**. The bottom line is known as the **base line**. The point where the base line and the line corresponding to 90° meet is known as the **centre point**.

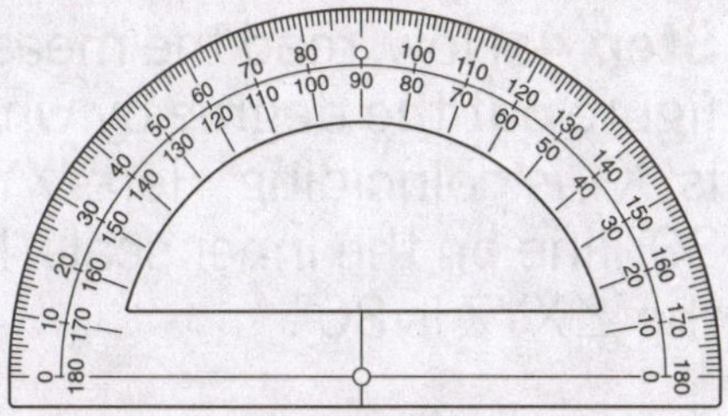

Do You Know?

The protractor which is there in the geometry box is known as **half-circle protractor**. There is also a **full-circle protractor**. It also has an inner scale and an outer scale marking from **0° to 360°**.

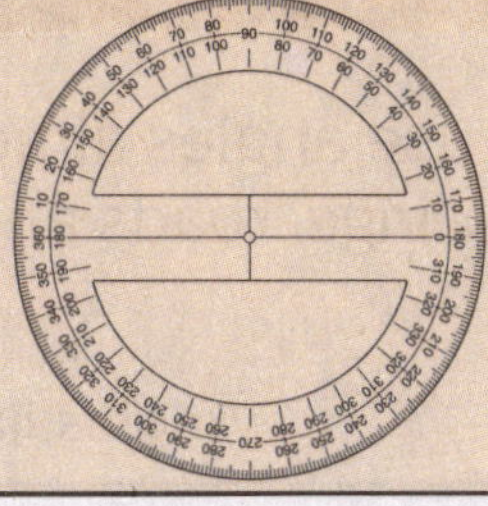

Measuring Angles Using Protractor

Let us measure the ∠XYZ given here using the protractor. Here, XY and YZ are the arms of the angle and Y is the vertex of the angle. Follow the steps given below for measuring ∠XYZ.

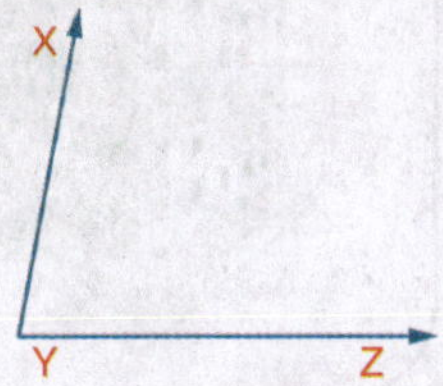

Step 1: Place the protractor over the angle to be measured, i.e., ∠XYZ, such that the centre point of the protractor coincides with the vertex of the angle, that is, Y.

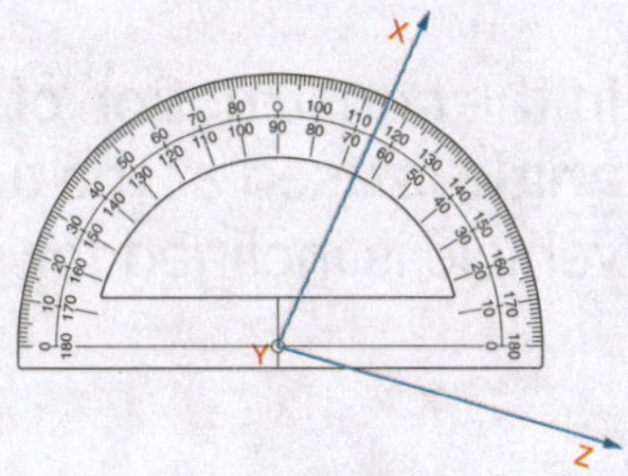

Step 2: Adjust the protractor such that the base line of the protractor coincides with the arm YZ of the protractor. Make sure that the vertex and the centre of the protractor lie on the same point.

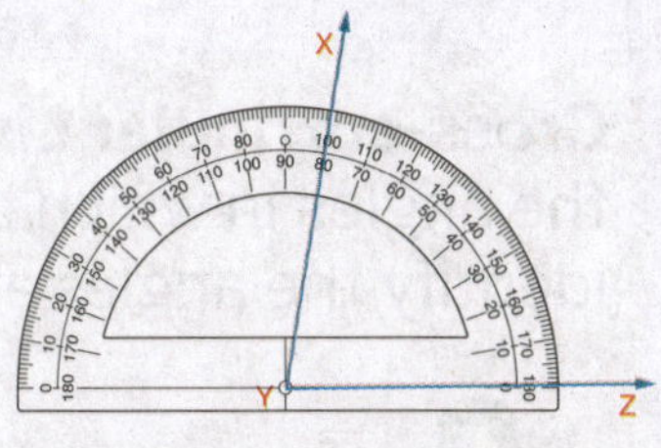

Step 3: Choose the scale (inner or outer) to be used. Look at the scale where the baseline arm is pointing to 0°.

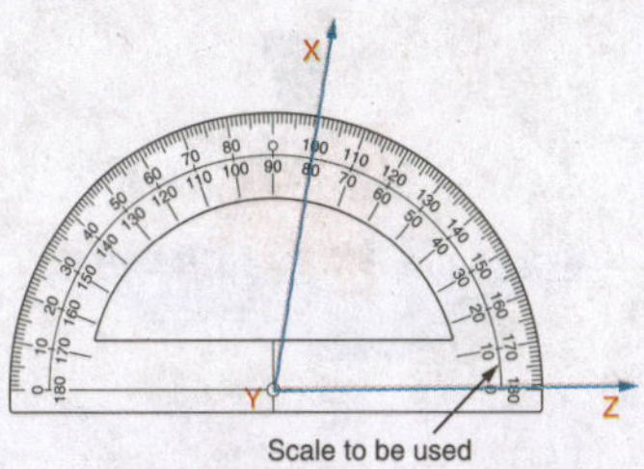

Angle Measurement

Step 4: Now, read the measure of the angle and figure out the degree by which the other arm, that is, XY is coinciding. Here, XY is coinciding with the 80° line on the inner scale. Hence, the measure of the ∠XYZ is 80°.

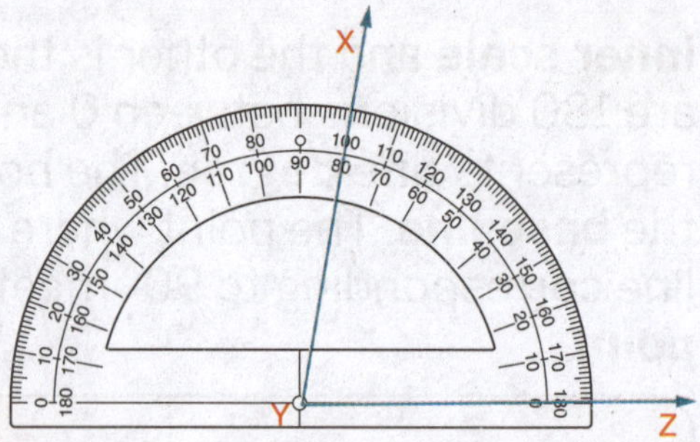

APPLICATIONS OF ANGLES IN REAL LIFE

We use angles almost everywhere in our everyday life from construction of buildings, roads and bridges, etc., to sports.

Angles in Construction

Angles in Sports

In the construction of roads, an angle called a **banking angle** is used at the turns. It is the angle at which the vehicle is inclined towards the inside of the turn.

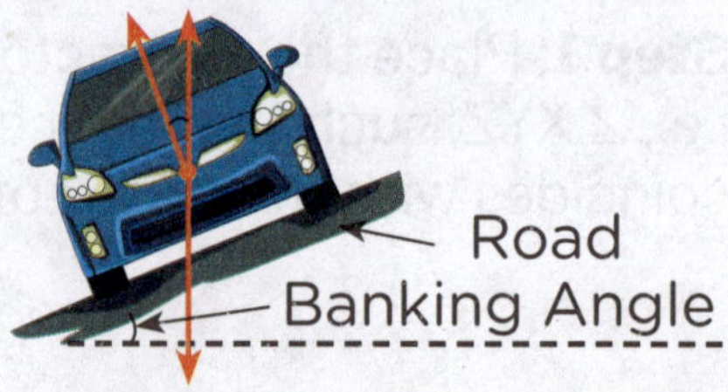

Cross-curricular Link: Collect some photos of Olympic sports events. Identify the angles in which the athletes hold their body or their arms or legs. Try to identify the angles at which they hold the equipment they use.

Exercise 5.3

1 **Measure the following angles using a protractor and write them in the boxes provided.**

(a)

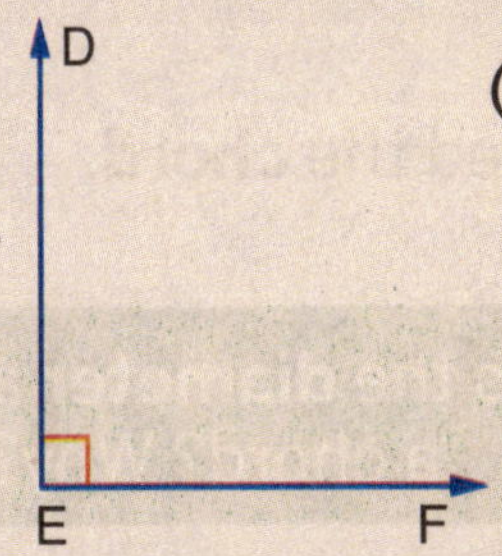

∠DEF =

(b)

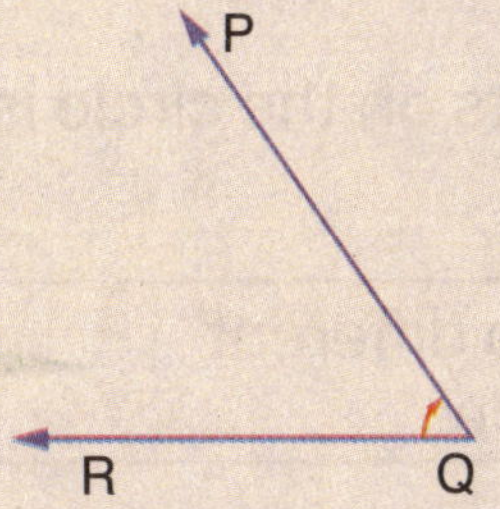

∠PQR =

(c)

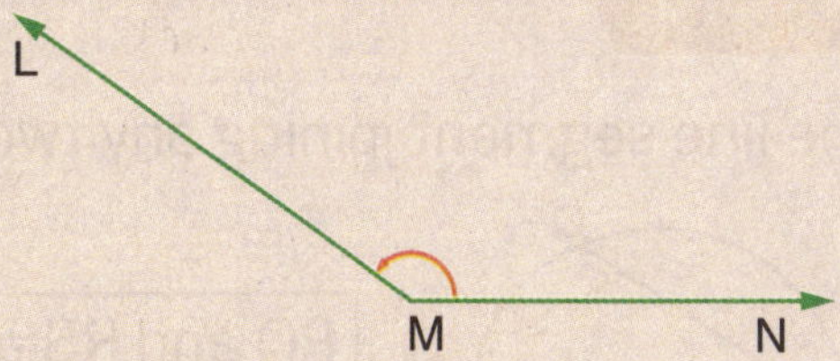

∠LMN =

2 **Identify the types of angles and write them in the boxes with their names.**

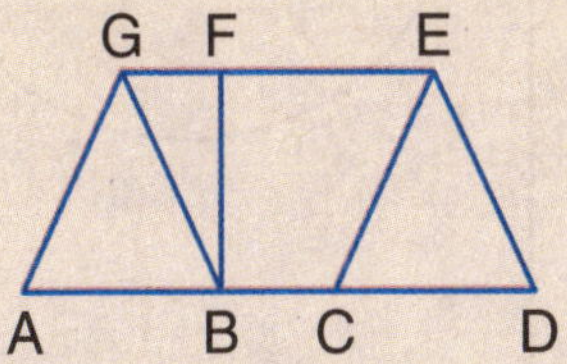

Acute Angles	Obtuse Angles	Right Angles

3 **Use a ruler and draw five angles (acute, obtuse and right angles) in your notebook. Measure them using a protractor and write their measurements.**

CIRCLE

Examples

A **circle** is a simple closed curve.

Parts of a Circle:

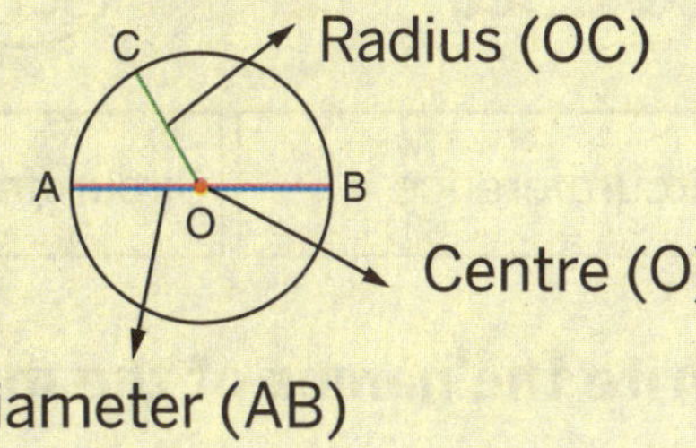

Circumference

Look at the circle shown here. How can we find the length of the boundary around this circle? Take a thread and wrap it along the edge once exactly.

Take out the thread and measure its length using the ruler. The length of the boundary of a circle is called the **circumference** of a circle.

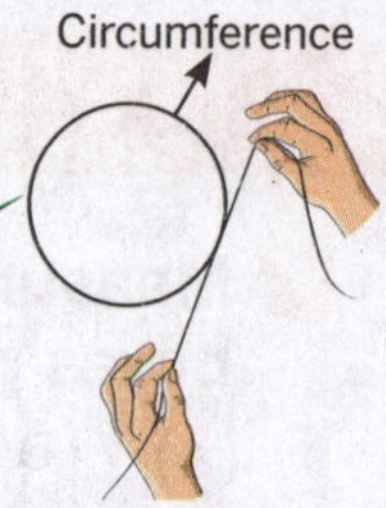

Can we also call it the **perimeter** of a circle?

Chord

The line segment joining any two points on the circle is called the **chord**.

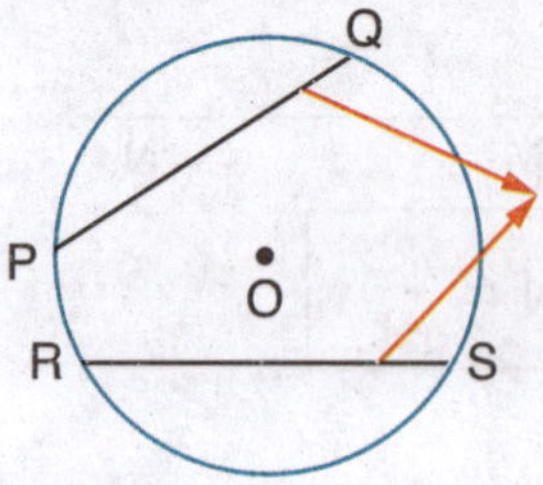

PQ and RS are two different chords of this circle.

Is the **diameter** also a chord? Why?

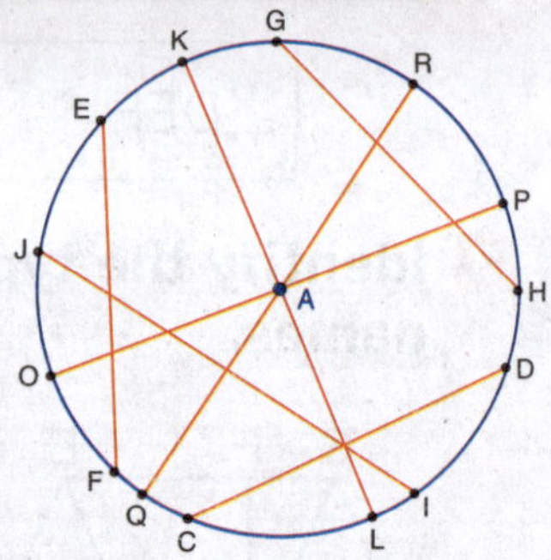

Identify the chords and the diameters in this circle. Measure their lengths. Record your results in the following table and write your observations.

Line Segment	Is it a Chord/ Diameter?	Length

You can observe that out of all the chords of a given circle, **diameter is the longest chord**.

Exercise 5.4

1 **Measure the circumference of the circles using a thread and a ruler.**

(a) 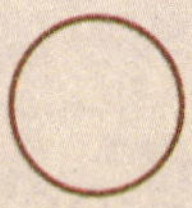 (b) 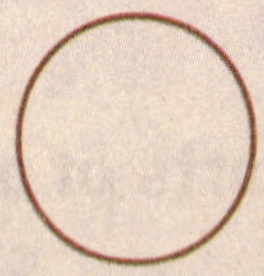 (c)  (d) 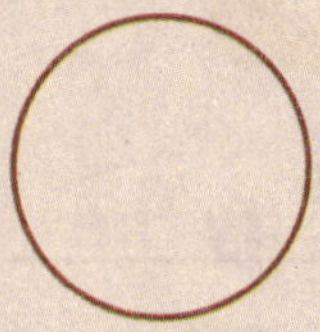

Circumference =	Circumference =	Circumference =	Circumference =

2 **Write the names of the marked parts of the circles given below.**

(a) 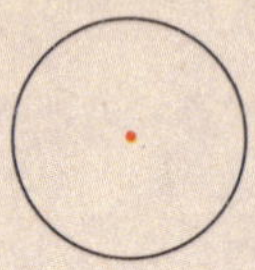 (b) 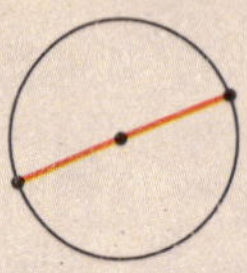 (c) 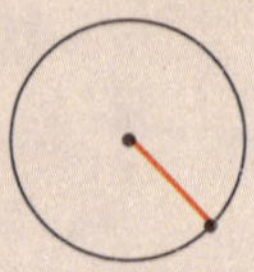 (d) 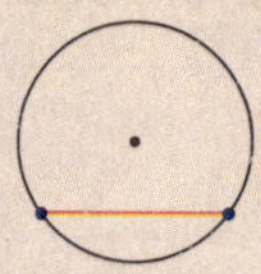 (e) 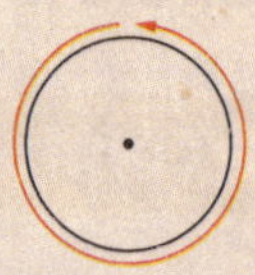

_______ _______ _______ _______ _______

3 **State whether the following statements are true (T) or false (F).**

(a) A diameter is also a chord of a circle. ☐

(b) Different chords of a circle can have different lengths. ☐

(c) The lengths of the radii of a circle are different. ☐

(d) A circle can have only one diameter. ☐

Revision Exercise

1 **Tick (✓) the rays among the following figures.**

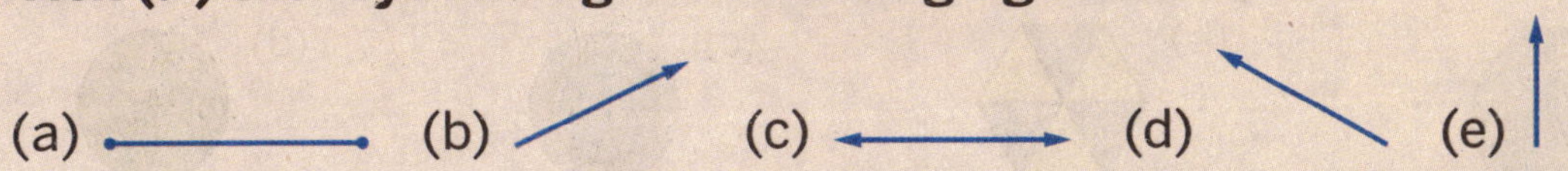

2 **Tick (✓) the figures which represent an angle among the following.**

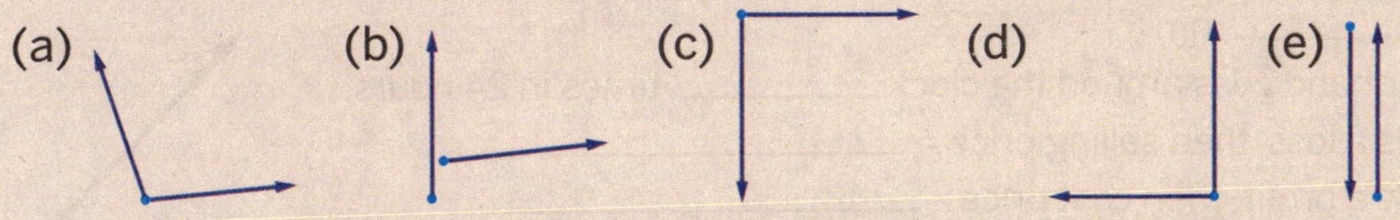

3 **Write the names of the following angles. Also, write the vertices and the arms of the angles.**

(a) 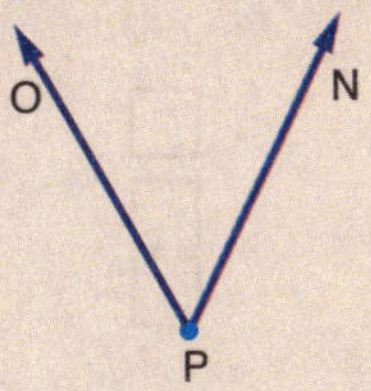

Name of the angle = ________

Vertex = ________

Arms = ________

(b) 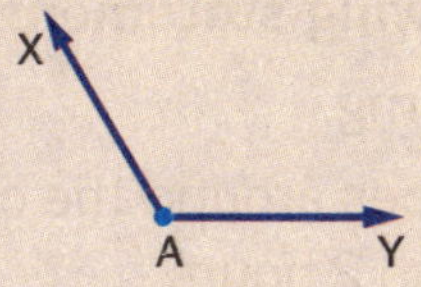

Name of the angle = ________

Vertex = ________

Arms = ________

4 **Identify the types of angles and write them in the boxes with their names.**

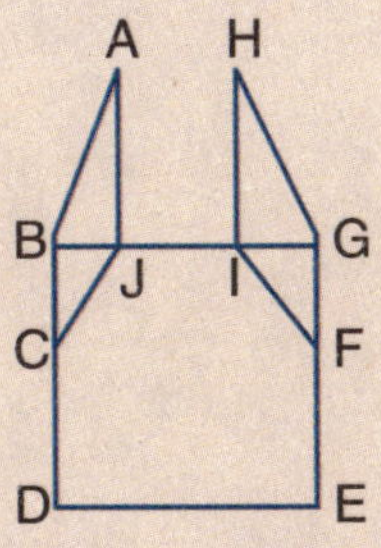

Acute Angles	Obtuse Angles	Right Angles

5 **Draw a circle and mark its different parts (radii, diameters, circumference and chords).**

ASSESSMENT 1

Chapters 1-5

A Choose the correct option for each of the following.

1. 7 ℓ – 650 mℓ =

   (a) 6.35 mℓ (b) 6350 mℓ (c) 63500 mℓ (d) Answer cannot be found

2. 3 hours before 1:00 a.m. is

   (a) 4:00 a.m. (b) 10:00 p.m. (c) 4:00 p.m. (d) 10:00 a.m.

3. The number of days from 13th March to 10th August is

   (a) 147 days (b) 163 days (c) 150 days (d) 151 days

4. Mr Dixit bought 4 photo frames for ₹27 each. He earned an overall profit of ₹100 while selling them. What was the selling price of each?

   (a) ₹52 (b) ₹25 (c) ₹73 (d) ₹31.75

5. Which of the following figures does not look the same after one-third turn?

   (a)  (b)  (c)  (d) 

B Fill in the blanks.

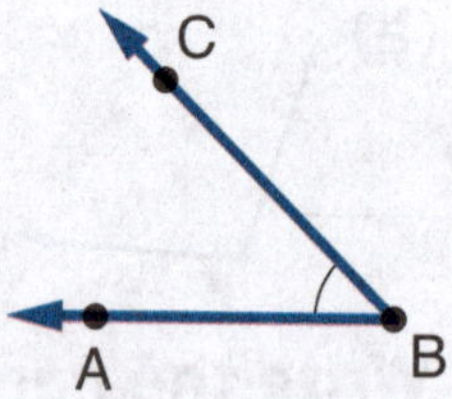

1. 1 m = ________ mm
2. The hour hand goes around the clock ________ times in 24 hours.
3. If there is a loss, then selling price = ________________.
4. If there is a profit, then cost price = ________________.
5. The measure of the angle ABC shown here is ________. (Use a protractor)

C State whether the following statements are true (T) or false (F).

1. The basic unit of mass is mg. ☐
2. When the second hand goes around the clock once, 1 minute passes by. ☐
3. There are 3600 seconds in 2 hours. ☐
4. If a seller wants to make a profit on an object, then the selling price of the object will be the difference between cost price and profit. ☐
5. I bought an umbrella for ₹137 and sold it for ₹150. My profit is ₹23. ☐

D Match the following.

Column A	Column B
(a) 79 km	(i) 7900 m
(b) 7.9 km	(ii) 790 m
(c) 	(iii) 79000 m
(d) 	(iv) Straight angle
(e) 	(v) Right angle
	(vi) Obtuse angle

6 Area and Perimeter

Learning Objectives

- To find the perimeter and area of a rectangle and a square
- To find the area of a triangle by completing the rectangles
- To learn about different units of area
- To solve problems on perimeter and area of rectangle and square

Let's Get Started

Walk along the boundary of your classroom until you reach the starting point. The distance covered by you is called the perimeter of your classroom.

Perimeter is the distance covered along the boundary of a figure when you go around it once. It can be found by adding the lengths of all the sides of a figure.

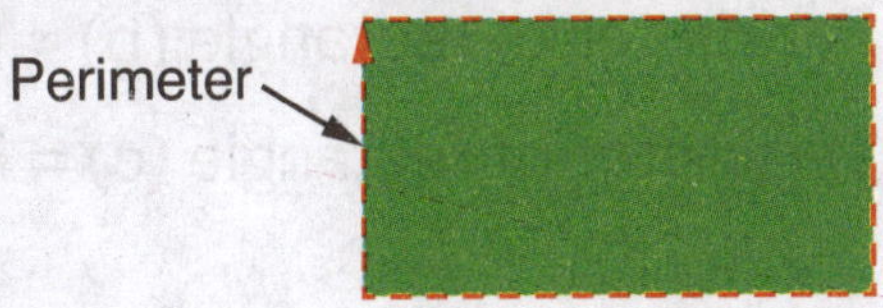

Observe the following figures and their perimeters.

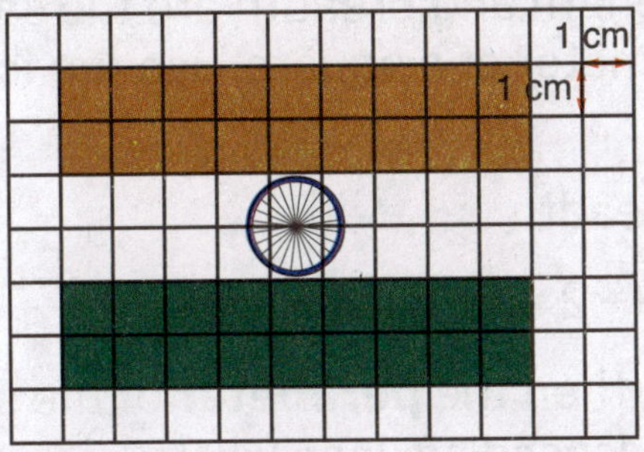

Perimeter = 9 cm + 6 cm + 9cm + 6 cm = 30 cm

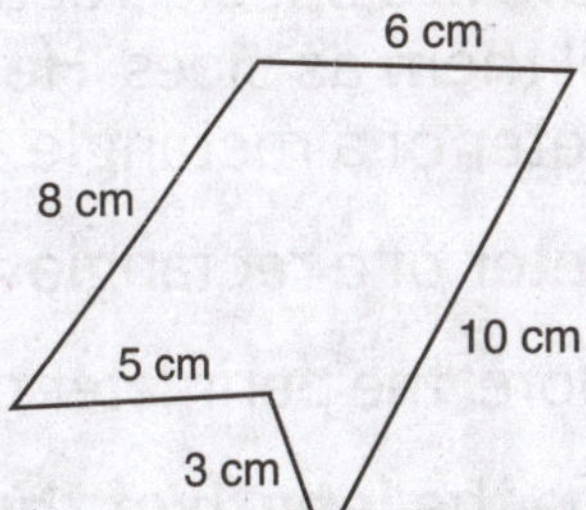

Perimeter = 8 cm + 6 cm + 10 cm + 3 cm + 5 cm = 32 cm

PERIMETER OF A RECTANGLE

Observe the following rectangles and their perimeters.

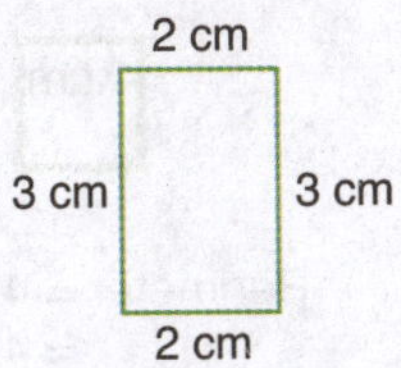

(a)

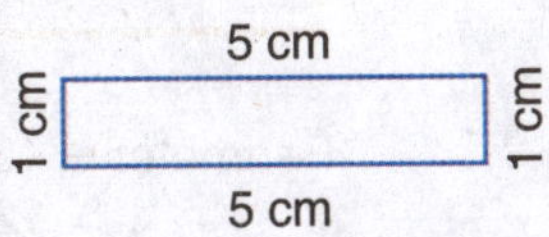

(b)

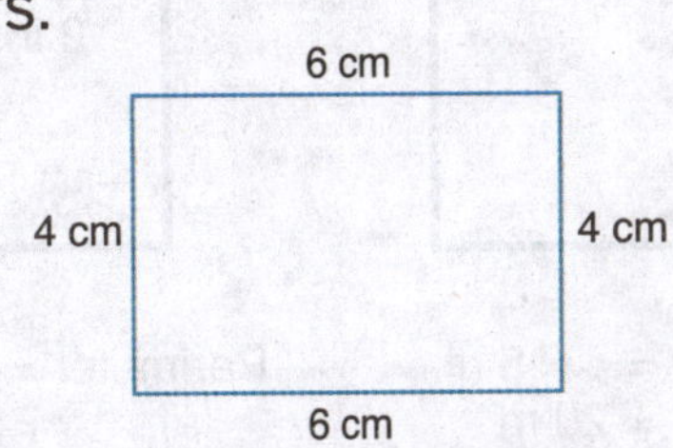

(c)

The perimeter of rectangle (a) = 2 cm + 3 cm + 2 cm + 3 cm = 10 cm

The perimeter of rectangle (b) = 1 cm + 5 cm + 1 cm + 5 cm = 12 cm

The perimeter of rectangle (c) = 6 cm + 4 cm + 6 cm + 4 cm = 20 cm

To find the perimeter of a rectangle, we add its length 2 times and its breadth 2 times.

Therefore, the perimeter of a rectangle = length + breadth + length + breadth

= 2 × length + 2 × breadth = 2 × (length + breadth)

Let ℓ be the **length** of the rectangle and ***b*** be the **breadth** of the rectangle, then the **perimeter** of the rectangle is given by **P = 2(**ℓ **+ *b*)**.

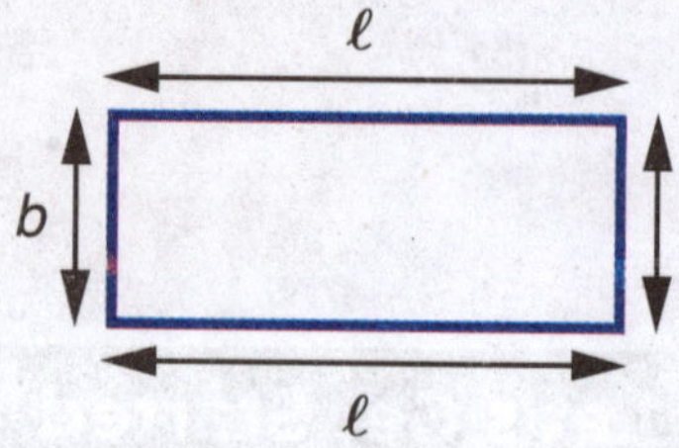

Let us calculate the perimeters of the above rectangles using the formula.

Perimeter of rectangle (a) = P= $2(l + b) = 2(3 + 2) = 2(5) = 10$ cm

Perimeter of rectangle (b) = P= $2(l + b) = 2(5 + 1) = 2(6) = 12$ cm

Perimeter of rectangle (c) = P= $2(l + b) = 2(6 + 4) = 2(10) = 20$ cm

PERIMETER OF A SQUARE

A square is a special rectangle in which the length and breadth are the same and we call them as sides. Hence, to find the perimeter of a square, use the formula for perimeter of a rectangle.

Perimeter of a rectangle = 2 × length + 2 × breadth

Therefore, the perimeter of a square = 2 × side + 2 × side = **4 × side**

Let ***s*** be the **length of the side** of the square, then the **perimeter** of the square is given by ***P*** **= 4*s*.** The units of perimeter are cm, m, etc., depending upon whatever unit is being talked about in the question.

Let us find the perimeters of some squares.

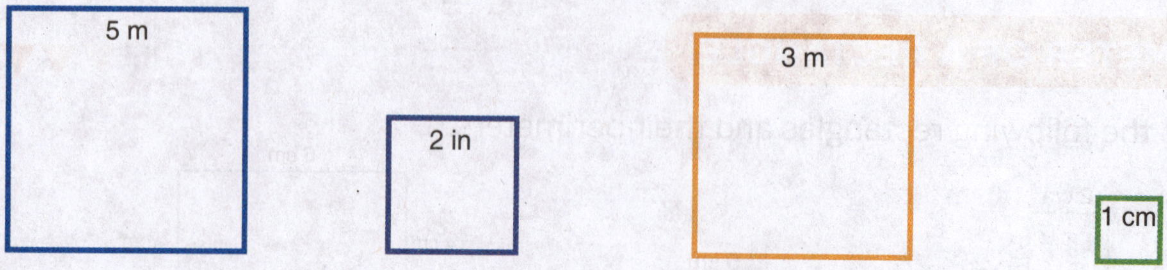

Perimeter = 4 × 5 m = 20 m

Perimeter = 4 × 2 in = 8 in

Perimeter = 4 × 3 m = 12 m

Perimeter = 4 × 1 cm = 4 cm

Exercise 6.1

1 **Find the perimeter of the following objects using the correct formulae.**

(a) 125 cm, 125 cm

(b) 15 cm, 15 cm

(c) 52 in, 30 in

(d) 10 in, 10 in

(e) 18 cm, 7 cm

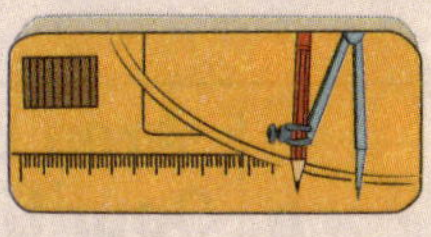

(f) 24 in, 24 in

2 **Find the missing sides in the following figures.**

(a) Perimeter = 48 cm

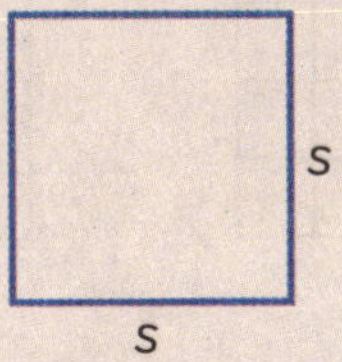

(b) Perimeter = 30 cm

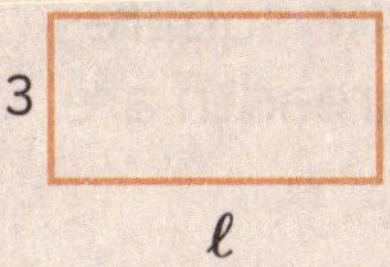

(c) Perimeter = 32 cm

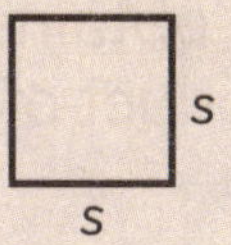

(d) Perimeter = 80 cm

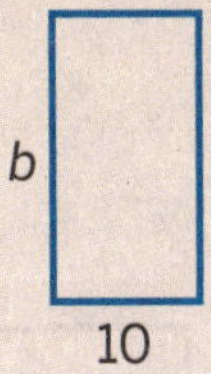

(e) Perimeter = 150 cm

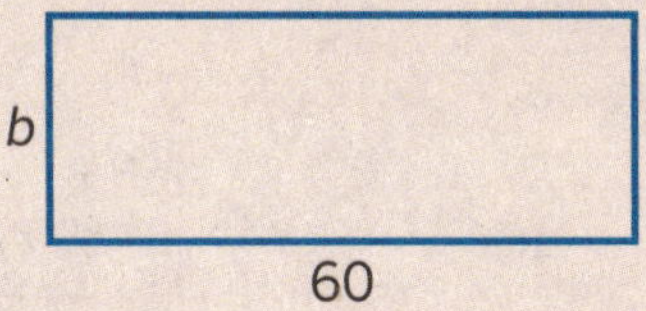

(f) Perimeter = 104 cm

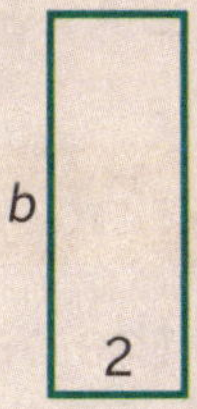

AREA

Place different objects such as a book, paper, eraser, etc. on your bench. Each of them occupies certain region on the bench.

The amount of surface or region covered by an object is called its area.

In your previous classes, you have learned how to find the area of certain figures by counting the number of unit squares they occupy. For example, the area covered by the doormat shown here is 28 sq. units.

Let us find the areas of rectangle and square by deriving formulae.

Area of a Rectangle

Rakesh wants to put tiles on the floors of different rooms of his home. Find the area covered by the tiles in each place by counting the number of tiles. The floors in all the rooms are rectangular in shape. Find the length and the breadth of each floor and fill the table given below.

Room	Length (ℓ)	Breadth (b)	$\ell \times b$	Area by Counting Squares
Drawing Room				
Kitchen				

Drawing Room

Kitchen

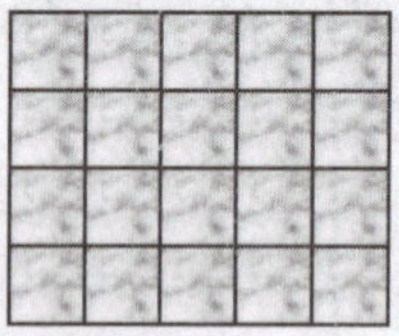

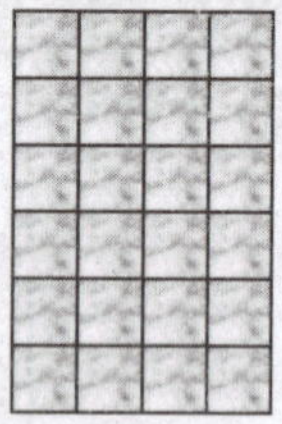

From the table, we can observe that the area of a rectangle obtained by counting the squares and the product of its length and breadth are the same.

Therefore, area of the rectangle = length × breadth

Let ℓ be the length and b be the breadth of the rectangle, then the area of the rectangle is given by $\mathbf{A = \ell \times b}$.

Area of a Square

As we found the perimeter of a square using the perimeter of a rectangle, we can also find the area of a square using the formula for area of a rectangle. We can do that by substituting the sides of square in place of length and breadth of the rectangle with the sides of the square.

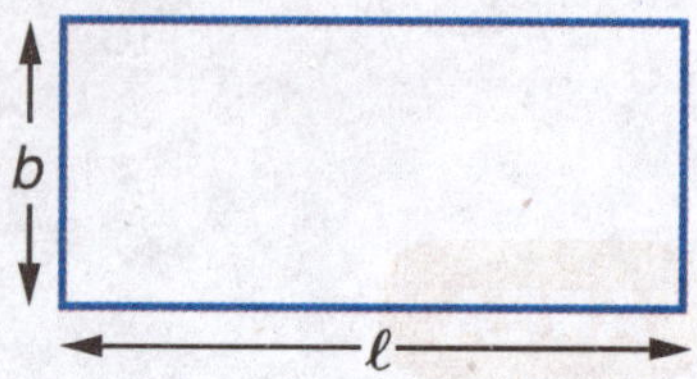

Area of a rectangle = length × breadth

Therefore, area of a square = side × side

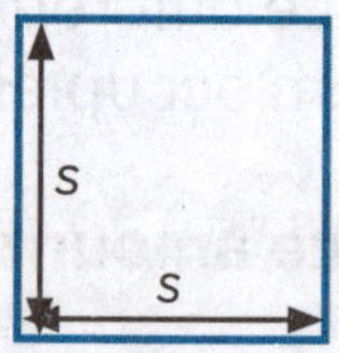

Let s be the side of a square, then its area is given by $\mathbf{A = s \times s}$. The units of area are sq. cm (square centimetre), sq. m (square metre), etc., depending upon whatever unit is being talked about in the question.

Exercise 6.2

1 **Find the areas of the following objects using the correct formulae.**

(a) 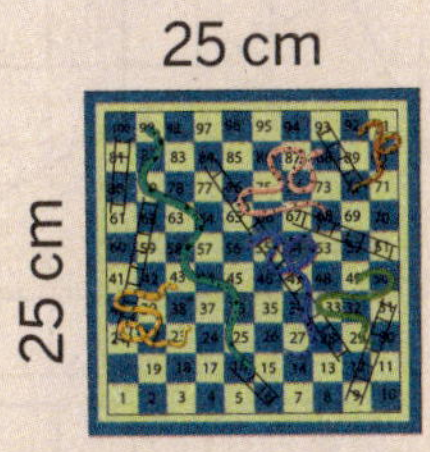

(b) 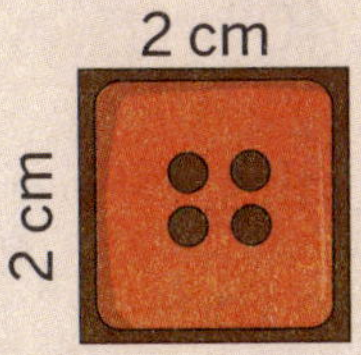

(c) 

(d) 

2 **Find the areas of the following figures.**

(a) 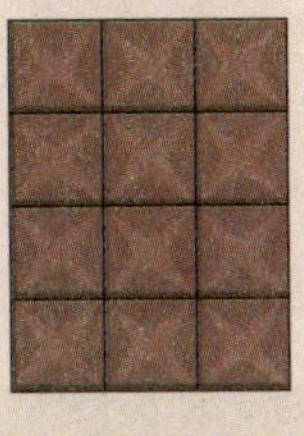

(b) 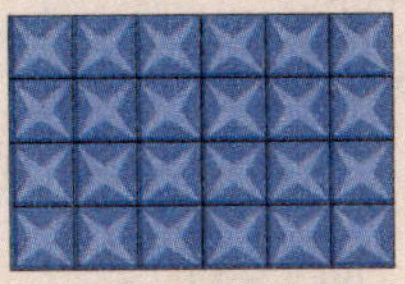

(c) 

(d) 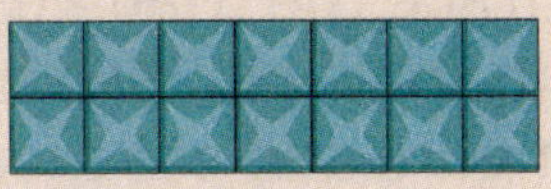

3 **Find the missing sides in the following figures.**

(a) Area = 1500 sq. units

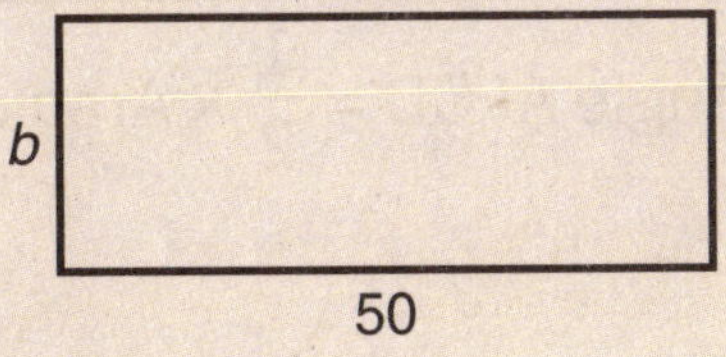

(b) Area = 100 sq. units

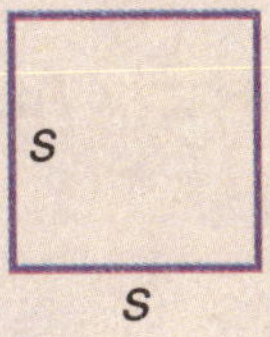

(c) Area = 75 sq. units

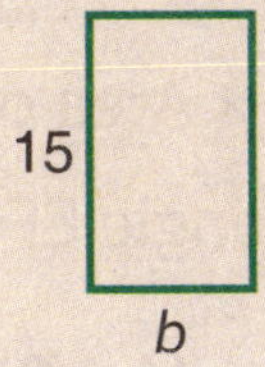

Area of a Triangle

You already know how to find the area of a rectangle if its length and breadth are known. We can use it to find the area of a triangle. Complete the rectangle as shown in the following figure.

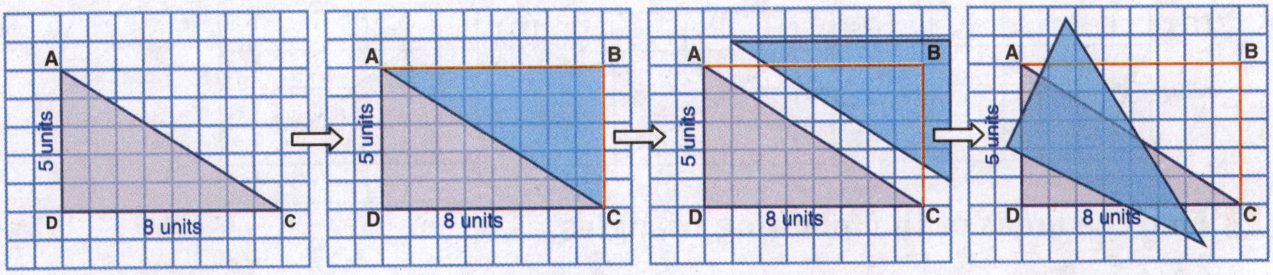

Trace this rectangle on a transparent sheet. Cut the two triangles. Place one triangle over the other. The two triangles overlap each other. So, they are of the same area and the sum of the areas of these two triangles is equal to the area of the rectangle. Therefore, the area of one triangle is half of the area of the rectangle.

Area of the triangle ADC $= \frac{1}{2} \times$ area of the rectangle ABCD

$$= \frac{1}{2} \times (8 \times 5) = \frac{1}{2} \times 40$$

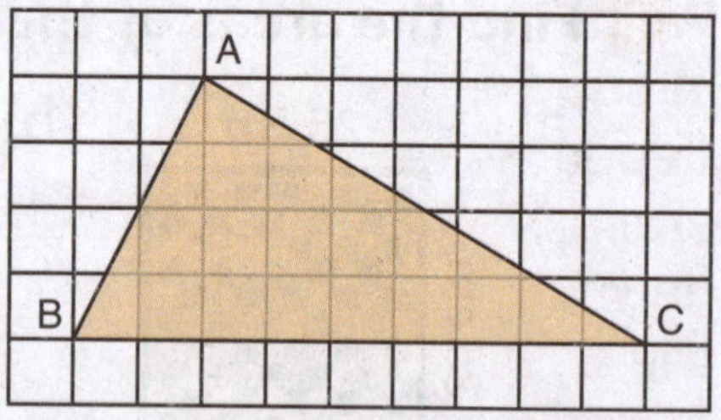

Therefore, area of the triangle ADC = 20 sq. units.

Consider the triangle shown here. Can you use the same method to find the area of this triangle? Yes. Follow the steps given below to find its area.

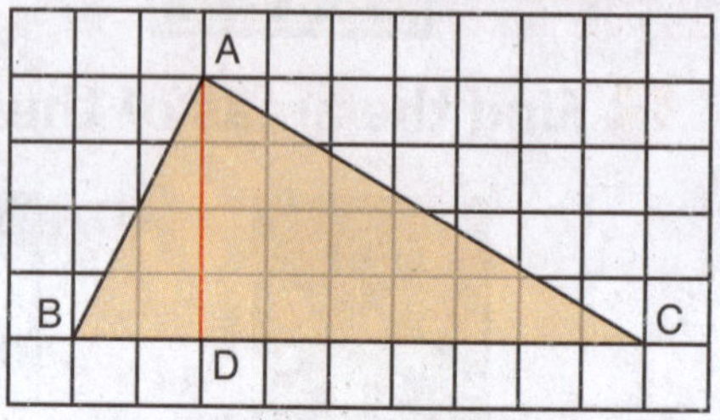

1. Trace the triangle on another sheet. Divide the triangle into two triangles as shown in the second figure and cut them.
2. Then flip the two cut out parts and keep on the sides of the triangle in the reverse order as shown in the third figure.. Then you will get the nearest rectangle containing this triangle.

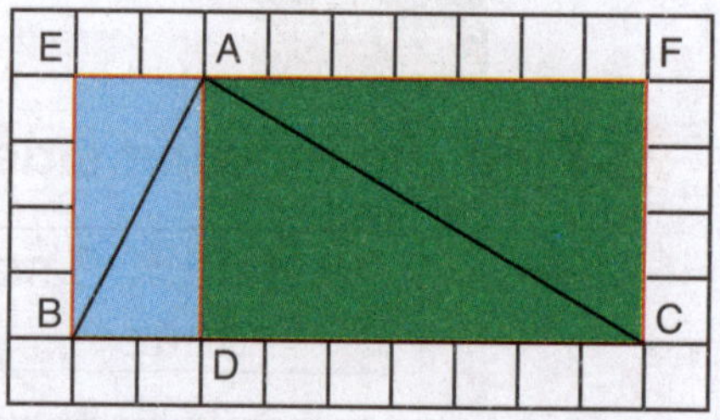

Area of the triangle ABC = Area of the triangle ABD + Area of the triangle ADC

$= \frac{1}{2} \times$ Area of rectangle AEBD $+ \frac{1}{2} \times$ Area of rectangle AFCD $= \frac{1}{2} \times$ Area of rectangle EFCB

$= \frac{1}{2} \times (4 \times 9)$

Therefore, area of the triangle ABC = 18 sq. units.

Exercise 6.3

1 **Find the areas of the following triangles without counting the squares.**

(a)

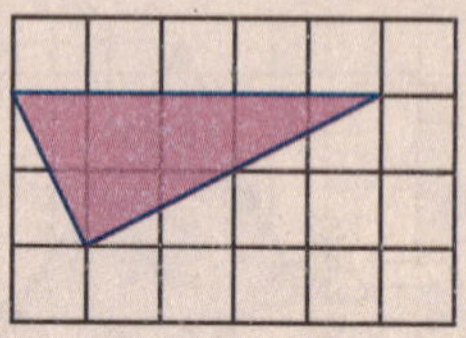

(b)

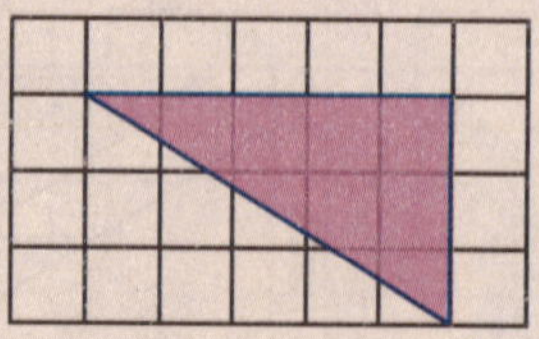

(c)

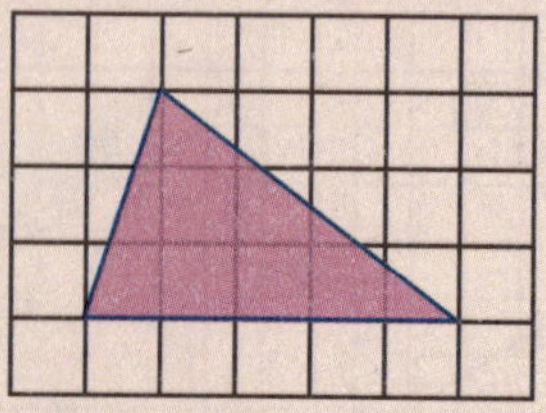

2 **Find the areas of the following triangles.**

(a)

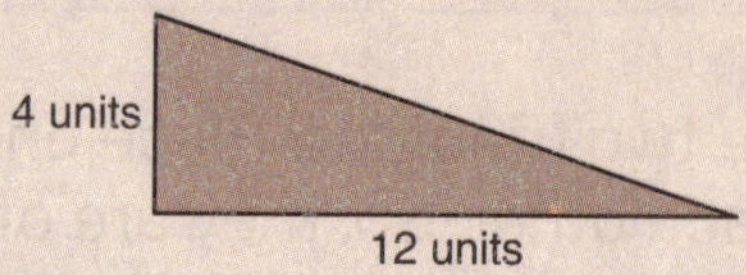

(b)

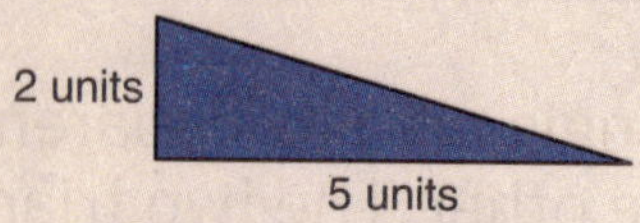

DIFFERENT UNITS OF AREA

We have been expressing area in terms of square units. Area is always measured in **square units**. The units can be mm, cm, m, km, miles, etc. The unit to be used depends on the size of the area that is being measured. The area of half of your eraser or half of a sim card can be of 1 sq. cm; the area of 25 textbooks, three newspaper sheets put adjacent to each other or 1 single bed sheet can be of 1 sq. m; the area twenty times of a school playground can be of 1 sq. km. Observe the areas of the following.

Area of the book = 500 sq. cm

Area of classroom = 150 sq. m

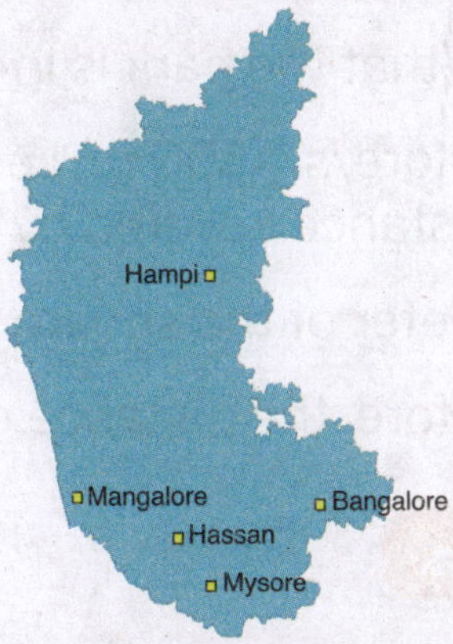

Area of Karnataka state = 1,91,976 sq. km

Smaller areas such as book, bench, etc. are measured in square centimetres. Medium areas such as classroom, playground, etc. are measured in square metres. Larger areas such as area of the town, state, etc. are measured in square kilometres.

Cross-curricular Link: Collect information on the dimensions of the different playing courts such as volleyball court, basketball court, kho-kho court, etc. and find their areas and perimeters.

WORD PROBLEMS

Perimeter

Example 1: Pramod has got a beautiful garden which is rectangular in shape. Its length is 20 m and breadth is 12 m. Find the perimeter of the garden and the cost of fencing the garden if it costs ₹300 per metre.

Given that the length (ℓ) of the garden = 20 m and breadth (b) of the garden = 12 m.

Therefore, the perimeter of the rectangular garden. $P = 2(\ell + b) = 2(20 + 12) = 2(32) = 64$ m

The cost of fencing the garden per metre = ₹300

Therefore, the cost of fencing the garden = **perimeter of the garden × cost of fencing per metre** = 64 × 300 = ₹19,200

Example 2: Pradeep goes for a walk in a nearby park which is in square shape. Length of its side is 100 m. If he walks three rounds, what is the distance covered by him?

Given that the park is in the shape of a square and its side is 100 m.

Therefore, *s* = 100 m. Let us first find the perimeter of the park which gives us the distance covered by Pradeep in one round.

Perimeter of the square park = 4 × s = 4 × 100 m = 400 m.

Therefore, the distance covered by Pradeep in three rounds is 3 × 400 m = 1200 m.

Area

Example 1: Shalini wants to decorate a wall of her reading room with square charts of side 2 m. The wall is 6 m in length and 4 m in height. How many charts are needed to completely cover the wall?

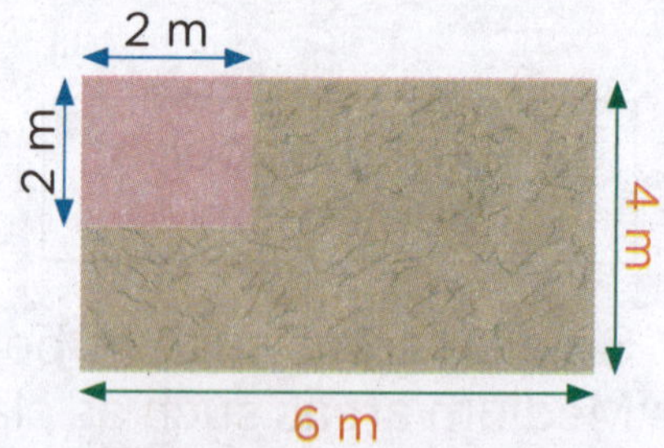

Given that the length (ℓ) of the wall is 6 m and breadth (*b*) of the wall is 4 m.

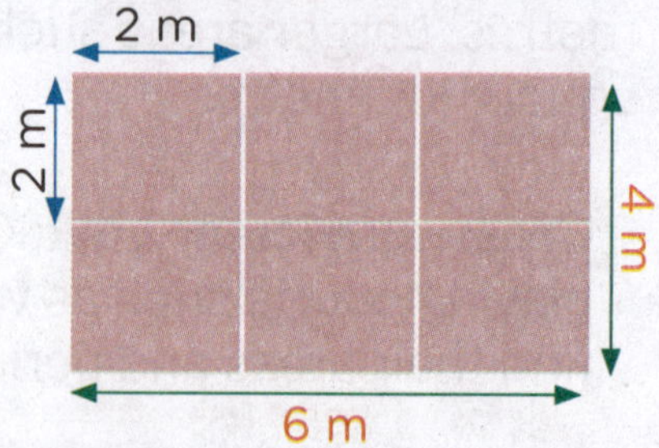

Therefore, area of the wall = $\ell \times b = 6 \times 4 = 24$ sq. m
It is also given that the side (*s*) of a square chart is 2 m.

Therefore, area of the chart = $s \times s = 2 \times 2 = 4$ sq. m

To find out the number of charts required to completely cover the wall, we need to divide the area of the wall by the area of the chart.

Therefore, the number of charts required = $\dfrac{\text{area of the wall}}{\text{area of the chart}} = \dfrac{24}{4} = 6.$

Example 2: Rajesh wants to paint a wall of his son's room. The wall is in the shape of a square of side 8 m. The cost of painting the wall is ₹95 per sq. m. It includes the cost of the paint and the labour charges. How much does Rajesh have to spend to paint his wall?

Given that the wall is in the shape of a square and its side (s) is 8 m.

Therefore, the area of the wall is given by $8 \times 8 = 64$ sq. m.

It is also given that it costs ₹95 per sq. m to paint the wall. Therefore, the total cost of painting the wall is given by area of the wall × cost per sq. m.

Therefore, total cost of painting the wall = 64×95 = ₹6080.

Exercise 6.4

1. Arvind has bought a computer. The length and the breadth of the computer monitor are 30 inches and 20 inches respectively. Find the perimeter of the computer monitor.

2. Hari bought a rectangular-shaped cake of length 30 cm and breadth 25 cm for his sister's birthday. He wants to decorate it by putting a ribbon along its edges. What is the length of the ribbon required by Hari? (*Hint:* Find the perimeter.)

3. Harshini has a square pillow of side 45 cm. She wants to put a lace border around it. What is the length of the lace required by her? (*Hint:* Find the perimeter.)

4. Murthy has a rectangular wooden box whose length is 7 m and breadth is 5 m. He wants to cover the top surface of it with a nice cloth. The cost of the cloth is ₹50 per sq. m. How much will it cost Murthy to cover the wooden box? (*Hint:* Find the area of the top surface of the box.)

5. A square field has a perimeter of 640 m. Find the length of its sides and also its area.

6. Find the area of a tile of dimensions 6 cm by 5 cm.

7. The breadth of a rectangular field is 40 m. Its length is twice its breadth. Find the area of the field.

8. Find the area of a rectangular region of dimensions 150 cm by 100 cm.

Revision Exercise

1 Find the perimeter and area of each of the following figures.

(a) 8 cm, 8 cm

(b) 20 cm, 20 cm

(c) 13 cm, 7 cm

2 Take a ₹5 note and a ₹10 note. Use a ruler and measure their lengths and breadths. Find and compare their areas and perimeters.

3 Find the areas of the following triangles.

(a)

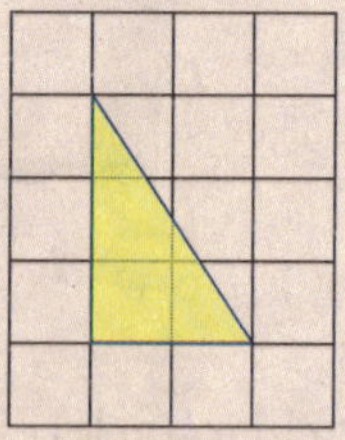

(b)

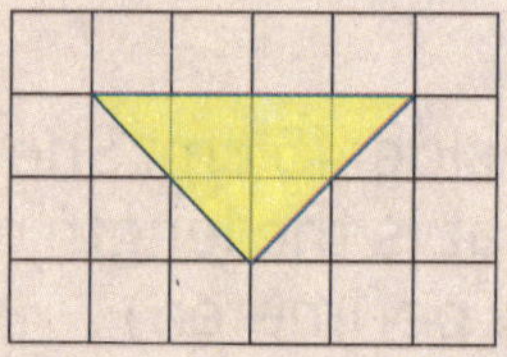

(c)

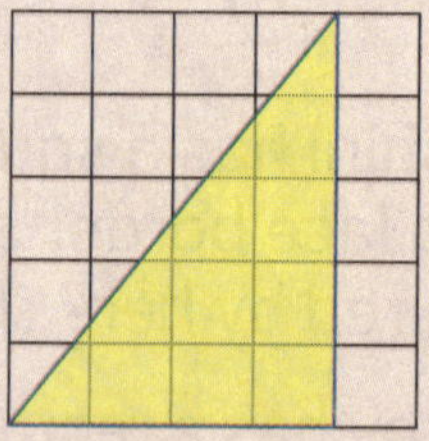

4 Write the appropriate units (sq. cm/sq. m/sq. km) for the areas of the following.

Blackboard		Arabian Sea		TV screen	
Tiffin box		Mobile		Cricket field	
Forest		Plate		Desert	

5 Find the cost of painting a compound wall which is 100 m long and 7 m high at ₹15 per square metre. (*Hint:* Find the area of the compound wall.)

6 The perimeter of a rectangular field is 400 m. If its length is 120 m, then find its breadth.

7 Ragini wants to lay tiles of size 20 cm × 20 cm on the floor of her kitchen which is 8 m in length and 4 m in breadth. How many tiles are required to completely cover the floor? (*Hint:* Divide the area of the kitchen by the area of the tiles.)

8 Find the perimeter and the area of a square field whose side is 15 m.

7 Volume and Nets

Learning Objectives

- To find the volume of a cube and a cuboid
- To draw solid shapes such as cubes and cuboids on isometric dot paper
- To draw the top view, front view and side view of different solids

Let's Get Started

In the previous class, you learned about how to find the volume of a box by counting the number of unit cubes it can hold. Let us find the volume of this empty box.

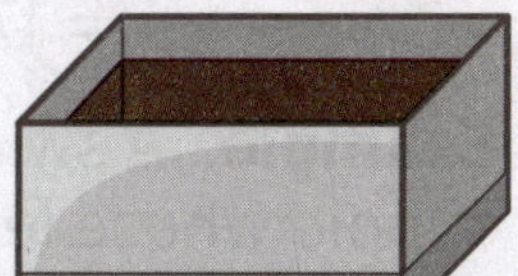

There are 5 rows in one layer and there are 6 cubes in each row.

Therefore, the number of cubes in one layer is 6 × 5 = 30.

Let us fill the box completely with centimetre cubes and count the number of layers.

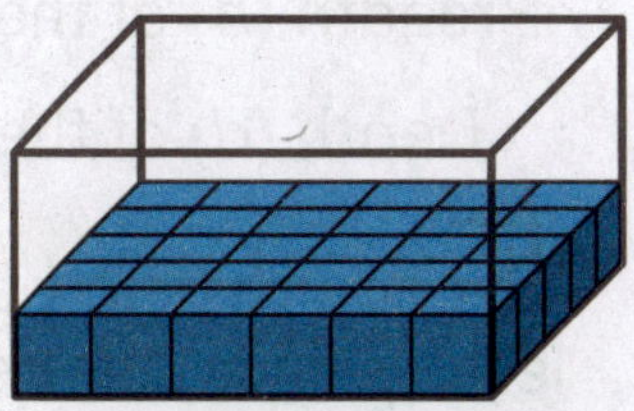

There are 3 layers. The total number of centimetre cubes filled in the box is (6 × 5) × 3 = 90. Therefore, the volume of this empty box is 90 cu. cm. We can use a short cut method to find the volume of any cuboid (as we did for finding the area of a rectangle). We need not count each time the number of unit cubes it will hold.

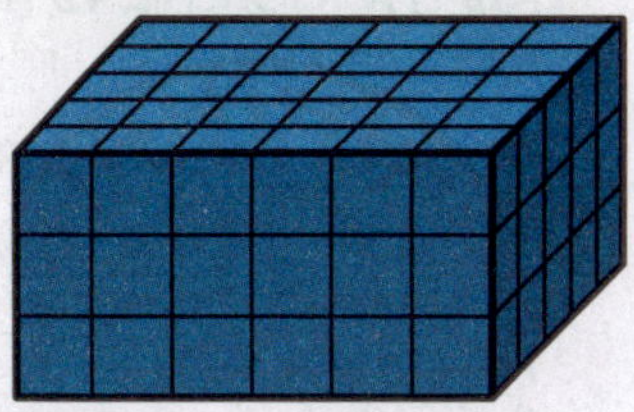

Volume of any cuboidal box = Number of cubes per layer × Number of layers

= Number of cubes in each row × Number of rows × Number of layers

Length (ℓ) × **Breadth (b)** × **Height (h)**

Therefore, the volume of a cuboid whose length is ℓ, breadth is b and height is h is given by:
Volume = length × breadth × height

$$V = \ell \times b \times h$$

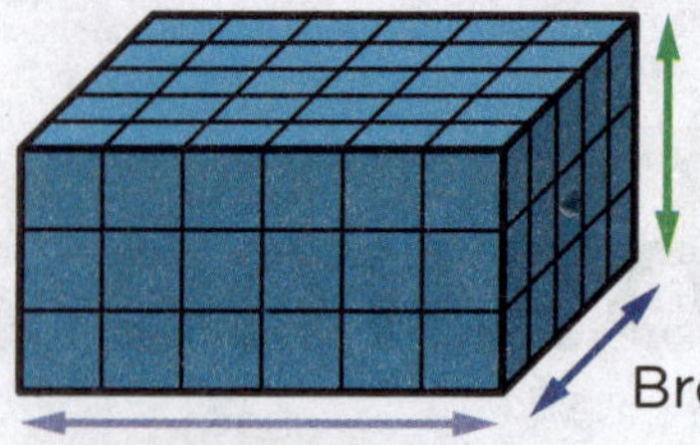

Volume of the wooden box is given by V = $\ell \times b \times h$

= 12 cm × 12 cm × 12 cm

= 1728 cu. cm

Volume of the ballot box shown here is given by

V = $\ell \times b \times h$ = 30 cm × 45 cm × 60 cm

= 81000 cu. cm

Example: A swimming pool is in the shape of a cuboid whose length is 50 m, breadth is 25 m and depth is 5 m. Find the volume of the pool.

Length (ℓ) of the swimming pool = 50 m

Breadth (b) of the swimming pool = 25 m

Depth (d) of the swimming pool = 5 m

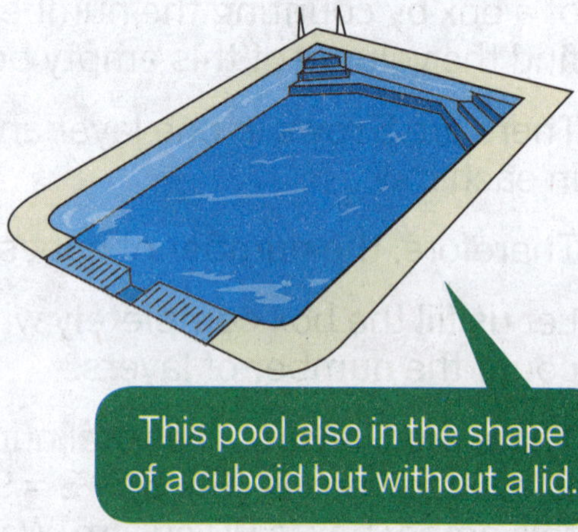

This pool also in the shape of a cuboid but without a lid.

The pool is below the ground level. Hence, the depth of a pool, not the height, is measured.

Therefore, the volume of the swimming pool = length × breadth × depth

= 50 m × 25 m × 5 m

= 6250 cu. cm

Activity

Use a ruler and measure the length, breadth and height of the available objects such as a notebook, a duster, a chair, a lunch box, etc. and find their volumes. Make a table in your notebook and record your observations. Write the appropriate units for volume.

Note: All the measurements of length, breadth and height should be in the same units.

Exercise 7.1

1 **Find the volumes of the following objects using the formula.**

(a)

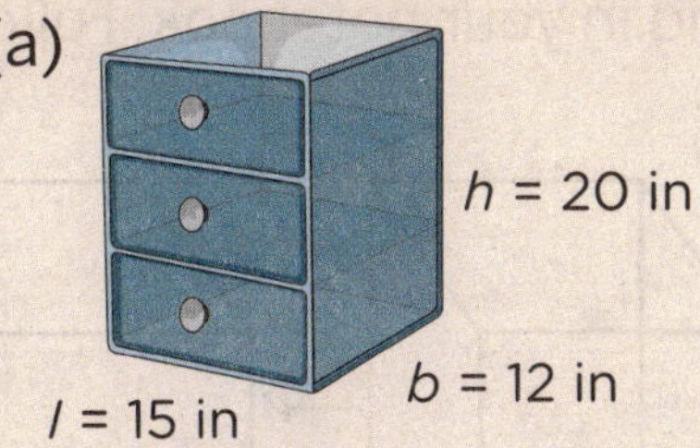

(b)

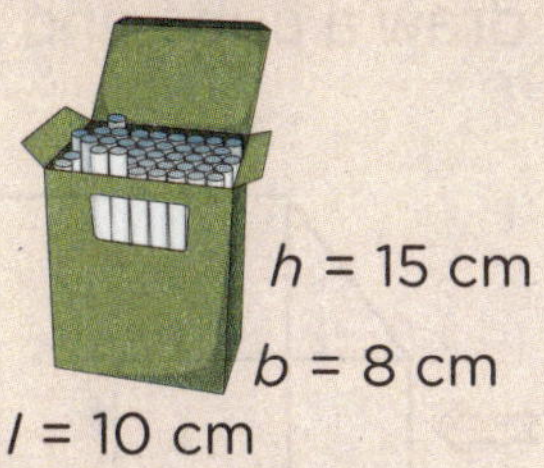

(c)

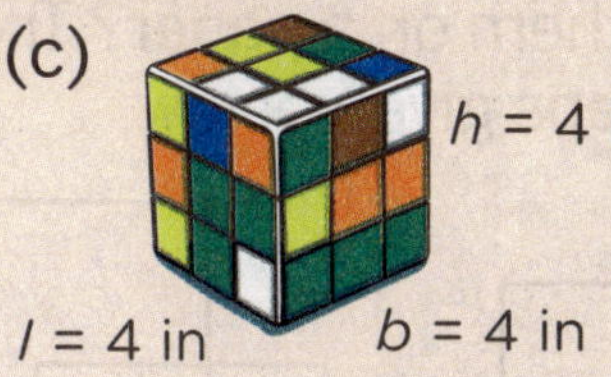

2 **Find the volumes of the solids given below.**

(a)

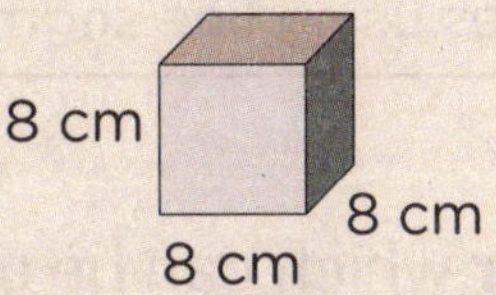

(b)

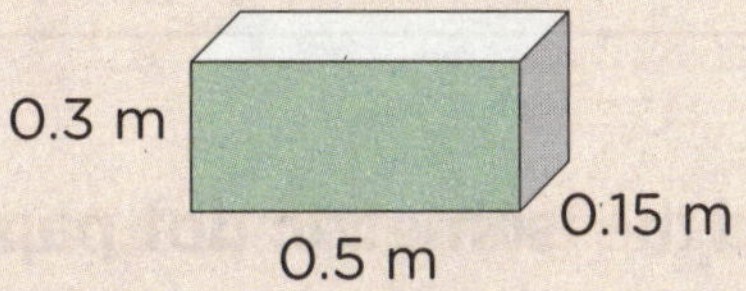

(c)

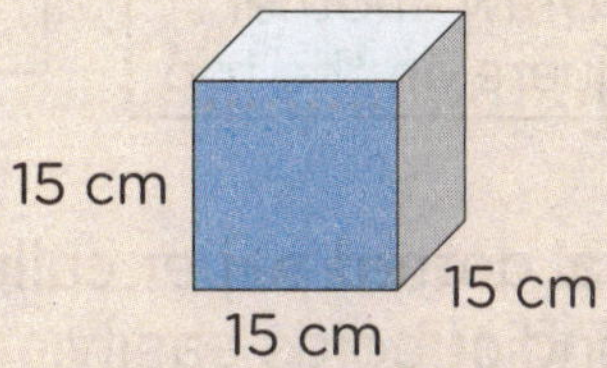

(d)

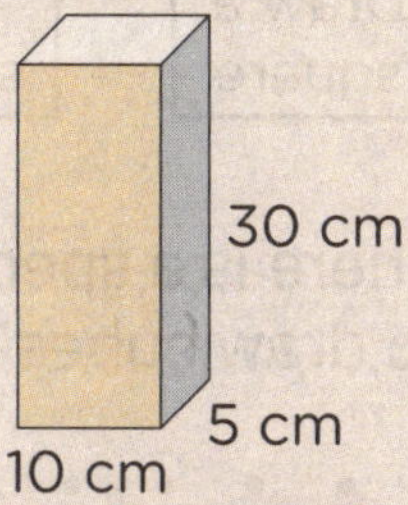

3 **Complete the table given below.**

S. No.	Length	Breadth	Height	Volume
(a)	7 cm	5 cm	2 cm	
(b)	3 m	7 m		84 cu. cm
(c)		2 mm	5 mm	30 cu. mm
(d)	150 cm	75 cm	50 cm	
(e)	10 m		12 m	2040 cu. m

4 A cuboid box of dimensions 30 cm × 20 cm × 6 cm has to be filled with matchboxes of dimensions 5 cm × 4 cm × 3 cm. Find the number of matchboxes it can hold. (*Hint:* Divide the volume of the cuboid box by the volume of a matchbox.)

5 A wooden piece which is in the shape of a cuboid has a length of 12 in, breadth of 8 in and thickness of 1 in. What will be the volume if 15 such wooden pieces are piled on top of each other?

6 A large container carrying bikes has the dimensions 20 ft × 10 ft × 8 ft. Find its volume.

DRAWING CUBES AND CUBOIDS

You might have seen many cubes and cuboids around you. Have you ever tried to draw them on a paper? Try to draw a cube and a cuboid in your notebook. Follow the steps given below.

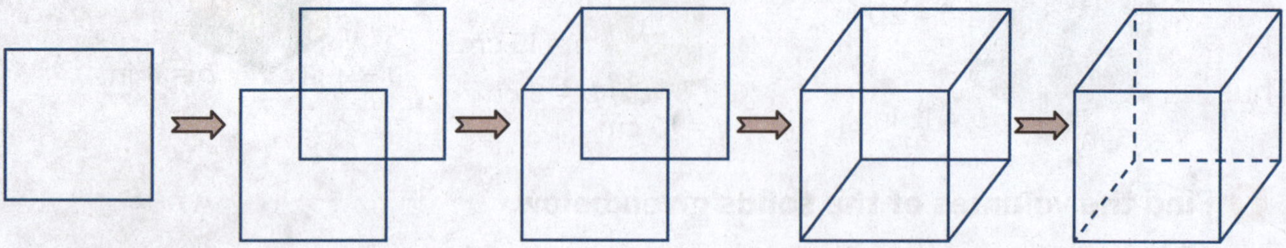

Draw a square → Draw another square on the top → Join the corresponding vertices using line segments.

There is a special dotted paper called the **isometric dot paper** which can be used to draw cubes and cuboids easily.

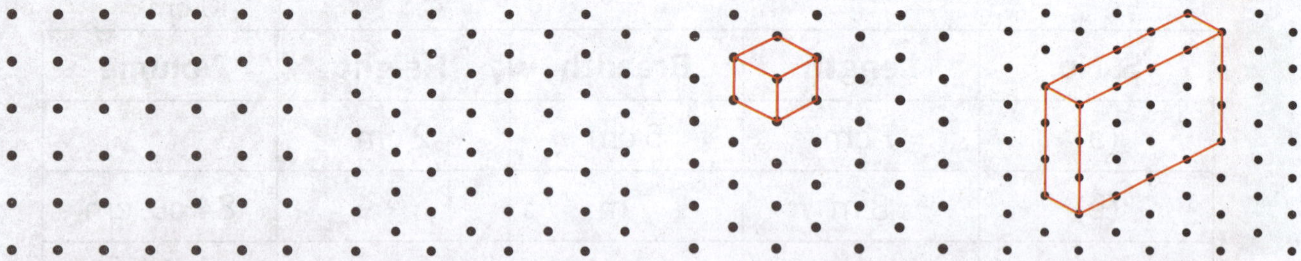

Dot paper | Isometric dot paper | Cube | Cuboid

DIFFERENT VIEWS OF SOLID SHAPES

Have you ever looked at your house from different angles? Does it look the same from all the angles? No, it looks different from the top, different from the front and different from the side. Here are the front, top and side views of a house.

Front view | Top view | Side view

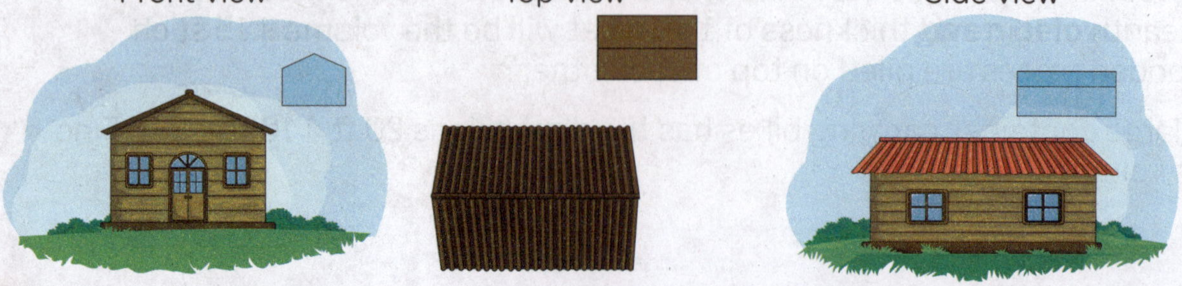

Look at the different views of a bus given below.

Front view

Side view

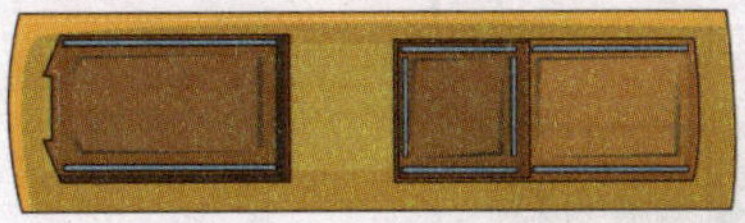

Top view

Thus, solid shapes also look different from different angles.

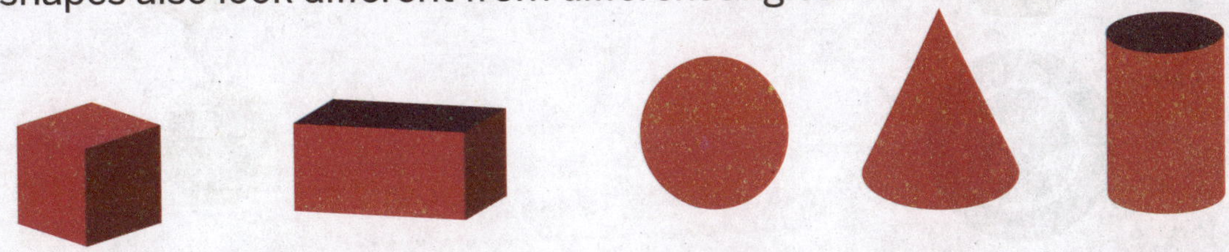

Cube *Cuboid* *Sphere* *Cone* *Cylinder*

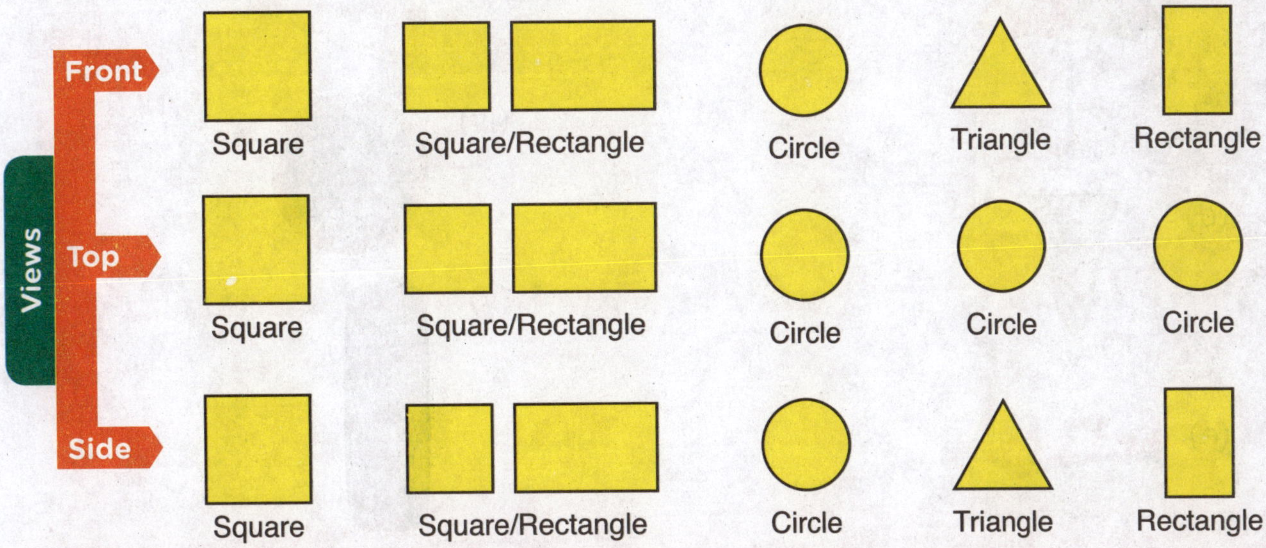

Exercise 7.2

1 Draw the remaining parts of cubes and cuboids given below.

(a)

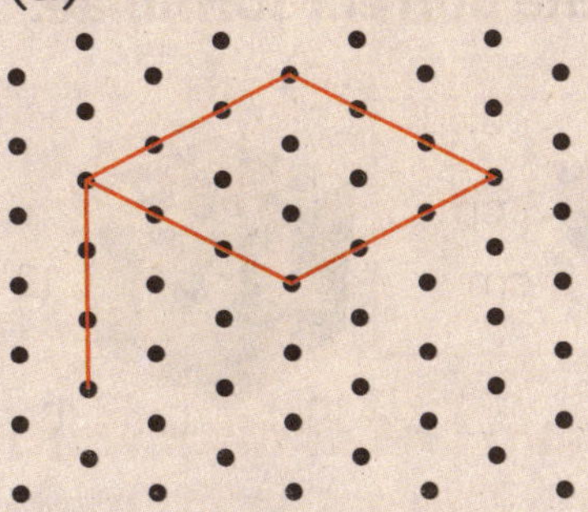

(b)

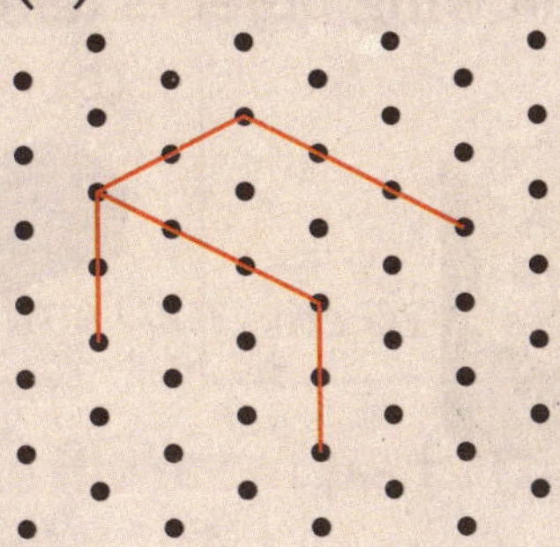

(c)

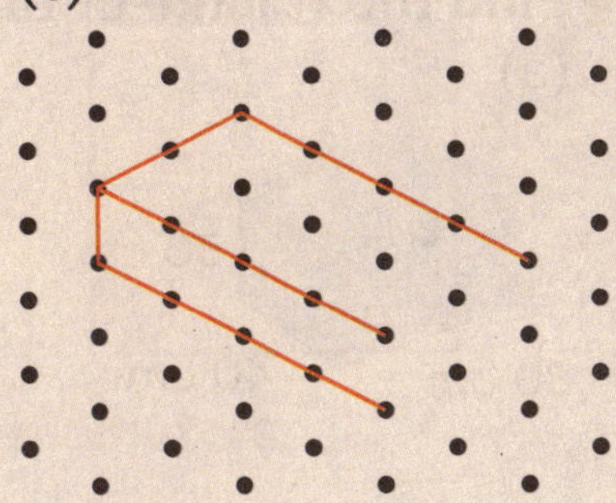

2 **Match the side view of the objects to their top views.**

Side View

(a) 

(b) 

(c) 

(d) 

(e) 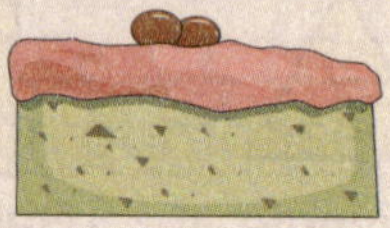

Top View

(i) 

(ii) 

(iii) 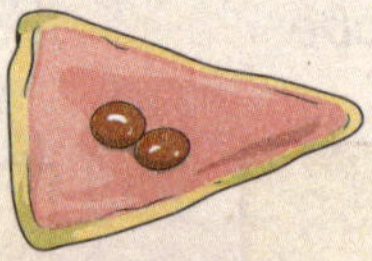

(iv) 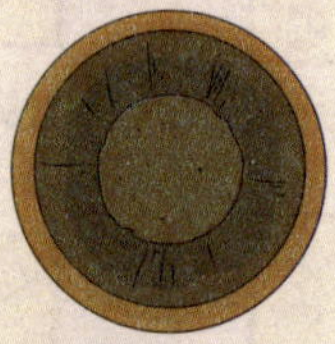

(v) 

Revision Exercise

1 **Find the volume of the following objects using the correct formulae.**

(a) 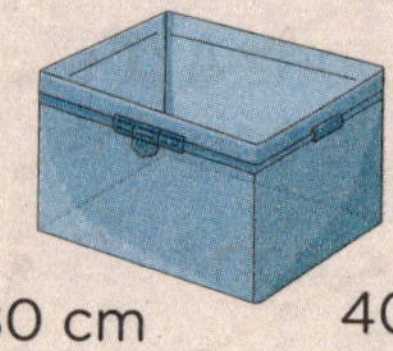

30 cm, 80 cm, 40 cm

(b) 

20 cm, 10 cm, 7 cm

(c) 

3 cm, 20 cm, 5 cm

(d) 

12 in, 12 in, 12 in

2 **The dimensions of some objects are given below. Find their volumes and write the appropriate units.**

(a)

Length (ℓ) = 5 mm
Breadth (b) = 3 mm
Height (h) = 2 mm
Volume (V) = ____

(b)

Length (ℓ) = 12 cm
Breadth (b) = 9 cm
Height (h) = 5 cm
Volume (V) = ____

(c)

Length (ℓ) = 3 m
Breadth (b) = 5 m
Height (h) = 7 m
Volume (V) = ____

3 **Match the shapes with their views.**

(a) 

(b) 

(c) 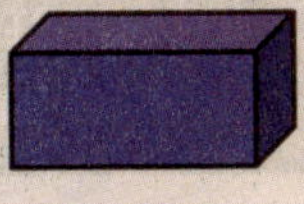

(d) 

(e) 

(i) The top and front views are rectangles.

(ii) The side view is a rectangle and the top view is a circle.

(iii) The top and front views are squares.

(iv) The top and front views are circles.

(v) The side view is a triangle.

HOTS (Higher Order Thinking Skills)

A rectangular container has length 20 cm, breadth 10 cm and height 30 cm. It is filled with water to a height of 10 cm.

How much more water should be added to fill the container completely?

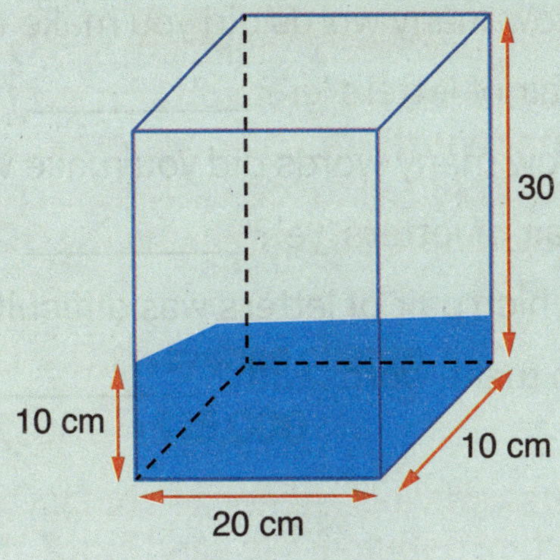

8 Data Handling

Learning Objectives

- To read circle graphs and line graphs
- To record data using tally marks

Let's Get Started

Write as many words as you can having the letters mentioned below.

1. Words having 'ea' together: For example–clear, rear
2. Words having 'ie' together: For example–quiet, field
3. Words having 'ei' together: For example–receive, eight
4. Words having 'ye' together: For example–yell, dye
5. Words having 'ey' together: For example – monkey, kidney

This exercise integrates Maths and English

Complete the bar graph using different colours.

Answer the following questions.

(a) With which pair of letters could you make the maximum words? __________

(b) How many words did you make with the pair of letters 'ei'? __________

(c) How many words did you make with the pair of letters 'ye'? __________

(d) Which pair of letters was difficult to make words with? __________

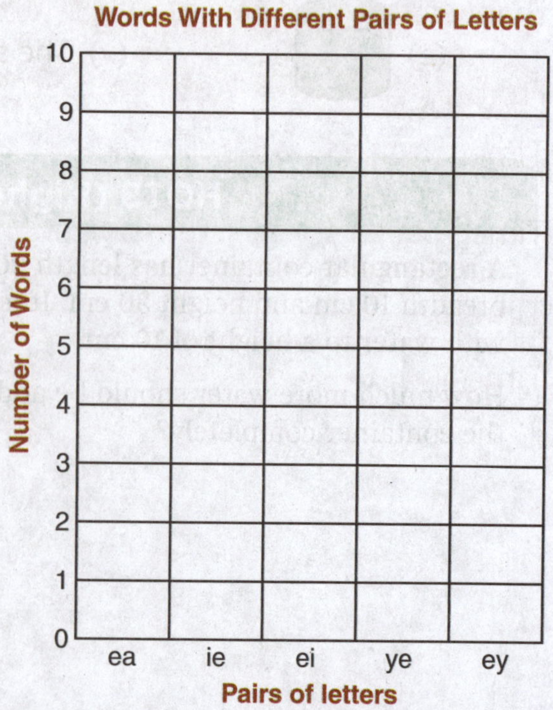

CIRCLE GRAPHS

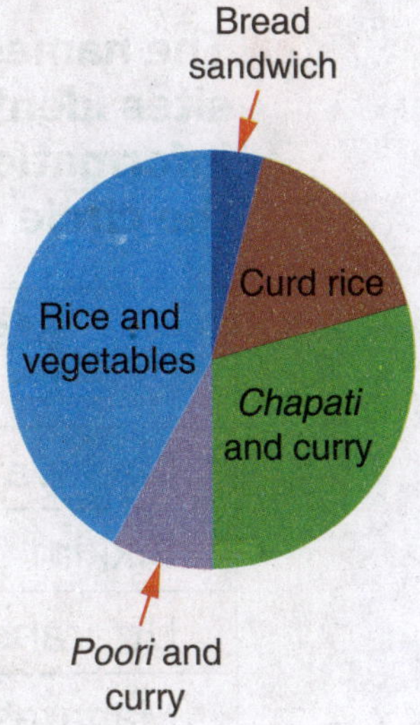

Circle graph is a circular chart divided into different sections. Different parts of the information are represented by these sections. It shows how different parts of information are related to the whole and to each other.

Example 1: The circle graph shown here represents information about different dishes in Amar's lunch box in a particular month.

(a) Which dish did he take the maximum number of times in this month? Rice and vegetables

(b) Which dish did he take the minimum number of times in this month? Bread sandwich

(c) Was curd rice taken more often than *chapati* and curry? (Yes/No) No

(d) Did Amar's box contain *poori* and curry the same number of times as curd rice? (Yes/No) No

Example 2: The number of hours spent by Monica after school on different activities in a particular week is listed below and represented in the circle chart. The circle represents 16 hours.

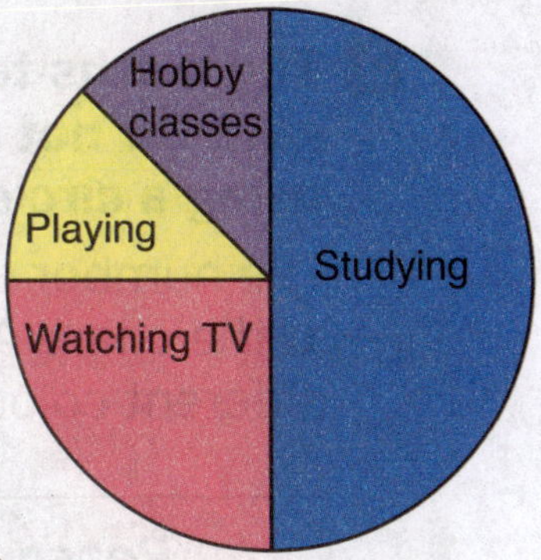

Let us find the number of hours spent by Monica on each activity.

The total number of hours spent by Monica on these activities in that week was 16 hours since the circle represents 16 hours.

From the circle graph, we can find:

Time spent on studying is $\frac{1}{2}$ of the total hours $= \frac{1}{2} \times 16 = 8$ hours

Time spent on watching TV is $\frac{1}{4}$ of the total hours $= \frac{1}{4} \times 16 = 4$ hours

Time spent on playing is half of $\frac{1}{4}$ of the total hours $= \frac{1}{2}\left(\frac{1}{4}\right) \times 16 = \frac{1}{8} \times 16 = 2$ hours

Time spent on hobby classes is same as time spent on playing, i.e., 2 hours.

Activity	Number of Hours
Studying	8
Watching TV	4
Playing	2
Hobby classes	2

Exercise 8.1

1 **The names of some Indian states and the number of world heritage sites identified by UNESCO in those states are listed below. The information is also represented in a circle chart. Complete labelling the circle chart by looking at the list.**

State	Number of World Heritage Sites
Madhya Pradesh	3
Sikkim	1
Uttaranchal	1
Maharashtra	4
Karnataka	2
Rajasthan	2
Assam	2
Uttar Pradesh	3

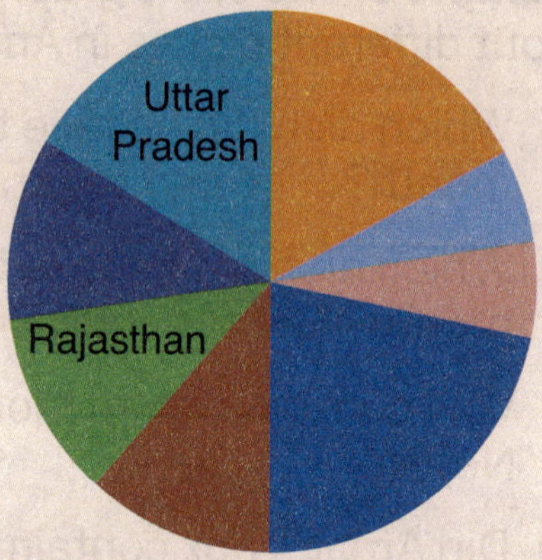

How many world heritage sites are there in these 8 states?

2 **The maths teacher made a list of all the reasons that the students gave for not being prepared for the test. She represented the reasons using a circle chart.**

The number of students in the class is 30. Complete the table by looking at the chart. Also, colour the different sections of the circle chart in different colours.

Reasons	Number of Students
Too much homework	15

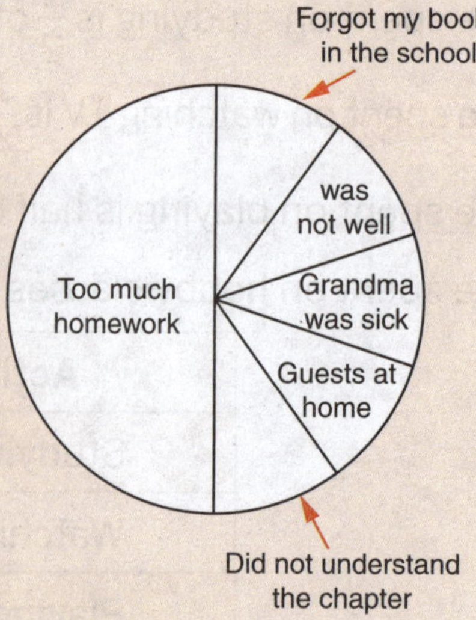

TALLY MARKS

Shyam collected data on the favourite colours of his classmates.

Red, Red, Blue, Green, Green, Green, White, White, Black, Yellow, Yellow, Red, Red, Blue, Red, Red, Green, Green, Blue, Black, Blue, Blue, Yellow, Green, Yellow, Yellow, White, White, Red, Green, Red, Red, White, Red, Green, Blue, Blue, Green, Yellow, Red

He used tally marks to record the data. Let us observe the table and answer the questions given.

Colours	Tally Marks	Number of Students
Red	𝍸 𝍸 𝍷	11
White	𝍸	5
Black	𝍷𝍷	2
Yellow	𝍸 𝍷	6
Blue	𝍸 𝍷𝍷	7
Green	𝍸 𝍷𝍷𝍷𝍷	9

(a) Which colour is liked by most of the students? Red

(b) Which colour is least liked by the students? Black

(c) Which colour is liked by 9 students? Green

(d) How many students are there in the class? 40

Choose the correct numbers to match the tally marks and write them in the spaces provided.

1	2	3	4	5	6	7	8	9	10	11	12	13	14

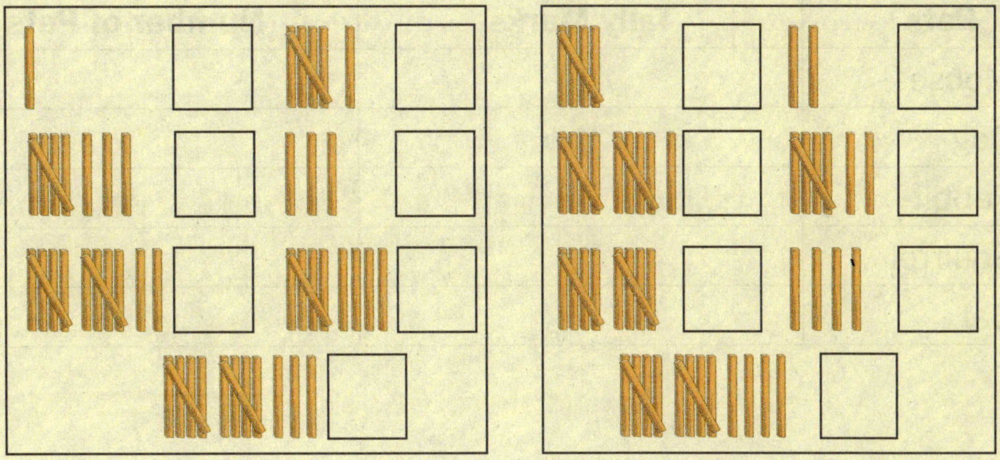

Exercise 8.2

1 **This is the warning board on the way to Hanakapiai Beach in Hawaiian Islands. The sandy shore is clearly visible during summer but during winter months, the dangerously powerful waves wash away the sandy shoreline.**

How many visitors have drowned according to this warning?

2 **Count the different pets in the given picture starting from the first one. As you count, draw a cross over the picture to show that it has been counted.**

Complete the tally chart for the number of pets.

Pets	Tally Marks	Number of Pets
Mouse	|	
Dog		
Rabbit		
Squirrel		
Cat		

LINE GRAPHS

The number of students in different years since the school began in 2007 is listed below. This data is recorded in a line graph by putting a dot on the chart every year, after the admissions are completed.

Year	Number of Students
2007	50
2008	200
2009	350
2010	400
2011	450
2012	500
2013	600

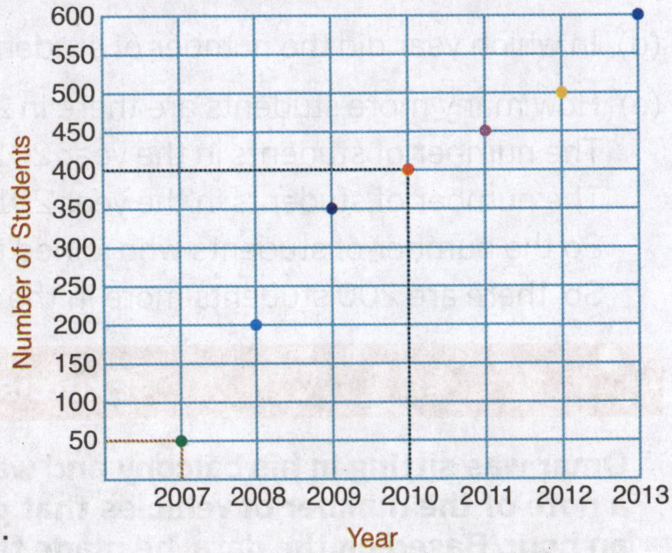

Let us see how the dots have been placed.

The red vertical line shows year 2007 and the red horizontal line shows 50 students. The green dot has been placed where the two red lines meet. It means that in the year 2007, when the school began, the number of students was 50.

The red dot is placed where the black vertical and horizontal lines meet. The red dot shows that in the year 2010, there were 400 students.

Similarly, find out what the other dots represent.

On joining the dots, you get a line graph.

Use a ruler to know exactly where the dots are placed.

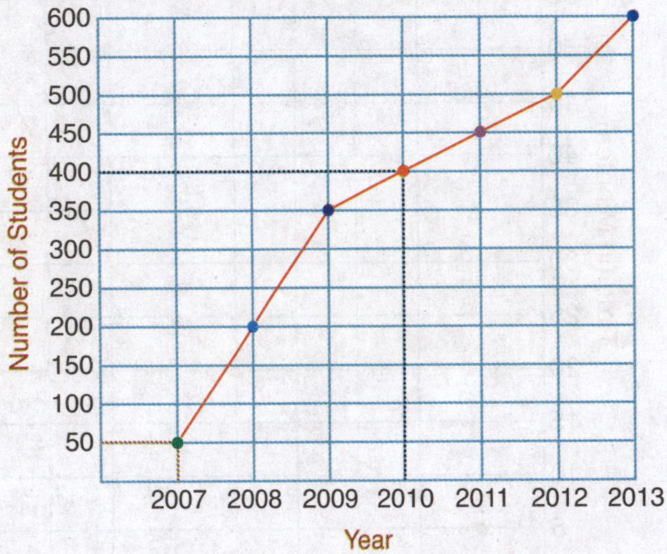

Answer the following questions.

(a) What was the number of students when the school began? 50

(b) What was the number of students in the year 2012? 500

(c) How many students joined in the year 2008?

The number of students in the year 2007 = 50

The number of students in the year 2008 = 200

So, the number of students who joined in 2008 = 200 – 50 = 150

(d) In which year did the number of students reach 450? 2011

(e) How many more students are there in 2013 than in the year 2010?

The number of students in the year 2013 = 600

The number of students in the year 2010 = 400

So the number of students who joined in 2008 = 600 – 400 = 200

So, there are 200 students more in the year 2013 than in the year 2010.

Exercise 8.3

Omar was sitting in his balcony and watching the vehicles go by. He made a note of the number of vehicles that passed by after every 5 minutes for an hour. Based on the data, he made the following line graph.

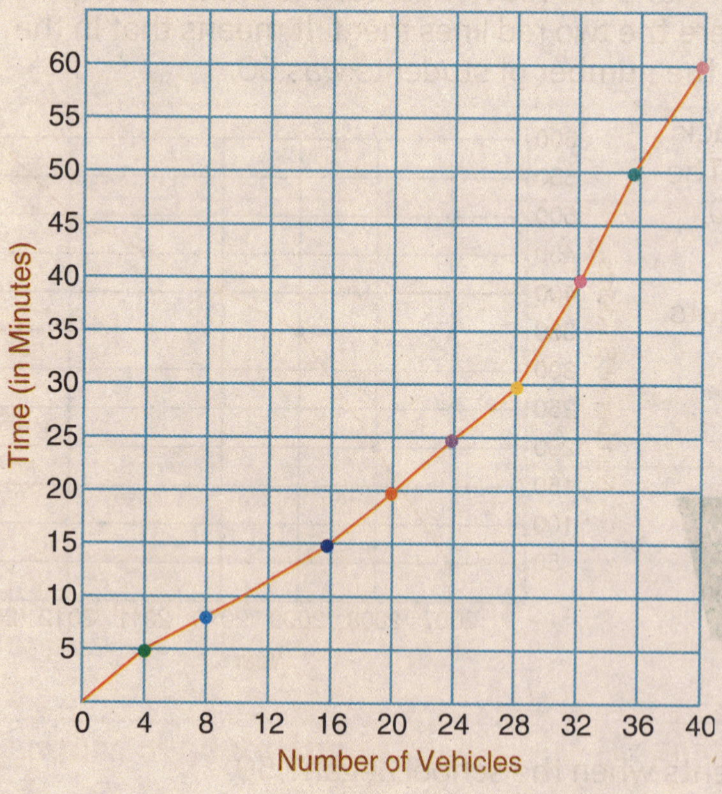

Answer the following questions.

1. When did 8 vehicles pass by?
2. How many vehicles had passed by the end of 25 minutes?
3. How many more vehicles had passed by the end of 30 minutes compared to 15 minutes?
4. When did the 40 vehicle pass by?

Revision Exercise

1 Choose the correct answers.

(a) 100 children were asked whether they liked to draw and paint. 75 children answered yes. What fraction of the circle chart will the yes section take up?

(i) $\frac{3}{4}$ (ii) $\frac{1}{2}$ (iii) $\frac{1}{3}$ (iv) $\frac{2}{3}$

(b) Which of the following graphs will be best at showing the temperature variations of a city over a week?

(i) Pictograph (ii) Circle chart (iii) Bar graph (iv) Line graph

(c) Tally marks are drawn in groups of

(i) 5 (ii) 4 (iii) 3 (iv) 2

(d) Which set of tally marks shows 30?

(i) 卌 卌 卌
(iii) 卌 卌 卌 卌 卌
(ii) 卌 卌 卌 卌 卌 卌
(iv) 卌

2 The population of different areas of a town is represented in the circle chart.

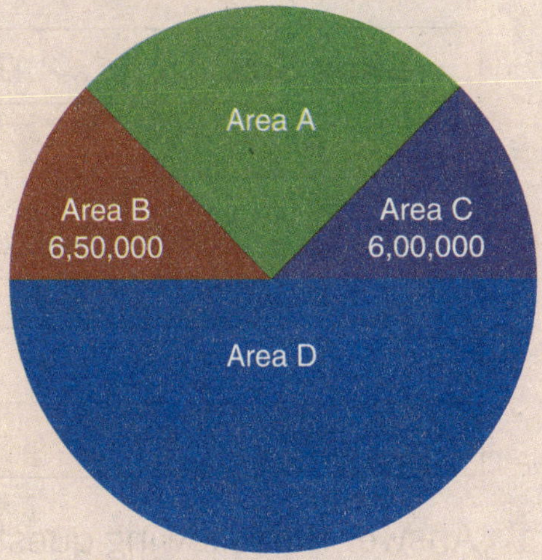

(a) What fraction of the whole population is the population of Area A?

(b) The population of Area A is

(i) 6,50,000
(ii) 6,00,000
(iii) 6,50,000 – 6,00,000
(iv) 6,50,000 + 6,00,000

(c) Population of Area D is __________ the population of the town.

(i) $\frac{1}{2}$ (ii) $\frac{1}{4}$ (iii) $\frac{3}{4}$ (iv) $\frac{1}{8}$

(d) What is the total population of the town?

3 The number of charts put up on the display board in Class 5 is shown in the bar graph.

Answer the following questions.

(a) What is the number of Hindi and English charts on the display board?

(b) How many fewer maths charts are there than science charts?

(c) Is the total number of English and Hindi charts the same as the number of maths charts?

(d) How many more science charts are there than social science charts?

(e) What is the total number of charts on the display board?

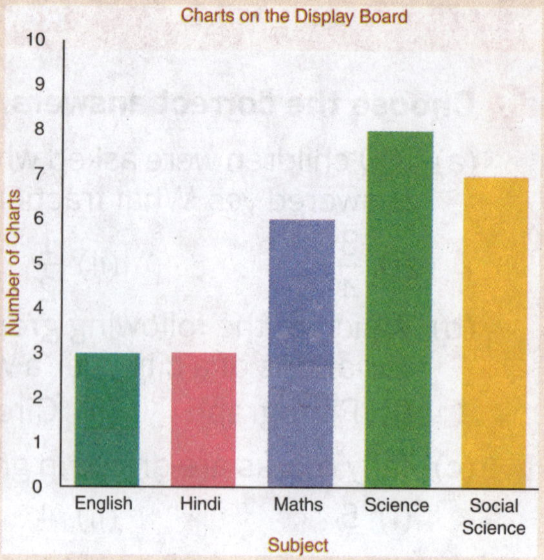

4 The following are the shoe sizes of different students of Class 5. Complete the tally chart for the data.

4	6	4	6	5	4	5
5	6	4	6	6	7	5
7	4	4	6	4	6	4
7	7	4	4	7	7	7
5	5	5	7	8	5	6

Shoe Size	Tally Marks	Number of Students
4		
5		
6		
7		
8		

Answer the following questions.

(a) Which shoe size is worn by the maximum number of students?

(b) Which shoe size is worn by the least number of students?

(c) How many students wear the maximum size?

(d) __________ students wear size 6.

(e) There are 42 students in Class 5. (True/False)

9 Symmetry

Learning Objectives

- To classify figures based on the lines of symmetry and learn about reflection symmetry
- To learn about rotational symmetry and identify figures with quarter, half and full turns
- To learn about rotational symmetry in English alphabets and words

Let's Get Started

A figure is said to be **symmetrical** if it has mirror halves. One half will be a reflection of the other.

The line which divides the figure into halves is known as the **line of symmetry**.

1. Tick (✓) the figures which are symmetrical among the following.

(a)  (b)  (c)  (d)  (e) 

2. Draw the line of symmetry for the following figures if they are symmetrical.

(a)  (b)  (c)  (d) 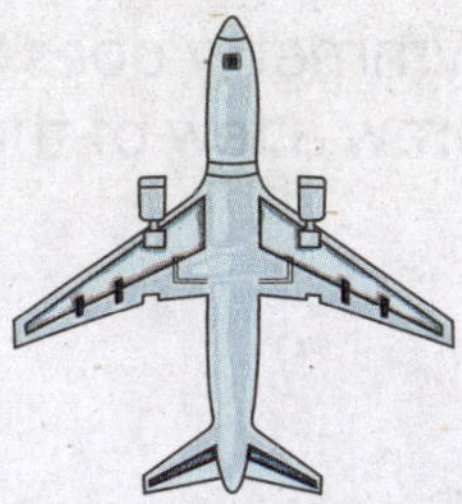

REFLECTION SYMMETRY

Look at the following buildings. Architects have used the concept of symmetry to construct these buildings. If you place a mirror along the dotted line in each of the figures, you can see that one-half is the mirror reflection of the other half.

The line along which the mirror is placed known as the line of symmetry. A figure is said to have **reflection symmetry** if one half of it is the mirror image of the other half. If you fold the image along the line of symmetry, each part exactly coincides with the other.

Merchandise Mart - Famous Building in Chicago River Bank

Eiffel Tower - Paris

Leaning Tower of Pisa - Italy

Sun Temple - Konark

All the above figures have only one line of symmetry. Can a figure have more than one line of symmetry? Yes. Look at the following figures which have more than one line of symmetry.

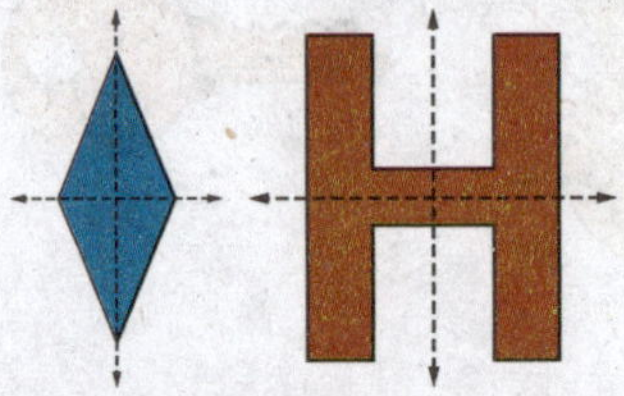
Figures with **two lines of symmetry**

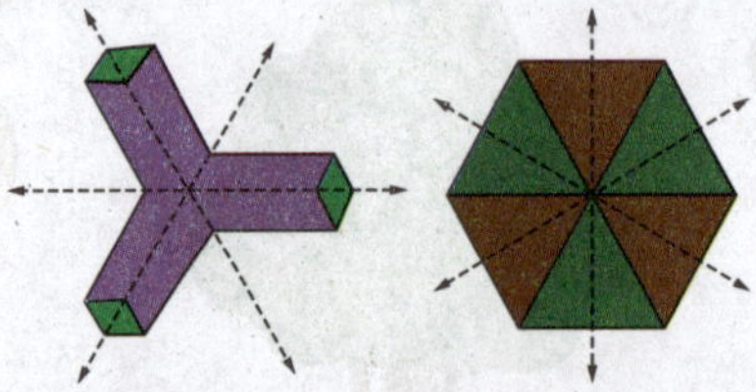
Figures with **three lines of symmetry**

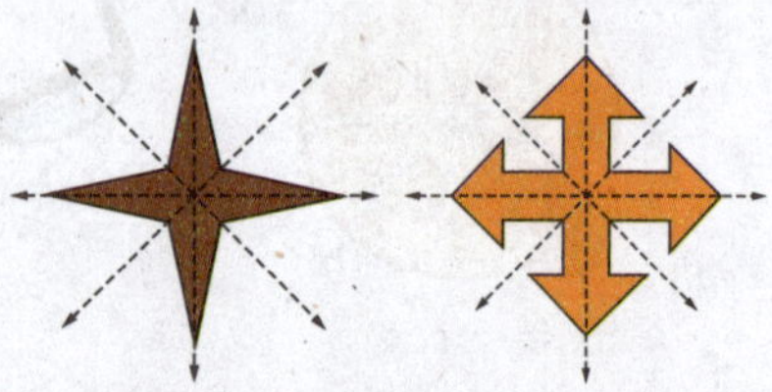
Figures with **four lines of symmetry**

Challenge: How many lines of symmetry does a circle have? Draw a few of them.

Do You Know?

Reflection symmetry is also known as line symmetry or mirror symmetry.

Look at the adjoining figures. Figure A is symmetrical and the dotted lines are the lines of symmetry, whereas Figure B is not symmetrical and the dotted lines are not the lines of symmetry. Though both of them have same shape (square), Fig B has a drawing inside which is not symmetrical. So, we have to consider not only the shape but also all parts of the figure. We cannot decide whether the figure is symmetric or not only by looking at its shape. We should consider all the parts of the figure.

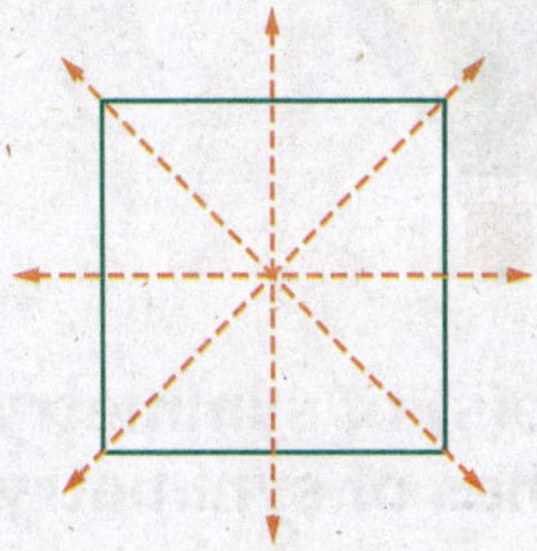

Figure A

Figure B

Symmetry in Symbols

The mathematical symbols (+, −, ×, ÷, =) also exhibit the line symmetry. Draw the lines of symmetry for them and identify the number of lines of symmetry for each symbol.

Symmetry in Face Masks

The following are different face mask designs. Draw the lines of symmetry for them.

Exercise 9.1

1 Which of the following pictures are symmetrical?

(a)

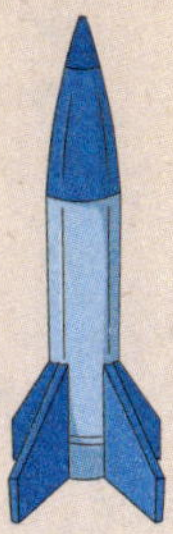

(b)

(c)  (d)  (e) 

2 **Draw the line(s) of symmetry for the following figures. Mention the number of lines of symmetry for each of them.**

(a) 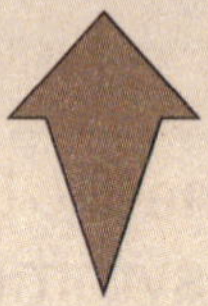 (b) 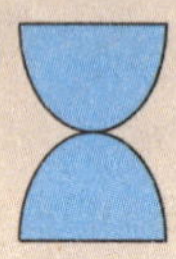 (c)  (d) 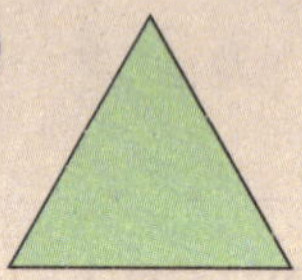 (e) 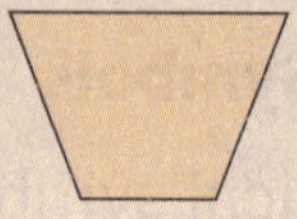 (f) 

3 **Which of the following dotted lines are lines of symmetry?**

(a)  (b) 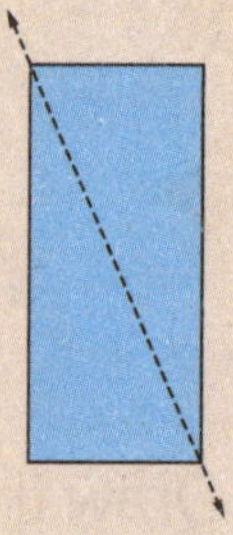 (c) 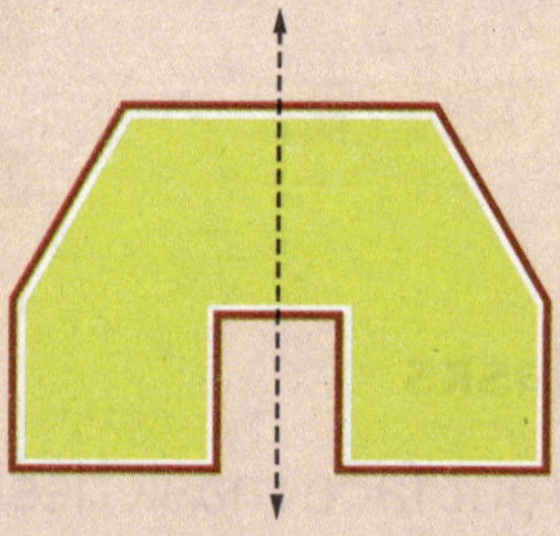 (d) 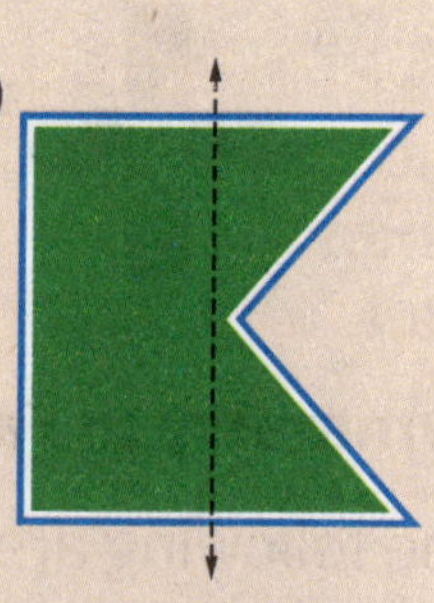

4 **Place the mirror along the yellow dotted line and draw the other half for each of the symmetrical figure given below.** (Note: Use a transparent sheet. Trace the figure, flip along the yellow dotted line and verify the figure you have drawn.)

(a)  (b)  (c) 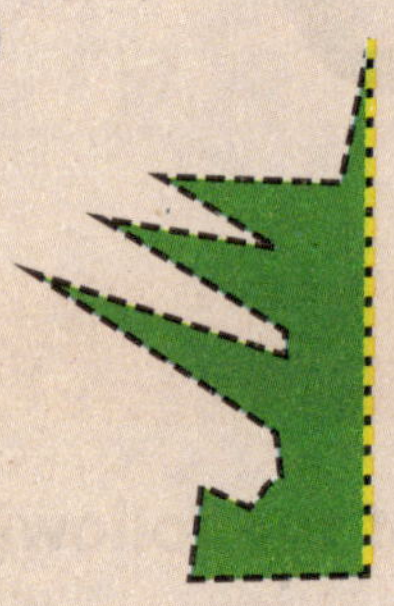

ROTATIONAL SYMMETRY

Look at the following figure. Is it symmetrical? Can you find the line(s) of symmetry?

This figure does not have any line of symmetry, but still it looks symmetrical.

There is another type of symmetry called **rotational symmetry**. This figure has rotational symmetry. A figure is said to have rotational symmetry if it fits exactly into itself when it is rotated by a certain amount of turn, that is, the figure looks exactly the same when it is rotated.

Before going into the details of rotational symmetry, let us learn about different turns.

Turns

Have you ever visited any village fair and sat on the giant wheel?

Consider the cabin in which you are sitting as the reference. When the giant wheel is rotated and when you come back to the same position from where you have started you would have completed one **full turn**. When you are exactly in the opposite position, then you would have completed **half turn**. Full turn, half turn and quarter turn are shown below.

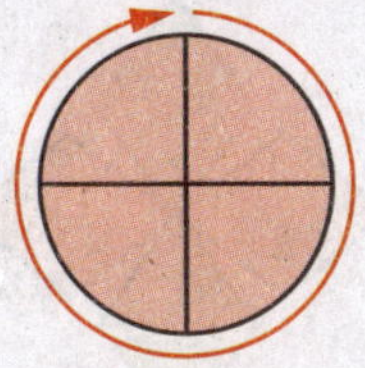

Full Turn

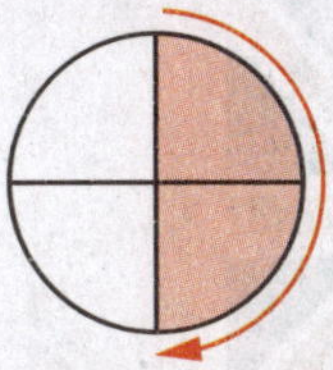

Half Turn or ½ Turn

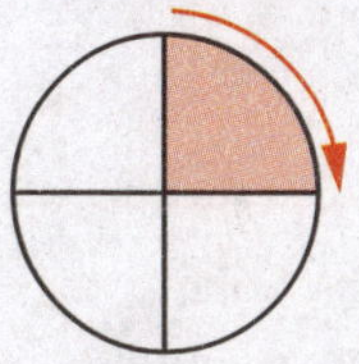

Quarter Turn or ¼ Turn

Let us see by how much turn the above picture has to be rotated to fit exactly into itself.

Activity

Copy this image on a transparent sheet. Insert a pin at the centre. Put a dot (red) for reference on both the images. Turn the image which is traced through the pin. Observe the original image and the traced image. Observe when the image will exactly fit into itself. Also observe how many times it coincided with itself in one full turn.

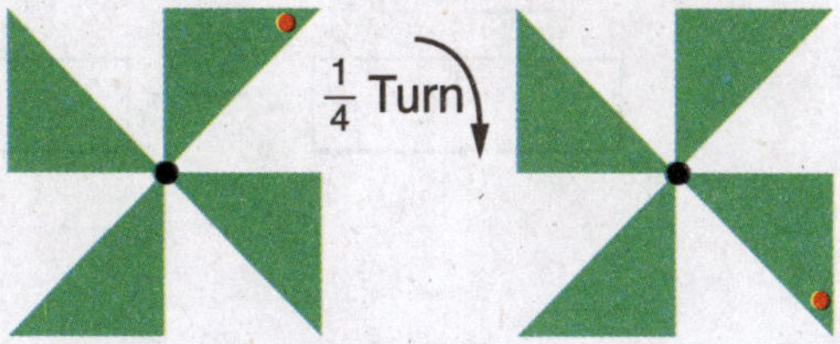

You can observe that the image fits exactly into itself after a quarter turn. It coincides with itself four times in one full turn.

ACTIVITY

Trace the following figure on a transparent sheet and repeat the same steps as mentioned above.

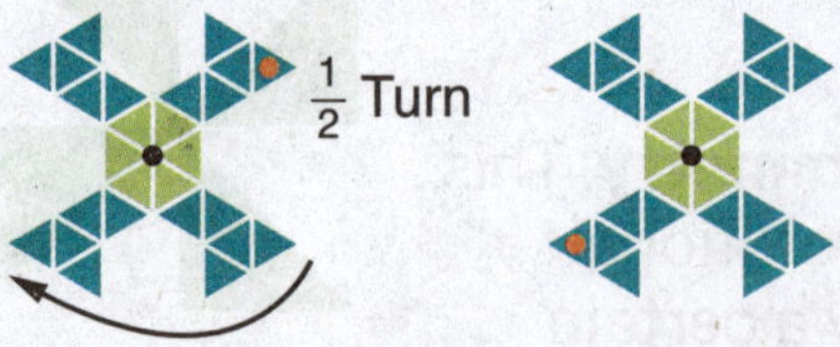

You can observe that the figure fits exactly into itself after a half turn. It coincides with itself exactly twice in one full turn.

Exercise 9.2

1 Tick (✓) the shapes which look the same after a quarter turn.

(a)  (b)  (c)  (d)  (e) 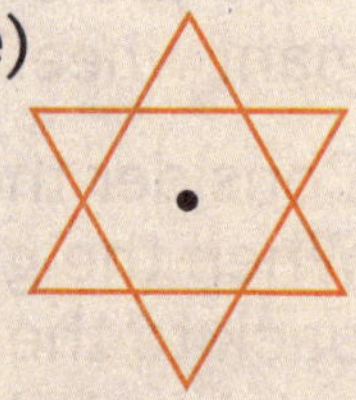

2 Tick (✓) the shapes which look the same after a half turn.

(a) 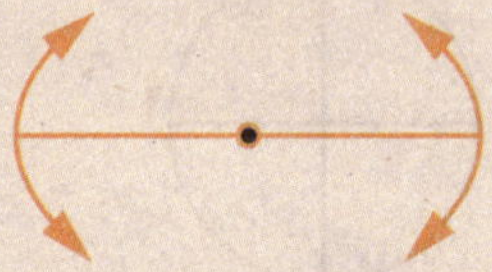 (b)  (c)  (d) 

3 For the shapes below specify the turn after which they will look the same.

(a) 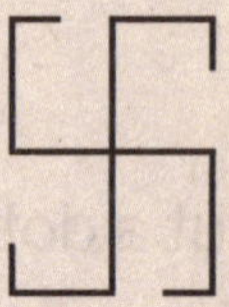 (b)  (c)  (d) 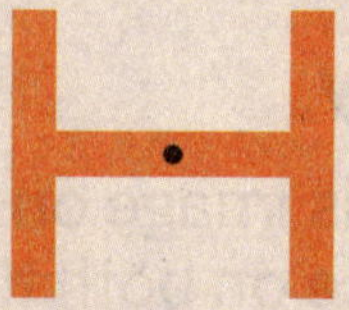

Rotational Symmetry in English Alphabets and Words

Rotational Symmetry in Alphabets

The letters of the English alphabet show rotational symmetry. They fit exactly into themselves when they are rotated by a half turn.

H I N O S X Z

Rotational Symmetry in Words

Observe the words shown here. They look the same when they are rotated by a half turn. Find out more such words.

SIS NOON

Real-life Examples of Symmetry

There are many real-life examples which exhibit rotational symmetry. A few examples are given below.

Windmill

Car wheel

Periwinkle flower

Giant wheel

Revision Exercise

1 **Draw the line(s) of symmetry for the following figures, if they are symmetrical. Also, write the number of lines of symmetry for those which are symmetrical.**

  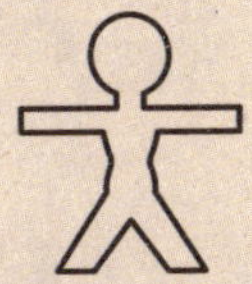 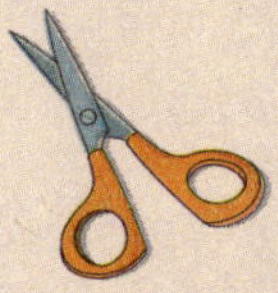   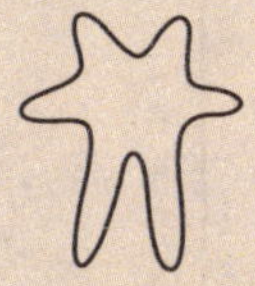

2 **Write the number of turns needed for each of the following figures to come back to its original position.**

(a) 

(b) 

(c) 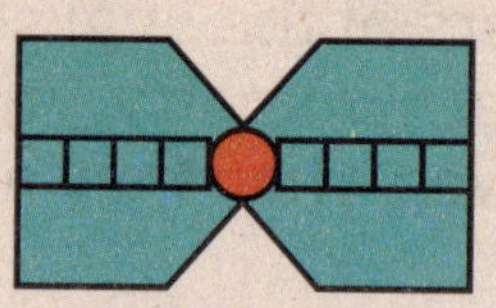

(d) 

(e) 

(f) 

3 **Draw the line of symmetry for the letters of the English alphabet. Also, specify the number of lines of symmetry for the letters having more than one line of symmetry.**

A B C D E H I M O

T U V W X Y

4 **The adjacent figures do not have rotational symmetry. Modify the figures such that they have rotational symmetry.**

5 **Draw two figures which fit exactly after a half turn.**

10 Mapping Skills

Learning Objectives

- To identify the location of different places in a map using the given directions
- To learn about symbols or legends in the map
- To find the actual distance between places based on the scale used in a map

Let's Get Started

Jahnavi is a news reporter working for a news channel in Delhi. She has come to Mumbai and is staying near Chhatrapati Shivaji Terminus. She has to go to Andheri East for covering some news. She wants to know the distance from Chhatrapati Shivaji Terminus to Andheri East, which is the best route to take, etc. As she is travelling there for the first time, she is taking the help of the Mumbai road map to get all the information she wants.

A **map** is a drawing that shows the position of things such as countries, cities, towns, streets, rivers, mountains, etc. There are different kinds of maps which are meant for different purposes.

Did You Know?

One of the first maps of the world was drawn around 510 B.C. by a Greek traveller, Anaximander. But that map is lost and there is no evidence of the existence of the map he created.

DIRECTIONS IN MAPS

The picture gives different directions that start from North and move in clockwise direction.

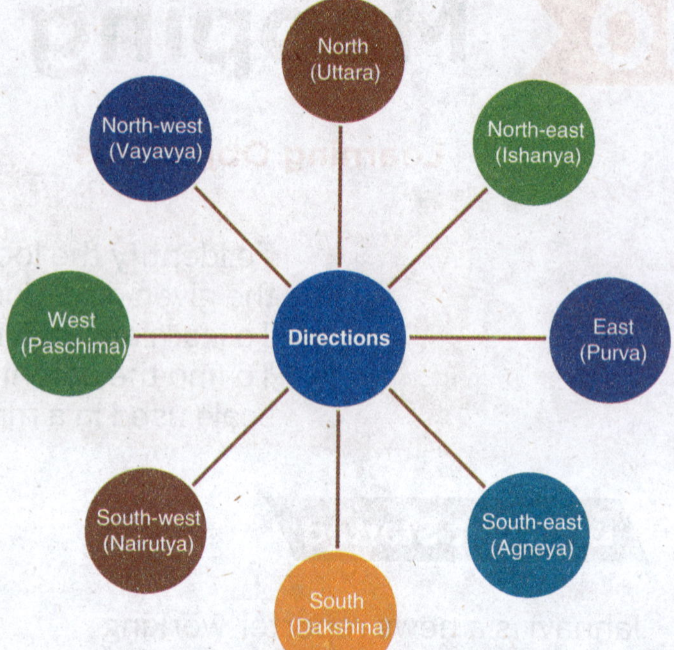

Look at the road map shown here. Let us mark the direction from Bus Stand to Jai Niwas Guest House. Move straight towards East and take second left towards North till you reach Gopinath Marg. From there, take a right turn towards East and the first left turn towards North to reach Jai Niwas Guest House.

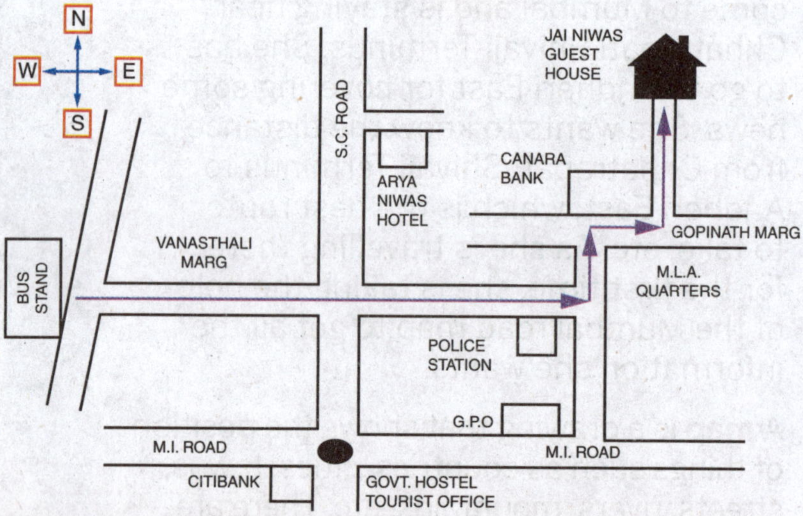

Exercise 10.1

1 Write the appropriate direction for each of the following. The first two have been done for you.

(a) If you are facing West, what direction is to your right? North

(b) If you are facing South, what direction is to your left? East

(c) If you are facing North, what direction is behind you?

(d) What direction is halfway between East and South?

(e) What direction is halfway between North and West?

(f) What direction is halfway between South and West?

(g) What direction is exactly opposite to South-east?

2 **In the map given below, mark the directions from Sunflower School to The New Horizon High School, and explain in words how you reached from Sunflower School to New Horizon School. Is there only one way to reach? If there are more, then mark a few other paths also.**

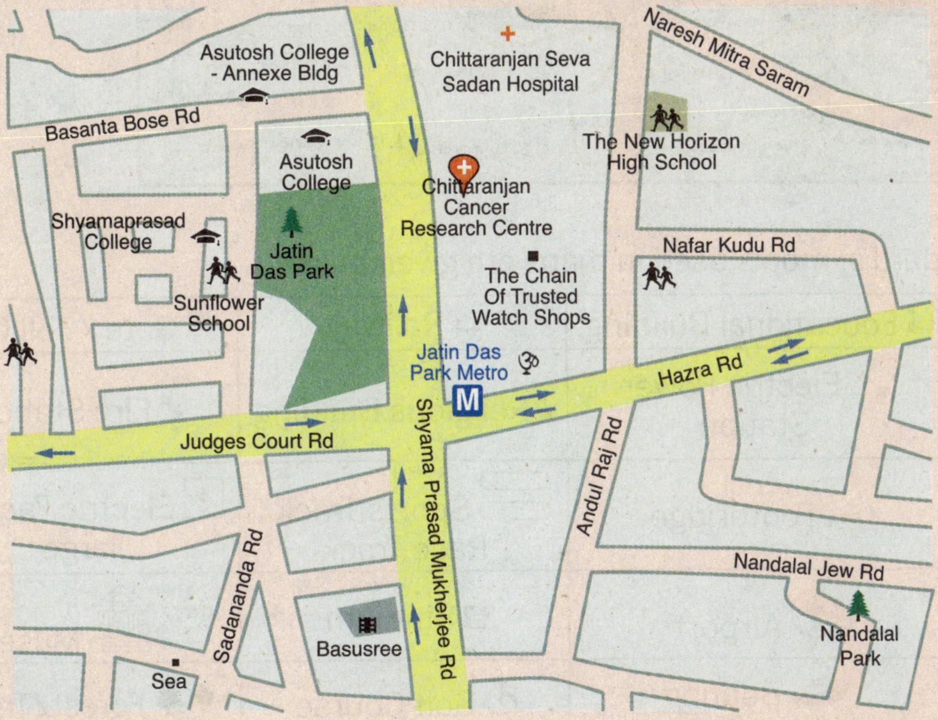

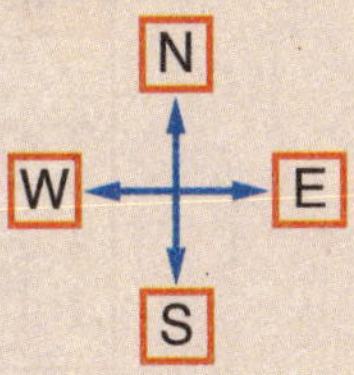

SYMBOLS OR LEGENDS IN THE MAP

Look at the tourist map of Ooty shown here. There are some symbols used in the map, which represent a specific location. They are also called **map legends**. If we use symbols in a map, we need to specify which symbol stands for what at the end of the map. This is called the **key**. Observe the symbols used for highway, railway, hotel, hospital, educational building, etc. in the map.

Some of the standard symbols used in maps are given below.

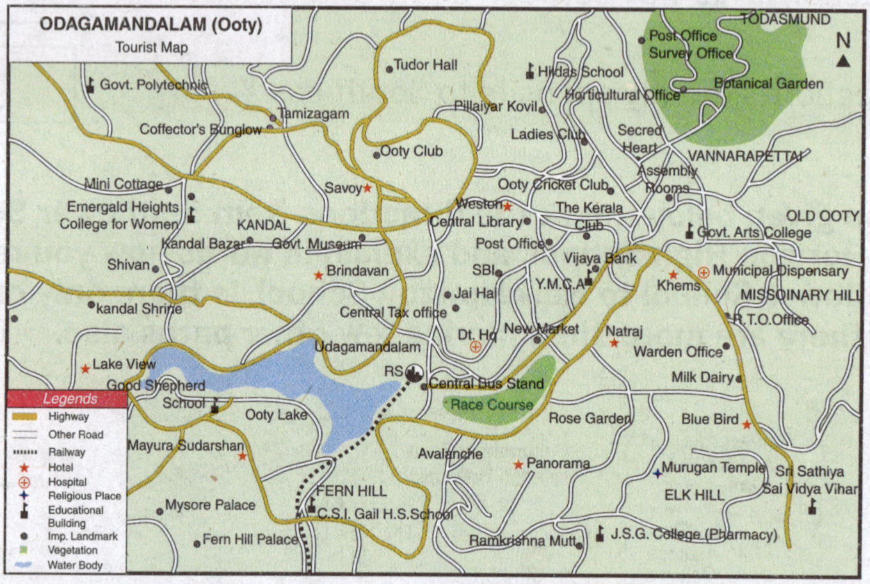

Some of the standard symbols used in maps are given below.

Bridge	Educational Building	Railway	Gate / Toll Gate
Highway Route Number	Electric Power Station	Religious Building	Fire Station
Tunnel	Footbridge	Sports Track/ Race Track	Electric Facility: large
Telephone Line	Airport	Stadium	Museum
Restaurant	Boating	Golf Course	Forest/Trees
Hospital	Hotel/Guest House	Library	Parking
Post Office	Rest Rooms	Fuel/Gas/Petrol	Telephone

SCALE IN THE MAP

Look at the pictures of a bicycle, an elephant and a giraffe. Are these the original sizes of them? No, the sizes of the pictures have been reduced in some proportion in order to draw it in our books.

We use scale while drawing maps. *The **scale** of a map is defined as the relation between the distance on the ground and the corresponding distance on the map.*

Look at the map of India shown here. One inch grid is used to draw the map. Scale used is **1 in = 700 km**. Let us find the distance between Hyderabad and Bhubaneswar. Connect the two places using a line segment and measure its distance, which is 3.8 cm = 1.5 in.

Therefore, the actual distance between Hyderabad and Bhubaneswar = 1.5 × 700 km = 1050 km.

Similarly, the distance between Jaipur and Bangalore is 2.83 × 700 km = 1981 km.

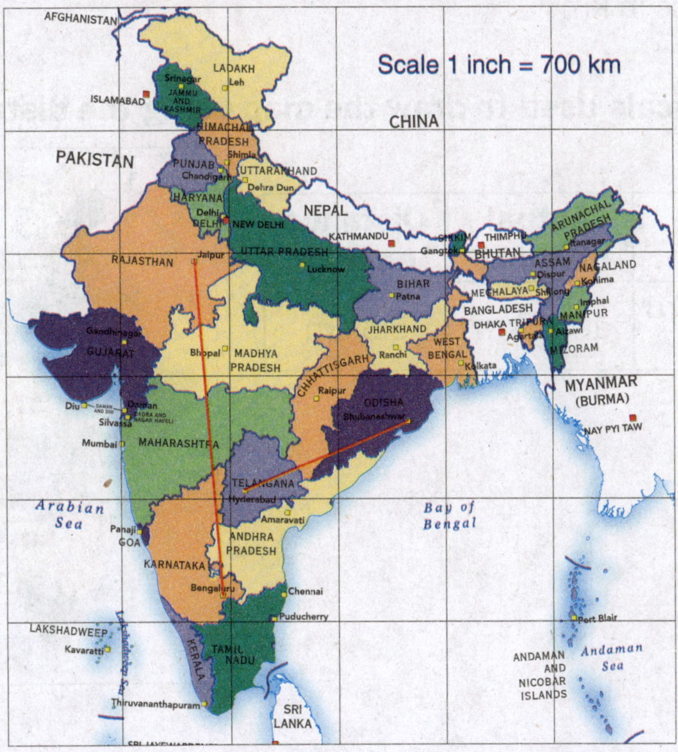

Exercise 10.2

1. Draw your school campus in a chart. Create and use your own symbols to represent different places such as library, classrooms, office room, playground, etc. in the chart.

2. **Refer the map of India shown and answer the following questions.**

   (a) Which are the neighbouring states to Madhya Pradesh?

   (b) Find the distance between the capital of Madhya Pradesh and the capitals of each of its neighbouring states.

   Given below are the distances on the map.

   Bhopal to Mumbai: 0.94 in

   Bhopal to Gandhinagar: 0.86 in

   Bhopal to Jaipur: 0.62 in

   Bhopal to Lucknow: 0.95 in

   Bhopal to Raipur: 0.89 in

   (c) Which is the nearest capital place to Bhopal among them and what is the distance in km?

3. **Find out the scale used to draw the map using the distance information given.**

Places	Actual distance	Distance on map
From Bengaluru to Lucknow	1855 km	5.3 cm

Revision Exercise

1 **You are going on a trip and you want to know the nearest hotel to stay. Which symbol will you look for in the map?**

(a) 

(b) P

(c) 

(d) 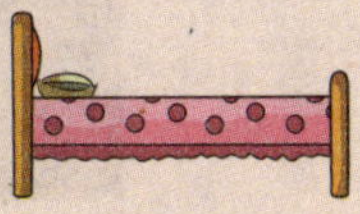

2 **Find the actual length of the following objects using the scales specified.**

(a)

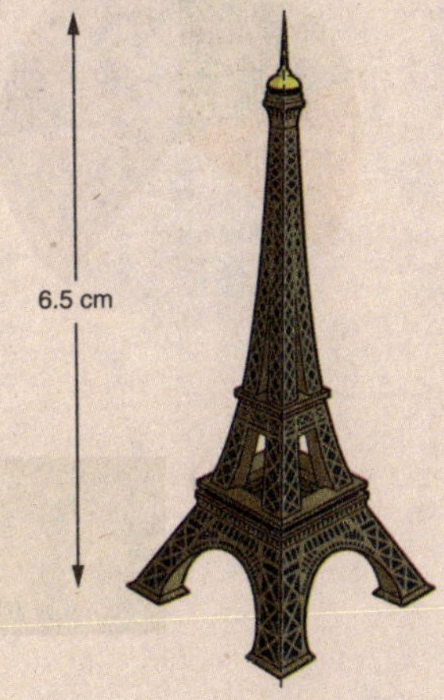

Scale: 1 cm = 58.9 m

Actual Height =

(b)

Scale: 1 in = 2.5 cm

Actual Length = Actual Width =

ASSESSMENTS

ASSESSMENT 2

Chapters 6-10

A Choose the correct option for each of the following.

1. Which of the following figures has a perimeter of 22 units?

(a) 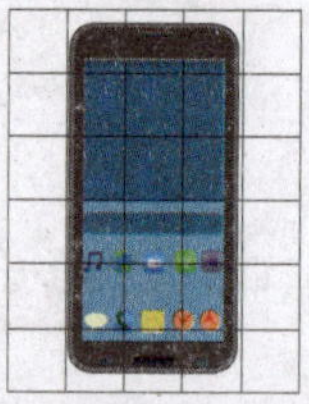
(b) 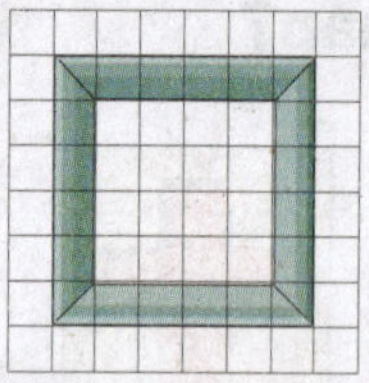
(c) 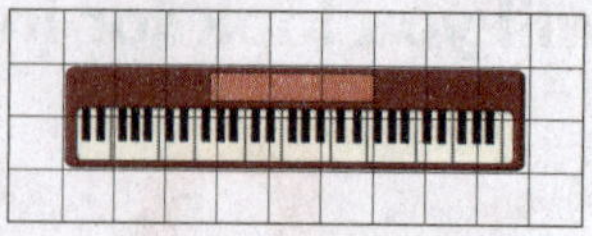
(d) 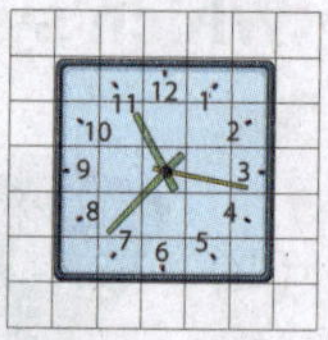

2. If the volume of a cuboid is 400 cu. m and its length and width are 10 m and 8 m respectively, what is the height of the cuboid?

(a) 500 mm (b) 0.5 m (c) 5 m (d) 50 cm

3. The circle graph given here shows the number of children participating for playing different games in a sports camp.

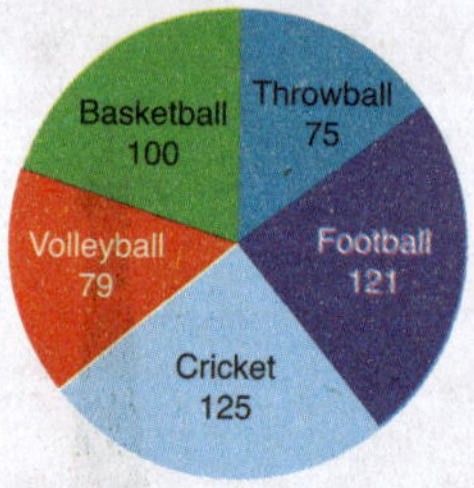

How many children are there in the sports camp?

(a) 421 (b) 375
(c) 500 (d) 425

4. Identify the asymmetrical figure among the following?

(a) 
(b) 
(c) 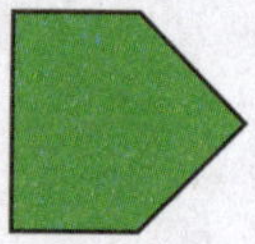
(d) 

5. Which is the nearest place to Goa among the following?

(*Hint:* Use the scale and find the distances.)

(a) Raipur (b) Hyderabad (c) Bhopal (d) Gandhinagar

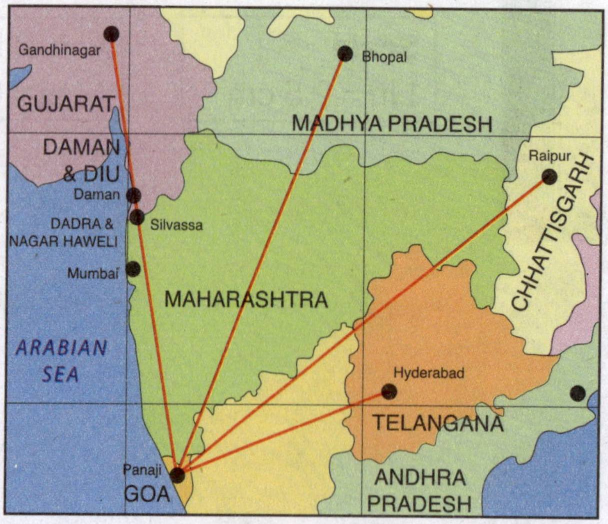

B Fill in the blanks.

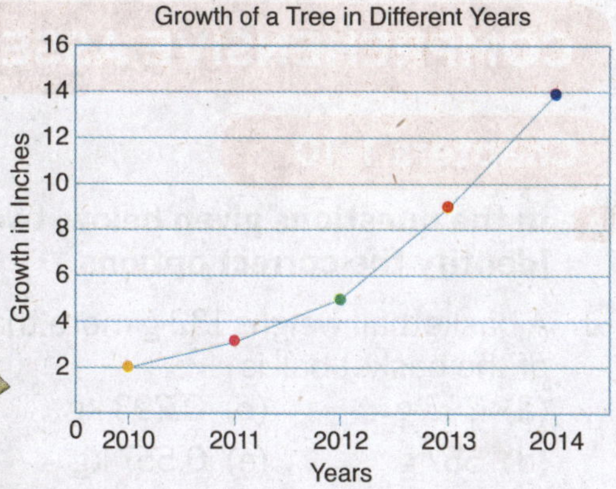

1. The solid shape whose front, top and side views are circles is a ________________.
2. In the given graph, the tree was ______ inches tall in the year 2014.
3. There are ___________ lines of symmetry for the division symbol (÷).
4. The windmill shown here looks the same after ____________ turn.

5. The relation between the distance between two places on the ground and their corresponding distance on the map is called ____________ of the map.

C State whether the following statements are true (T) or false (F).

1. A line graph represents information that is related to the whole and to each other. ☐
2. Tally marks are drawn in groups of 5. ☐
3. The figure shown here is symmetrical and it has two lines of symmetry. ☐

4. The same scale is used to draw all maps. ☐
5. The distance between the two places increases when we increase the size of the map. ☐

D Match the following.

Column A

(a) Area of Indian Ocean

(b) Area of a geometry box

(c) Area of a playground

(d)

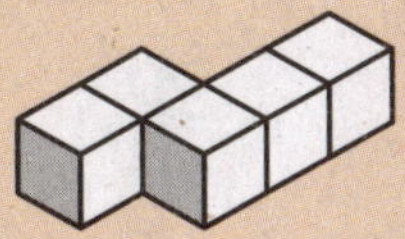

(e)

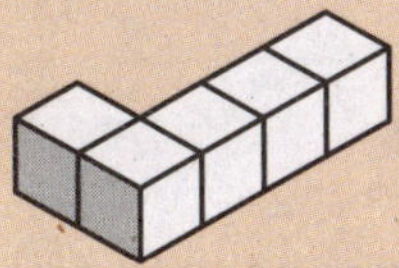

Column B

(i) Square millimetres

(ii) Square centimetres

(iii) Square kilometres

(iv) Square metres

(v)

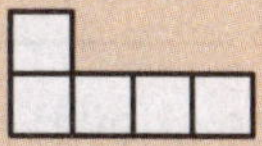

(vi)

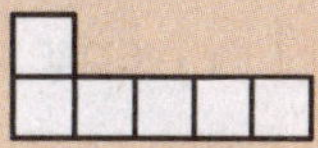

(vii)

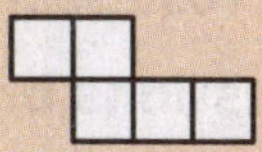

(viii)

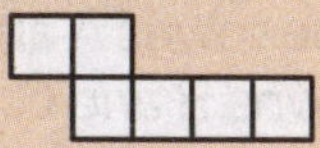

COMPREHENSIVE ASSESSMENT

Chapters 1–10

A In the questions given below, two options are correct for each question. Identify the correct options.

1. A basketball weighs 132 g more than a football. If the football weighs 425 g, then the weight of the basket ball is
   (a) 293 g (b) 0.293 kg (c) 2,93,000 kg
   (d) 557 g (e) 0.557 kg (f) 5,57,000 kg
2. In a sale, 4 pairs of shoes cost ₹1000 and 4 pairs of socks cost ₹160. Then
   (a) 1 pair of shoes costs ₹500 and 1 pair of socks costs ₹80
   (b) 1 pair of shoes costs ₹250 and 1 pair of socks costs ₹80
   (c) 1 pair of shoes costs ₹250 and 1 pair of socks costs ₹40
   (d) 2 pairs of shoes cost ₹250 and 2 pairs of socks cost ₹80
   (e) 2 pairs of shoes cost ₹250 and 2 pairs of socks cost ₹40
   (f) 2 pairs of shoes cost ₹500 and 2 pairs of socks cost ₹80

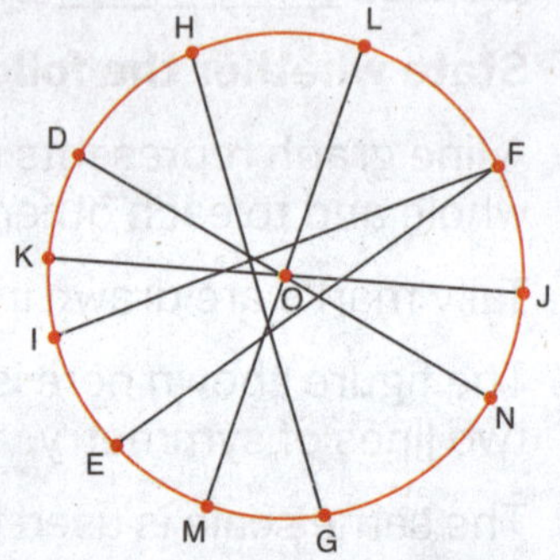

3. Tell without measuring, which of the following chords in the figure shown have the same lengths?
   (a) DN (b) IF (c) ML (d) KJ (e) HG (f) EF
4. Which among the following figures have the same area?

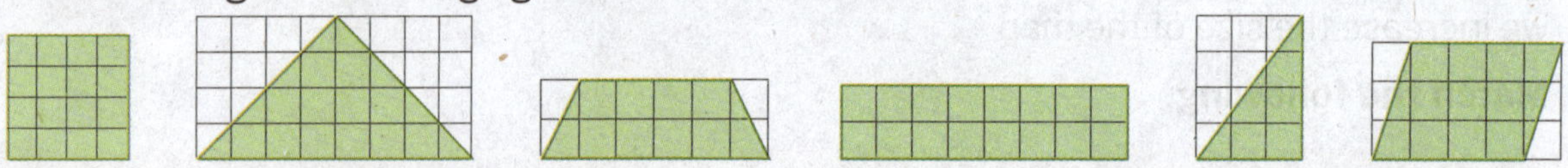

   (a) (b) (c) (d) (e) (f)

5. Which graphs will be the most appropriate to represent the increase in carbon dioxide levels in the atmosphere?
   (a) Circle graph (b) Pictograph (c) Bar graph (d) Line graph (e) Both circle graph and pictograph (f) Both pictograph and line graph

B Fill in the blanks.

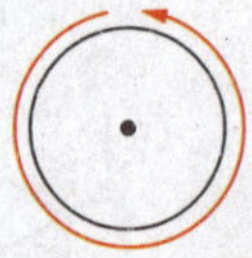

1. The basic unit of capacity is ___________.
2. The marked part of the circle shown in this figure is ___________.
3. The set of tally marks 卌 ||| represents ___________.
4. The figure shown here is a cross-section of a fruit. It has ___________ lines of symmetry.

C Answer the following questions briefly.

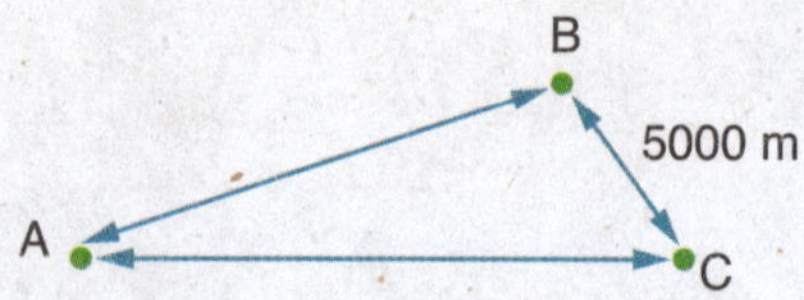

1. The distance between the towns A and B is twice than the distance between the towns B and C. Find the distance between A and C if the distance between them is 9 km more than the distance between A and B. Express your answer in km.
2. Shikha is making a painting of the ocean floor. She began at 8:20 am and worked on it for 5 hours. At what time did she complete the painting?

3. How many ice cubes of dimensions 2 cm × 2 cm × 3 cm can be put in a box of dimensions 20 cm × 5 cm × 3 cm.
4. Identify the turn by which the following shapes have to be rotated to look the same.

(a) (b) (c) (d)

5. Draw all the possible lines of symmetry for the figure shown and mention the number of lines of symmetry.

D Answer the following questions.

1. A mega sale started on 15th July and lasted till 2nd October. How many days did the sale last?
2. Jingha bought 55 kg onions for ₹400. He sold it at ₹10 per kg. What was his profit or loss %?
3. Measure the following angles and arrange them in the increasing order of their measures.

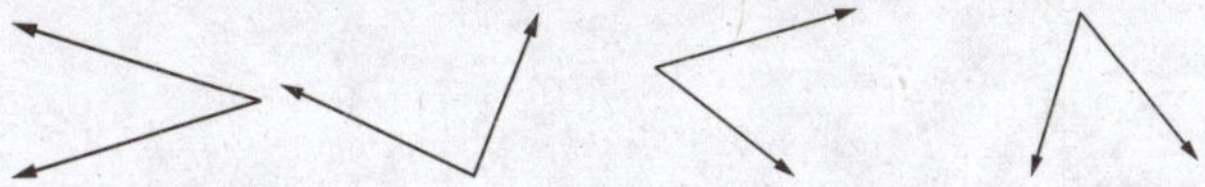

(a) (b) (c) (d)

4. Draw the cuboids of dimensions 6 units by 4 units by 3 units on the isometric dot paper given.

5. The number of students who were absent in different months in a school is shown in the circle graph. Answer the following questions.

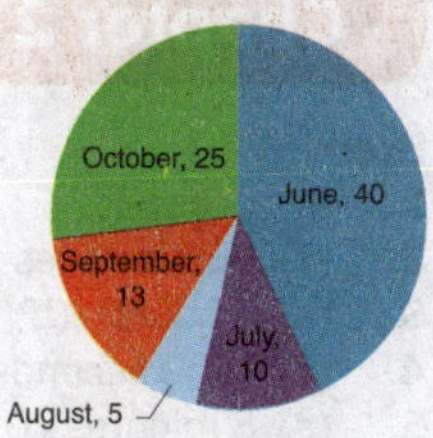

(a) In which month was the minimum number of students absent and how many?
(b) In which month was the maximum number of students absent and how many?
(c) The number of students absent in the month of September is 3 times less than in June. (True/False)

E Answer the following questions in detail.

1. (a) Krishna wants to put a new carpet in his drawing room. He asks his father to buy the new carpet. His father asks him to calculate the cost of carpeting his room at the rate of ₹130 per square feet. If the dimensions of his room are 10 ft by 8 ft, what is the cost of carpeting Krishna's room?
   (b) A tennis ball court with its dimensions is shown. Find the area and the perimeter of the tennis court.

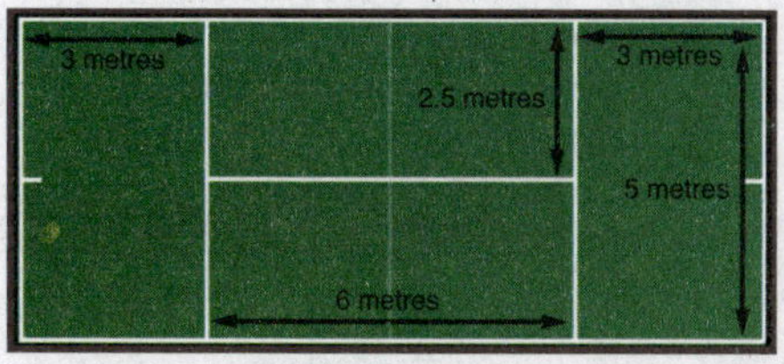

2. Find the scale used to represent the distance from Jaipur to Lucknow in a map of scale 1 cm = 300 km using the distance information provided below:

Places	Actual Distance
From Jaipur to Lucknow	566 km

ANSWERS

Chapter 1

Exercise 1.1

1. (a) 1650 (b) 1200 (c) 0.75 (d) 2.45
2. (a) 300 cm (b) 8,00,016 cm (c) 0.879 hm (d) 2,70,000 mg (e) 0.000924 kg (f) 3.94 dag (g) 120000 mℓ (h) 70000 dℓ (i) 0.27 ℓ
3. (a) 45 g (b) 700 g (c) 0.15 kg (d) 0.715 kg
4. (a) 220 mℓ (b) 5250 mℓ (c) 0.325 ℓ (d) 5.25 ℓ

Exercise 1.2

1. (a) 33 m 3 cm (b) 8 kg 200 g (c) 2 ℓ 150 mℓ (d) 12 cm 1 mm (e) 3 kg 100 g (f) 9 ℓ 200 mℓ
2. (a) 7 m 60 cm (b) 1 kg 900 g (c) 2 ℓ 150 mℓ (d) 1 cm 6 mm (e) 3 kg 250 g (f) 7 ℓ 750 mℓ
3. (a) 23.135 hm (b) 228.75 kg (c) 585481 m (d) 255.51 m (e) 7176.6 dag (f) 691.04 hℓ
4. (a) 1591 mℓ b) 900 kg (c) 106 g (d) 2460 m (e) 3.045 km (f) 2.908 gm

Exercise 1.3

1. 2.1 km **2.** 0.76 km **3.** 1.42 m **4.** 60 **5.** 67500 g **6.** 8 **7.** 80 potatoes **8.** 75,000 mℓ **9.** 2.250 litres. Yes **10.** 12

Exercise 1.4

1. 9 m **2.** 8 m **3.** 150 g **4.** 30 g **5.** 10 mℓ **6.** 250 mℓ

Revision Exercise

1. (a) (iv) 1025 m (b) (ii) 65 mm (c) (i) 2.250 ℓ (d) (iv) 6 kg 2 g (e) (i) 8.750 kg
2. 189 cm
3. Total length = 23.5 m, 2350 cm
4. (a) Cheng Yi (b) Ali and Deepak
5. (a) 1.27 kg (b) 426 g, 142 g, 45 g, 57 g, 600 g (c) Basketball (d) Golf bail (e) 0.369 kg
6. Yes, can be used for 8 days.
7. (a) mℓ (b) kg (c) cm (d) ℓ (e) g

HOTS (Higher Order Thinking Skills)

If all the bags had coins of 1 g, then the weight would have been 55 g. If bag 1 has forged coins then the weight will be 55.1 g, if bag 2 has forged coins the weight would be 55.2, if bag 3 has forged coins then the weight would be 55.3 and so on.

Chapter 2

Exercise 2.1

1 (b) seconds (c) minutes (d) minutes (e) hours
2. (a) 360 minutes (b) 495 minutes (c) 540 minutes (d) 274 minutes (e) 600 minutes (f) 465 minutes
3. (a) 5 hours (b) 5 hours 80 minutes (c) 4 hours 40 minutes (d) 1 hour 40 minutes (e) 9 hours (f) 3 hours 30 minutes
4. (a) 1500 seconds (b) 3000 seconds (c) 915 seconds (d) 765 seconds (e) 660 seconds (f) 1980 seconds
5. (a) 8 minutes 20 seconds (b) 7 minutes (c) 3 minutes 54 seconds (d) 2 minutes 38 seconds (e) 12 minutes 40 seconds

Exercise 2.2

1. (a) 5 minutes 50 seconds (b) 4 hours 20 minutes (c) 17 years 3 months (d) 9 minutes (e) 6 hours 15 minutes (f) 5 years 9 months
2. (a) 1 minute 37 seconds (b) 50 minutes (c) 8 years 3 months (d) 4 years 6 months

Exercise 2.3

1. (a) 3:20 a.m. (b) 6:30 p.m. (c) 11:40 a.m. (d) 1:10 p.m. (e) 12 midnight (f) 01:40 p.m.
2. (a) 2:40 p.m. (b) 2:50 p.m. (c) 6.45 p.m. (d) 1.10 a.m. (e) 3.30 a.m. (f) 9.03 p.m.

Exercise 2.4

1. 240 minutes **2.** 135 seconds, 30 candles **3.** 6 hours 30 minutes **4.** 2 minutes 4 seconds **5.** 9:40 a.m. **6.** 20th May **7.** 5 months, 7 months **8.** 11:25 a.m. **9.** 9:20 a.m. **10.** 7:20 a.m.

Revision Exercise

1. (a) T (b) F (c) F (d) T (e) T
2. (a) (iv) (b) (v) (c) (i) (d) (ii) (e) (iii)
3. (a)

Hours	Minutes	Seconds
$2\frac{1}{4}$	135	8100
$1\frac{3}{4}$	105	6300
2	120	7200

(b)

Starting Time	Duration	Finishing Time
11:15 a.m.	1 h 40 min	12:55 p.m.
11:15 a.m.	4 h 20 min	3:35 p.m.
12:05 p.m.	5 h 40 min	5:45 p.m.

(c)

Starting Date	Duration	Finishing Date
23rd January	2 months 2 days	25th March
15th December	30 Days	13th January
17th May	50 Days	5th July

4. (a) (i) July (b) (i) 2:00 a.m. (c) (iv) 0700 hours (d) (iv) 2 hours 50 minutes (e) (iii) 3 months 25 days
5. (a) 214 years (b) 78 years (c) 25 years

Chapter 3

Exercise 3.1

1. 5 2. 2 3. 30 g 4. 3 cm 5. $\frac{13}{3}$
6. $\frac{24}{11}$ 7. $\frac{55}{23}$ 8. $\frac{11}{10}$ 9. 7 10. 3

Exercise 3.2

1. 34°C 2. 40 cm 3. 120 cm 4. 5
5. $\frac{13}{18}$ 6. 45 min 7. ₹25 8. 50 runs

Revision Exercise

1. (a) 11 cm (b) 875 mℓ or 0.875 ℓ (c) 300 g or 0.3 kg (d) 575 cm or 5.75 m
2. (a) (iii) (b) (iv) (c) (i) (d) (ii) 3. 22 4. 35 5. 1.00 kg

HOTS (Higher Order Thinking Skills)

1. 9 2. $\frac{73}{80}$

Chapter 4

Exercise 4.1

1. (a)

Sl. No.	Profit/Loss	Profit/Loss Amount
(i)	S.P. < C.P. = Loss	₹50
(ii)	Profit	279
(iii)	Loss	369
(iv)	Loss	85

(b)

Sl. No.	C.P.
(i)	S.P. + Loss = 1542 + 200 = ₹1742
(ii)	54,061
(iii)	4156
(iv)	14,288

(c)

Sl. No.	S.P.
(i)	C.P. + Profit = 8642 + 200 = ₹8842
(ii)	3750
(iii)	1248
(iv)	11,727

2. ₹27 profit 3. C.P. = ₹5175 4. S.P. = ₹398 5. S.P. = ₹1920

Exercise 4.2

1.

	Cost Price (₹)	Selling Price (₹)	Profit%	Loss%
(a)	100	150	50	–
(b)	1000	900	–	10
(c)	1500	1050	–	30
(d)	3000	2400	–	20
(e)	1800	2160	20	–

2. Profit, 25%
3. Loss of ₹50, 10%
4. 5% 5. 20%
6. Profit% = 20% 7. Loss = ₹2200, 20%
8. Selling price = ₹480, 20%
9. ₹3000 10. ₹500

Revision Exercise

1. (a) loss (b) profit (c) C.P. + Profit (d) S.P. + Loss
2. (a) T (b) F (c) F (d) T 3. Profit of ₹222
4.

Cost Price (CP) in ₹	Selling Price (SP) in ₹	Profit (₹)	Loss (₹)	Profit %	Loss %
100	110	10	–	10	–
5000	4500	–	500	–	10
800	960	160	–	20	–

5. 6% 6. 10%

HOTS (Higher Order Thinking Skills)

1. Let the CP of 1 fan be ₹1

CP of 8 fans = ₹8

SP of 8 fans = CP of 12 fans = ₹12

Profit = 12 – 8 = ₹4

$$\text{Profit\%} = \frac{\text{Profit}}{\text{CP}} \times 100 = \frac{4}{8} \times 100 = 50$$

Hence, Profit% = 50%

Chapter 5

Exercise 5.1

1. (a) Ray (b) Line (c) Line segment
   (d) Point (e) Line
2. **Rays**: $\overrightarrow{OS}$, $\overrightarrow{OR}$, $\overrightarrow{OP}$, $\overrightarrow{OW}$, $\overrightarrow{OV}$, $\overrightarrow{OU}$, $\overrightarrow{OQ}$, $\overrightarrow{OT}$

   Lines: $\overleftrightarrow{TP}$, $\overleftrightarrow{VR}$, $\overleftrightarrow{SW}$, $\overleftrightarrow{UQ}$
3. **(a)**  **(b)**  **(c)**  **(d)** 
4. **(a)** 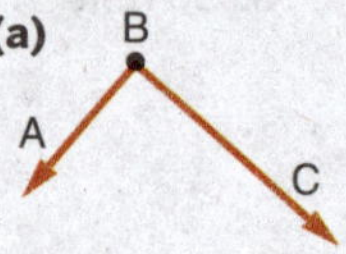

   Angle: ∠ABC or ∠CBA
   Vertex: B
   Arms: $\overrightarrow{BA}$ and $\overrightarrow{BC}$

   (b) 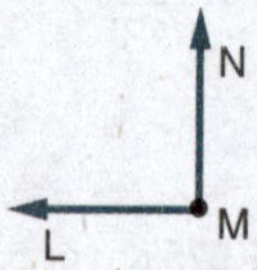

   Angle: ∠LMN or ∠NML
   Vertex: M
   Arms: $\overrightarrow{MN}$ and $\overrightarrow{ML}$

   (c) 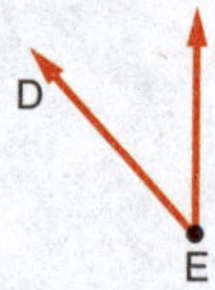

   Angle: ∠DEF or ∠FED
   Vertex: E
   Arms: $\overrightarrow{EF}$ and $\overrightarrow{ED}$

Exercise 5.2

1. (a) A (b) O (c) S (d) R (e) A (f) R (g) A (h) O (i) R
2. (a) R (b) A (c) A (d) R (e) O (f) O
3. Right angle- AOC, COD, FOD, AOF Acute angle- BOC, BOA, DOE, FOE Obtuse angle- BOD, BOF Straight Line - BOE, AOD, COF

Exercise 5.3

2. Acute angles: GAB, ABG, AGB, ECD, DEC, EDC, GBF, FGB, FCE
   Obtuse angles: GBC, BCE, AGF, DEF
   Right angles: GFB, BFE, FBC, FBA

Exercise 5.4

2. (a) Centre
   (b) Diameter (c) Radius (d) Chord
   (e) Circumference
3. (a) True (b) True (c) False
   (d) True

Revision Exercise

1. b, d and e
2. a, c and d
3. **(a)** Name of the angle = ∠OPN or ∠NPO, Vertex = P, Arms = $\overrightarrow{PO}$ and $\overrightarrow{PN}$

   (b) Name of the angle = ∠XAY or ∠YAX, Vertex = A, Arms = $\overrightarrow{AX}$ and $\overrightarrow{AY}$
4.

Acute Angles
∠BAJ
∠BCJ
∠IHG
∠IFG

Obtuse Angles	
∠ABC	∠HIF
∠AJC	∠HGF
∠JCD	∠JIF
∠CJI	∠IFE

Right Angles
∠CDE
∠AJI
∠DEF
∠HIJ

5. 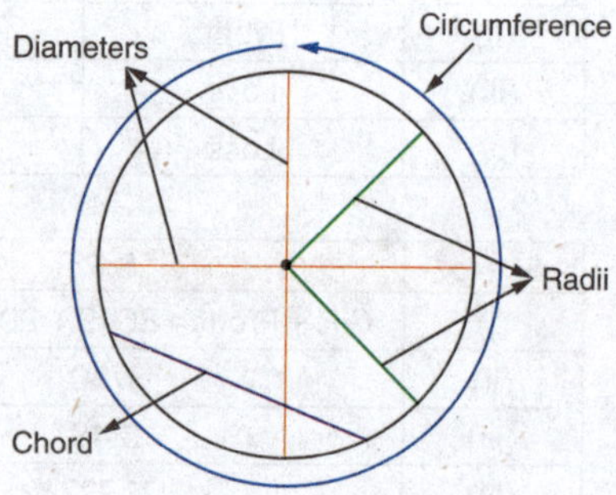

Chapter 6

Exercise 6.1

1. (a) 500 cm (b) 60 cm (c) 164 in (d) 40 in
   (e) 50 cm (f) 96 in
2. (a) s = 12 cm (b) l = 12 cm (c) s = 8 cm (d) b = 30 cm
   (e) b = 15 cm (f) b = 50 cm

Exercise 6.2

1. (a) 625 sq. cm (b) 4 sq. cm (c) 1500 sq. cm (d) 60 sq. cm
2. (a) 12 sq. units (b) 24 sq. units (c) 16 sq. units (d) 14 sq. units
3. (a) b = 30 units (b) s = 10 units (c) b = 5 units

Exercise 6.3

1. (a) 5 sq. units (b) 7.5 sq. units (c) 7.5 sq. units
2. (a) 24 sq. units (b) 5 sq. units

Exercise 6.4

1. 100 cm 2. 110 cm 3. 180 cm 4. ₹1750
5. Length of the side = 160 m, Area = 25,600 sq. m 6. 30 sq. cm 7. 3200 sq. cm 8. 15,000 sq. cm

Revision Exercise

1. (a) Perimeter = 32 cm, Area = 64 sq. cm (b) Perimeter = 80 cm, Area = 400 sq. cm (c) Perimeter = 40 cm, Area = 91 sq. cm
2. Five-rupee note 
   Length = 11.7 cm;
   Breadth = 6.2 cm
   Area = 72.5 sq. cm; Perimeter = 35.8 cm

   Ten-rupee note 

   Length = 13.6 cm;
   Breadth = 6.3 cm
   Area = 85.7 sq. cm; Perimeter = 39.8 cm
   Area and perimeter of a ten-rupee note are greater than the area and perimeter of a five-rupee note.

3. (a) 3 sq. units (b) 4 sq. units (c) 10 sq. units
4. Blackboard – sq. m; Arabian sea – sq. km; TV screen – sq. cm; Tiffin box – sq. cm; Mobile – sq. cm; Cricket field – sq. m; Forest – sq. km; Plate – sq. cm; Desert – sq. km.
5. ₹10,500
6. Breadth = 80 m
7. 800 tiles
8. Perimeter = 60 m; Area = 225 sq. m

Chapter 7

Exercise 7.1

1. (a) 3600 cu. in (b) 1200 cu. cm (c) 64 cu. in
2. (a) 512 cu. cm (b) 0.0225 cu. m (c) 3375 cu. cm (d) 1500 cu. cm
3.

S. No.	Length	Breadth	Height	Volume
(a)	7 cm	5 cm	2 cm	70 cu. cm
(b)	3 m	7 m	4 m	84 cu. m
(c)	3 mm	2 mm	5 mm	30 cu. mm
(d)	150 cm	75 cm	50 cm	5,62,500 cu. cm
(e)	10 m	17 m	12 m	2040 cu. m

4. 60 match boxes
5. 1440 cu. in
6. 1600 cu. ft

Exercise 7.2

1. (a)
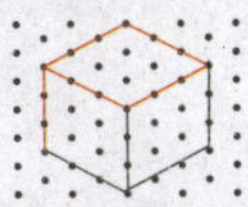
(b)
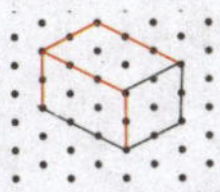
(c)
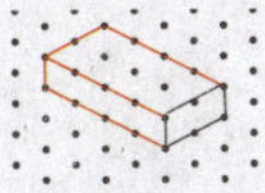

2. (a)-(iv) (b)-(v) (c)-(i) (d)-(ii) (e)-(iii)

Revision Exercise

1. (a) 96,000 cu. cm (b) 1400 cu. cm (c) 300 cu. cm (d) 1728 cu. in
2. (a) 30 cu. mm (b) 540 cu. cm (c) 105 cu. m
3. (a) – iv; (b) – v; (c) – i; (d) – iii; (e) – ii

HOTS (Higher Order Thinking Skills)

4000 cu. cm

Chapter 8

Exercise 8.1

1.
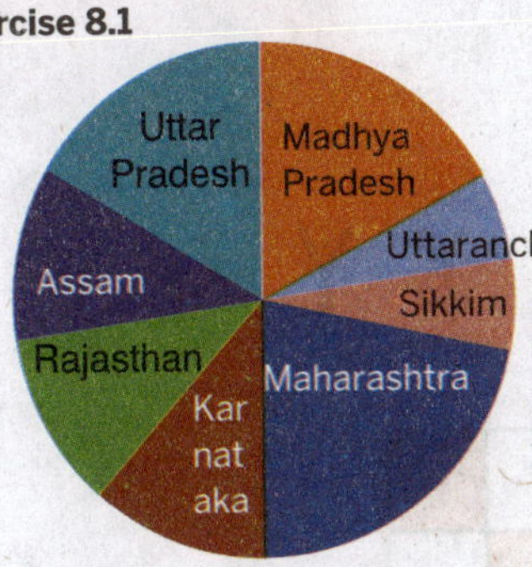

Total 18 world heritage sites are there in these 8 states.

2.

Reasons	Number of Students
Forgot my book in the school	3
Was not well	3
Grandma was sick	3
Too much homework	15
Guests at home	3
Did not understand this chapter	3

$\frac{30}{2} = 15$ students for too much homework

Rest $\frac{15}{5} = 3$ each

Exercise 8.2

1. 88 visitors have been drowned according to this warning
2.

Pets	Tally Marks	Number of Pets
Mouse	𝍸 IIII	9
Dog	𝍸	5
Rabbit	𝍸 III	8
Squirrel	𝍸 I	6
Cat	𝍸	5

Revision Exercise

Exercise 8.3

1. 10 minutes
2. 24 vehicles
3. 28 vehicles passed by end of 30 minutes, which is 12 more vehicles.
4. 60 minutes

1. (a) (i) (b) (iv) (c) (i) (d) ii
2. (a) $\frac{1}{4}$ (b) (iv) 6,50,000 + 6,00,000

   (c) $\frac{1}{2}$ (d) 50,00,000

ANSWERS

3. (a) 6 (b) 2 (c) Yes (d) 1 (e) 27

4.

Shoe Size	Tally Marks	Number of Students
4	𝍸 𝍸	10
5	𝍸 |||	8
6	𝍸 |||	8
7	𝍸 |||	8
8	|	1

(a) 4 (b) 8 (c) 1 (d) 8 (e) F

Chapter 9

Exercise 9.1

1. (a), (b) and (e)
2. Number of Lines of Symmetry

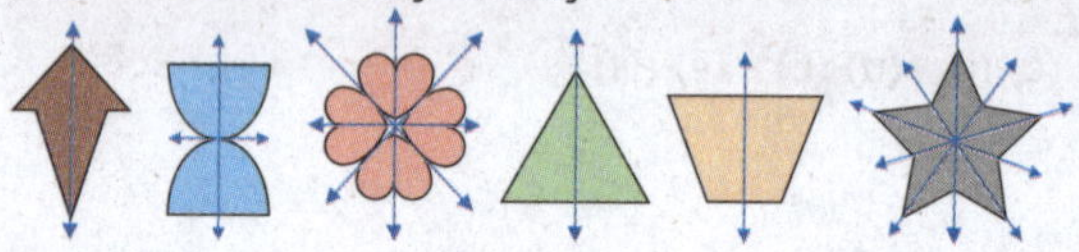

3. (a) and (c)

Exercise 9.2

1. (b), (c), (d) 2. (a), (b), (d) 3. a) $\frac{1}{4}$ turn b) $\frac{1}{2}$ turn c) $\frac{1}{4}$ turn d) $\frac{1}{2}$ turn.

Revision Exercise

1.

1 | 2 | 1 | 1 | 4 | 3 | 1

2. (a) Half (b) Quarter (c) Half (d) Quarter
   (e) Full (f) Half

3.

Letters with more than one line of symmetry are H, I, O and X.

4.

5.

Chapter 10

Exercise 10.1

1. (c) south (d) south east (e) north west (f) south west (g) north west

Exercise 10.2

2. (a) Maharashtra, Gujarat, Rajasthan, Uttar Pradesh, Chhattisgarh
   (b) Bhopal to Mumbai: 658 km
   Bhopal to Gandhinagar: 602 km
   Bhopal to Jaipur: 434 km
   Bhopal to Lucknow: 665 km
   Bhopal to Raipur: 623 km
   (c) Jaipur is the nearest capital place to Bhopal and the distance between them is 434 km.
3. 1 cm = 350 km

Revision Exercise

1. d
2. (a) Actual height = 383 m
   (b) Actual length = 20 cm, Actual width = 15 cm

SCIENCE

1. Our Lifelines: Air and Water 168

2. Rocks and Minerals 180

3. Earth, Sun and Moon 189

4. Our Environment 199

5. Natural Disasters 208

6. Light and Shadow 218

7. Force and Energy 225

LOOKING BACK 238

1 Our Lifelines: Air and Water

Learning Checklist

- Layers of the atmosphere
- Composition of air
- Properties of air
- Water
- Purification of drinking water

Let's Get Started

Rekha and Smita are sisters. They made a plan to celebrate their grandfather's birthday and bought balloons to decorate the house.

Look at the pictures and answer the question given below each.

What is Rekha blowing into the balloon?

____

Why did Smita's balloon burst?

____

Air and water are two of our basic necessities. In this chapter, we will learn about the composition and properties of air, and the ways to purify water.

LAYERS OF THE ATMOSPHERE

The Earth is surrounded by a thick envelope of air called the **atmosphere**. In order to study the atmosphere, scientists have divided it into five layers.

Troposphere: This is the first layer of the atmosphere, just above to the ground. Troposphere is where we live in and where most aeroplanes fly. The Weather changes take place in this layer.

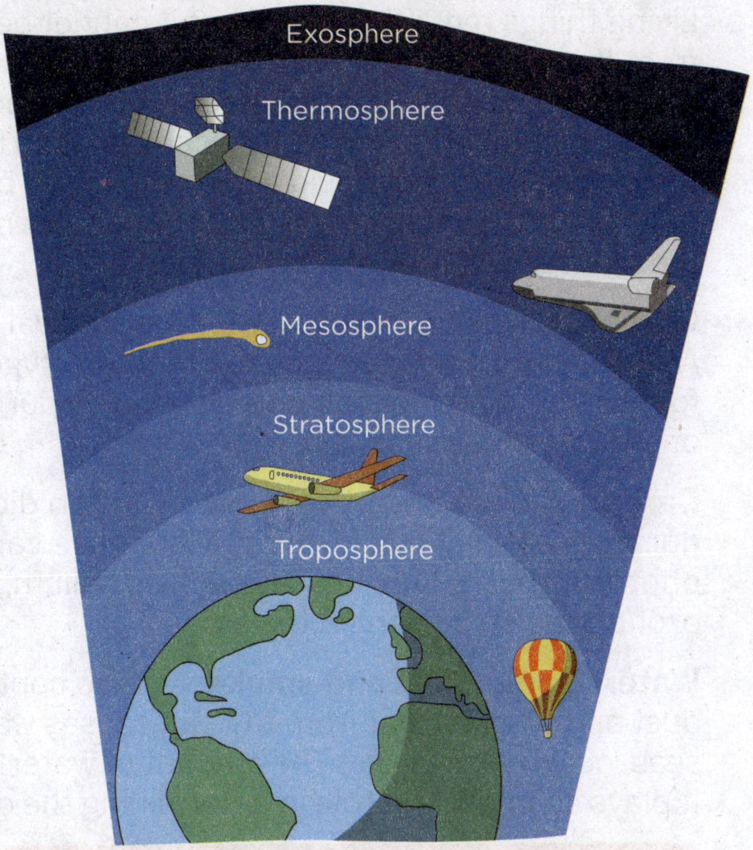

Layers of the atmosphere (not to scale)

Stratosphere: This is the second layer of the atmosphere. The ozone layer is a part of stratosphere. The ozone layer absorbs harmful radiations from the sun and stops them from reaching Earth's surface.

Jet planes fly in the stratosphere.

Mesosphere: This is the third layer of the atmosphere from the Earth's surface. This is the coldest among all the atmospheric layers.

Meteors[1] burn up in this layer while entering the Earth's surface. From the Earth, we see them as shooting stars.

Thermosphere: This is the fourth layer of the atmosphere from the Earth's surface. Space shuttles fly in this layer.

Exosphere: This is the uppermost layer of the atmosphere. There is no air beyond this.

> **Word Web**
>
> [1]**Meteors**: rocks from outer space that enter the Earth's atmosphere

The atmosphere is useful to us in many ways:

- It contains oxygen, which is essential for the survival of living things. It also contains carbon dioxide, which is required for photosynthesis.
- It helps to maintain the right temperature for the survival of living things.
- It has the ozone layer, which protects us from the harmful rays of the sun.

COMPOSITION OF AIR

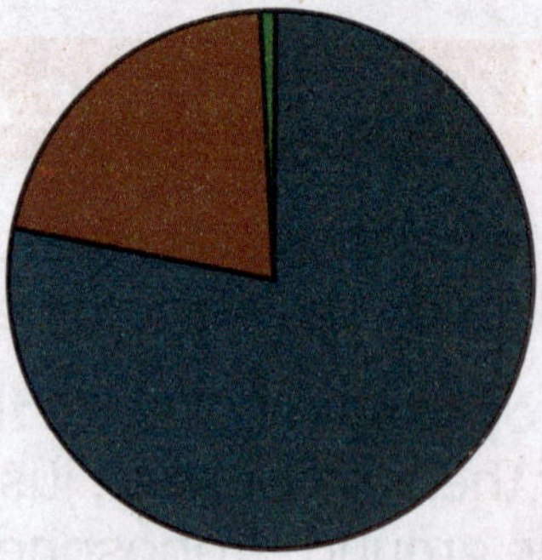

Air is a mixture of gases. It mainly consists of nitrogen (78%), oxygen (21%) and other components such as carbon dioxide and other gases (1%). Air also contains small quantities of water vapour, dust and smoke.

Nitrogen: It is the most abundant gas in the atmosphere. Living things require nitrogen but it cannot be taken directly from the air. Plants get nitrogen with the help of bacteria present in the soil. These bacteria fix the atmospheric nitrogen to different forms that can be taken up by the plants. Nitrogen is also added to the soil by means of fertilizers. Human beings and animals get nitrogen from the plant and animal sources of food.

Oxygen: Oxygen is necessary for the survival of living things. All living things need oxygen to breathe. Oxygen is also needed for burning. Green plants give out oxygen during the process of photosynthesis.

Carbon dioxide and other gases: Carbon dioxide is released into the atmosphere during breathing and burning. Plants use carbon dioxide for the process of photosynthesis. Other gases such as helium, neon, hydrogen, argon, krypton and ozone are also present in the air.

Water vapour, dust and smoke: Air also contains a small amount of water vapour, dust and smoke. Heat from the sun causes water to evaporate from the surface of seas, oceans, lakes, etc. The amount of water present in the air is called **humidity**. It plays an important role in determining the daily weather.

Activity 1

Aim: To show that oxygen is necessary for burning

Materials required: Two candles and a glass jar

Procedure:

1. Place the candles on a table and light them.
2. After a while invert the glass jar over one of the candles.

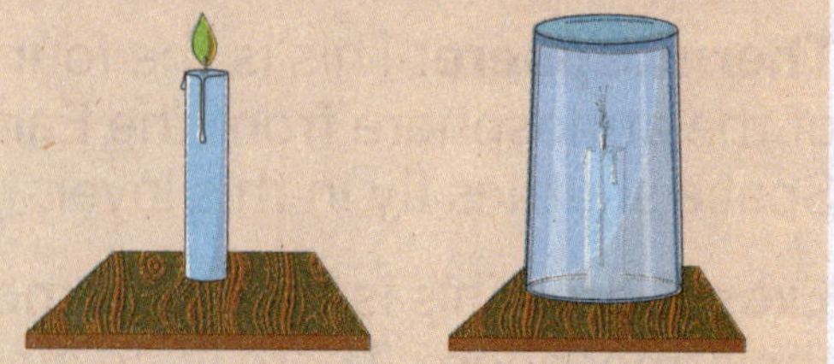

Observation: The candle that is exposed to air continues to burn, whereas the candle covered by the jar burns for a short while and then stops burning.

Reason: The flame of the candle in the jar goes off because covering the candle cuts off the oxygen supply.

Conclusion: This shows that oxygen is essential for burning.

Air is used in burning, breathing and also in a process called **rusting**. Objects made of iron get covered with a reddish brown substance called **rust**. This happens when iron objects come in contact with air and the water vapour present in the air.

PROPERTIES OF AIR

We know that air has weight and it occupies space. Let us do these simple activities to understand these properties of air.

Activity 2

Aim: To show that air has weight

Materials required: Two balloons, a needle, two pieces of thread and a scale

Procedure:

1. Blow air into both the balloons.
2. Tie the balloons with the help of threads to either side of the scale.
3. Lift the scale. Observe how the scale is positioned.
4. Now, burst one of the balloons with a needle.
5. Observe what happens.

Observation: On lifting the scale, it stays horizontal. But when one of the balloons is burst, the scale tilts towards the balloon that is still intact.

Reason: This happens because the intact balloon has air inside it, which makes it heavier. Hence, the scale tilts.

Conclusion: This shows that air has weight.

Activity 3

Aim: To show that air occupies space

Material required: A balloon

Procedure:

1. Hold the balloon in your mouth and blow into it.
2. Observe what happens.

Observation: The balloon increases in size when you blow into it.

Reason: The air we blow into the balloon occupies space. Hence, the balloon increases in size.

Conclusion: This shows that air occupies space.

Because of its weight, air pushes everything around it in all the directions. In other words, we say that air exerts pressure. This pressure is called the **air pressure**. Let us do a simple activity to show that air exerts pressure.

Activity 4

Aim: To show that air exerts pressure

Materials required: Plastic cup and index card (cardboard)

Note: It might be a good idea to try this over a sink.

Procedure:

1. Fill the plastic cup with water. Place the index card on top of the cup.
2. Hold the index card tightly against the mouth of the plastic cup and turn the cup upside down.
3. Carefully remove your hand holding the index card in place.

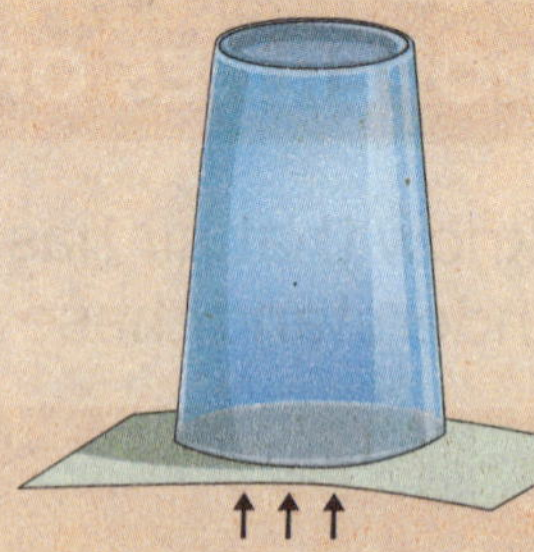

Observation: The index card does not fall.

Reason: The pressure of air outside the plastic cup is pushing the card up.

Conclusion: This shows that air exerts pressure on objects.

Not just upwards, air exerts pressure on all sides. When a balloon is blown over its maximum size, the air pressure increases. At some point, the air exerts too much pressure on the walls of the balloon and it bursts.

Some applications of air pressure in everyday life are given below:

Drinking through a straw

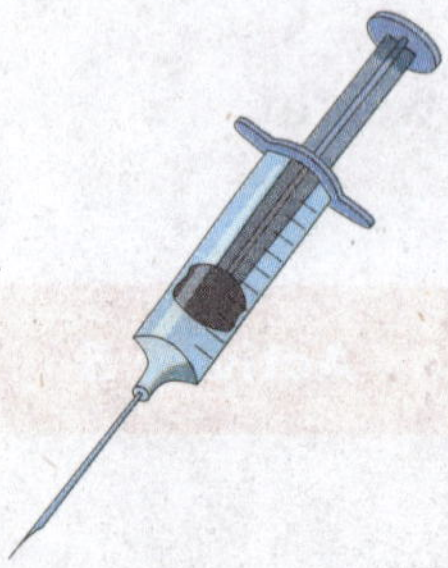

Filling up injection syringes

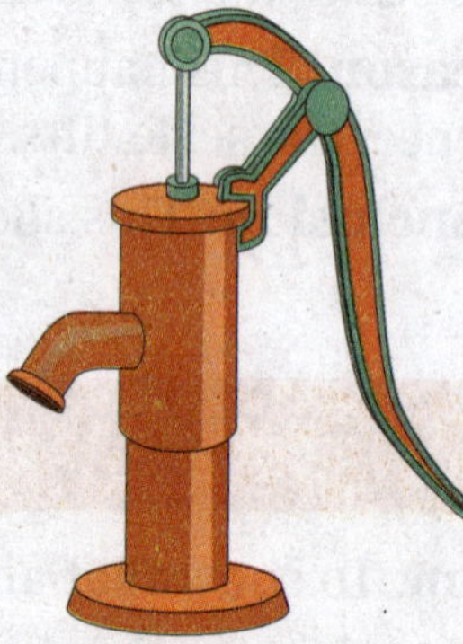

Getting water from a hand pump

Using a vacuum cleaner

Working of airplanes and sailboats

Revise and recall

Fill in the blanks using the correct words.

1. ________________ is added to the soil by means of fertilizers. (Nitrogen/Argon)
2. All living things need ________________ to breathe. (oxygen/nitrogen)
3. The layer of atmosphere where weather changes take place is ________________. (troposphere/stratosphere)
4. Space shuttles fly in ________________. (exosphere/thermosphere)
5. Air exerts ________________ on objects. (weight/pressure)

WATER

Like air, water is also essential for the survival of living things. We need water for drinking, cooking, bathing, etc. It is very important that we drink clean and pure water. Rainwater, rivers, ponds, lakes and wells are some main sources of water. Water from these sources contains substances such as sand, dirt and germs, which make the water impure and thus unfit for use.

Water needs to be purified to make it fit for human consumption[1]. Water that is fit for human consumption is called **potable water**.

Things that make the water impure are called **impurities**. Impurities can be soluble or insoluble. **Insoluble impurities** are the ones that do not dissolve in water. **Soluble impurities** are the ones that dissolve in water.

Word Web

[1]**Consumption**: eating or drinking

Removing Insoluble Impurities from Water

Insoluble impurities such as sand and mud can be removed by sedimentation and decantation, and filtration methods.

Activity 5

Aim: To understand the processes of sedimentation and decantation

Materials required: Two beakers, glass rod, sand and water

Procedure:

1. Take the beaker containing the mixture of sand and water.
2. Use the glass rod to mix the contents. Leave the beaker undisturbed for some time.
3. The heavier sand particles will settle at the bottom of the beaker as shown in the figure given alongside. This is called **sedimentation**.
4. Without disturbing the sediment of sand, carefully drain out only the clear water into another beaker as shown in the figure. This is called **decantation**.

Sedimentation

Decantation

The process of separating solid particles from a liquid medium using a filter paper is known as **filtration**.

Activity 6

Aim: To understand the process of filtration

Materials required: Two beakers, glass rod, filter paper, funnel, soil and water

Procedure:

1. Take some soil in a beaker and add some water to it. Use a glass rod to mix the contents.
2. Take a filter paper and make a cone as shown in the adjacent pictures.
3. Place the paper cone in the funnel. Now, place the funnel on the mouth of another beaker.
4. Gently pour the mixture of soil and water over the filter paper.
5. You will notice clear water dripping through the funnel into the beaker, while soil particles get retained in the filter paper.
6. The clear water that gets collected in the beaker after passing through the filter paper is called the filtrate.

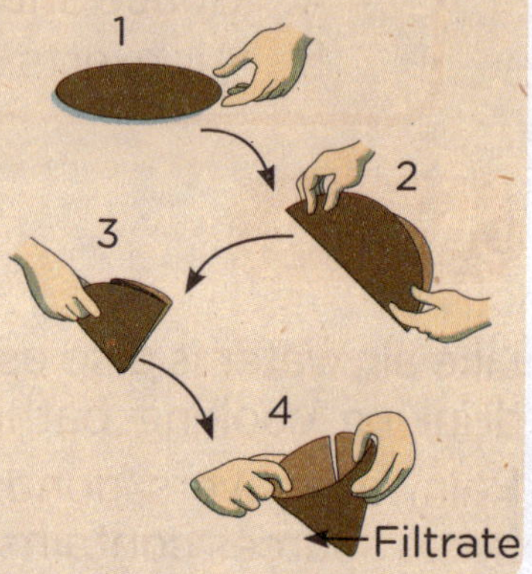

Applications of filtration in daily life

- Vacuum cleaners have filters to trap dust particles.
- Water taps usually have filters to purify water.
- Coffee makers have filters to keep coffee grounds out of coffee.
- Air conditioners have filter to trap the dust particles in the air.

Vacuum cleaner

Water tap

Coffee filter

Air conditioner

Removing Soluble Impurities from Water

The soluble impurities in water can be removed by evaporation and distillation methods.

Common salt (otherwise called sodium chloride) is extracted from seawater by the process of evaporation under the sun. Let us perform an activity to understand this process.

Activity 7

Aim: To understand the process of obtaining salt from seawater by evaporation

Materials required: A shallow dish, saltwater and Bunsen burner

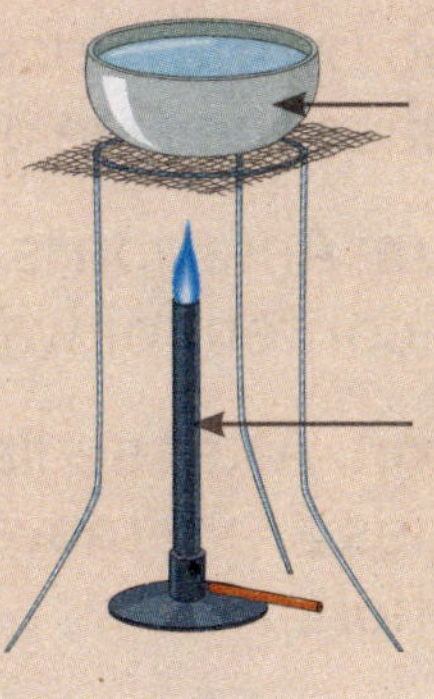

Procedure:

1. Set up the apparatus as shown in the picture.
2. Add saltwater to the shallow dish and heat it till all the water evaporates.

Observation: As the water evaporates, we can see salt getting deposited along the inner walls of the dish.

Distillation is a process that can be used to separate a pure liquid from a mixture of liquids due to the difference in their boiling points. The laboratory apparatus for distillation is shown below:

The process involves the following steps:

1. Impure water is heated in a round-bottom flask.
2. Water evaporates to form water vapour and the impurities are left behind.
3. Water vapour passes through the condenser and cools down to form water.
4. Pure water is collected in a separate container.

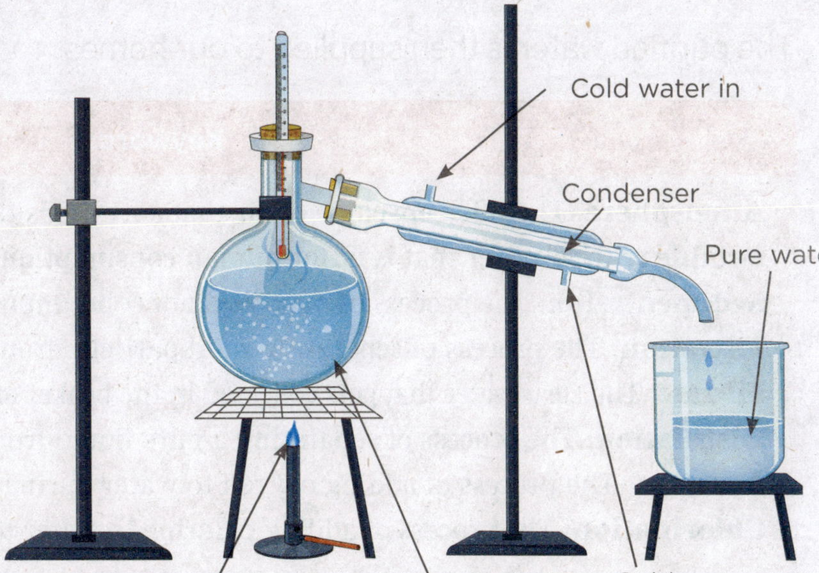

Apparatus for distillation of water

Distilled water is considered to be the purest form of water as it does not contain any impurities. It is used in science laboratories, car batteries and medicines.

PURIFICATION OF DRINKING WATER

Water purification is the process of removing germs and other harmful substances from water to make it fit for consumption.

At home, we can purify water by boiling it for about 10 minutes. It is the simplest way of purifying water.

The drinking water that is supplied to our homes is first treated to make it fit for drinking. The following steps are used in the process:

Sedimentation: Water is collected in large tanks where a lot of impurities are removed by the process of sedimentation. Chemicals such as alum are added to increase the rate of sedimentation.

Aeration: Aeration is a process in which the oxygen content of water is increased.

Filtration: After sedimentation, finer impurities are removed by the process of filtration.

Chlorination: It is the process of adding chlorine to water to kill harmful germs found in water. Chlorination can be done at any point during the water purification process.

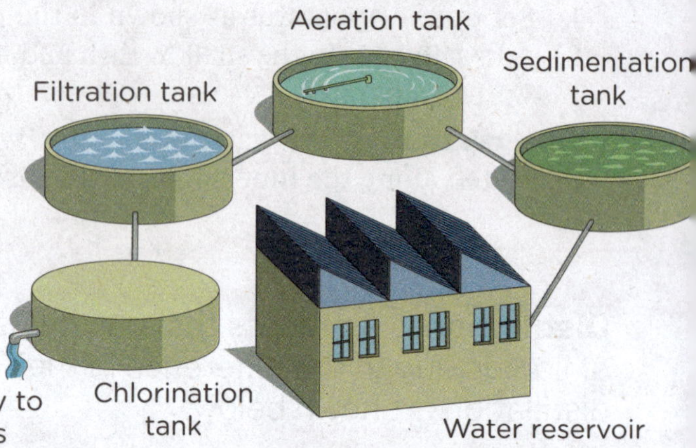

Purification of water

The purified water is then supplied to our homes.

Keywords

Atmosphere: The thick envelope of air that surrounds the Earth
Potable water: Water that is fit for human consumption
Sedimentation: The process of deposition of solid impurities present in a liquid
Filtration: The process of separating solid particles from a liquid using a filter paper
Filtrate: The clear water that gets collected in the beaker after passing through the filter paper
Distillation: The process of separating a pure liquid from a mixture of liquids
Aeration: The process of adding oxygen to water during the water purification process
Chlorination: The process of adding chlorine to water to kill harmful germs in water

Summary

1. Air is a mixture of gases.
2. Air has weight, occupies space and exerts pressure on all objects.
3. The thick envelope of air that surrounds the Earth is called the atmosphere.
4. The five layers of atmosphere are troposphere, stratosphere, mesosphere, thermosphere and exosphere.
5. Water can be purified by sedimentation, decantation, filtration and distillation methods.

EXERCISE

A Choose the correct option for each of the following.

1. The most abundant gas in the atmosphere is
   (a) Nitrogen (b) Oxygen (c) Carbon dioxide (d) Water vapour
2. ________________ is the gas that is used in photosynthesis.
   (a) Oxygen (b) Nitrogen (c) Carbon dioxide (d) Argon
3. Where is the ozone layer found?
   (a) Troposphere (b) Stratosphere (c) Mesosphere (d) Exosphere
4. In water purification, alum is added during the process of ________.
   (a) sedimentation (b) filtration (c) aeration (d) chlorination
5. Which of the following chemicals is used to kill germs during water purification?
   (a) Fertilizer (b) Alum (c) Chlorine (d) Argon

B State whether the following statements are true (T) or false (F).

1. Air exerts pressure always in the upward direction. ☐
2. Plants cannot use nitrogen directly from the atmosphere. ☐
3. Stratosphere is the coldest among all the atmospheric layers. ☐
4. Soluble impurities do not dissolve in water. ☐
5. Decanted water is the purest form of water. ☐

C Fill in the blanks with the correct words.

1. ________________ is responsible for rusting. (Water vapour/Dust)
2. The Earth is surrounded by a thick envelope of air called the ________________. (atmosphere/ionosphere)
3. The uppermost layer of the atmosphere is ______________. (troposphere/exosphere)
4. ________________ removes soluble impurities from water. (Filtration/Distillation)
5. ________________ is used to increase the rate of sedimentation. (Chlorine/Alum)

D Give two examples for each of the following.

1. Properties of air ________________ ________________
2. Gases present in the air ________________ ________________
3. Applications of air pressure ________________ ________________

4. Processes for removing insoluble impurities from water ____________ ____________
5. Uses of distilled water ____________ ____________

E Answer the following questions briefly.

1. What is air pressure?
2. Name the different layers of the atmosphere.
3. How does the ozone layer protect the Earth?
4. Why should we drink purified water?
5. Write any two applications of filtration method in our daily life.

F Answer the following questions.

1. What is the difference between troposphere and stratosphere? Explain.
2. How will you prove that air exerts pressure? Explain with the help of a diagram.
3. Define distillation and list the steps involved in this process.
4. Explain the steps involved in water purification before its supply to our homes.

G HOTS (Higher Order Thinking Skills)

1. You have to separate orange juice from its pulp. Which process out of these would you use: sedimentation and decantation or filtration? Why?
2. Iron grills in our windows and gates are painted.
   (Hint: Painting does not expose them to air)

H Label the parts of the distillation apparatus given below.

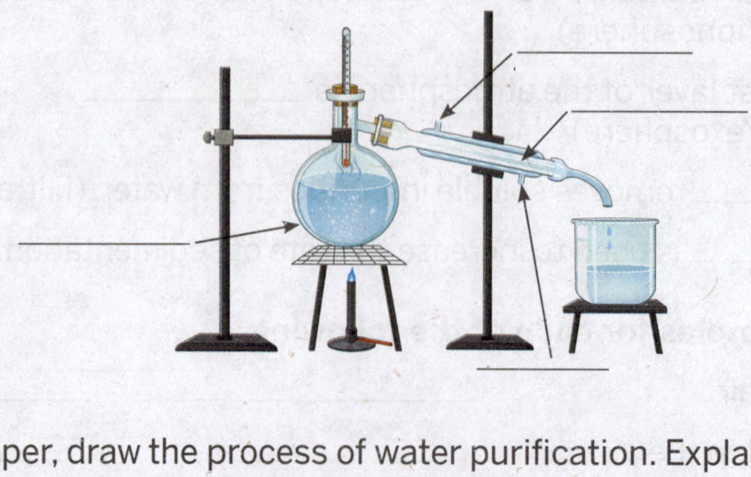

I Project

1. On a chart paper, draw the process of water purification. Explain each step.
2. Nowadays, a lot of water purifiers are available in the market. With the help of an elder, find out how they work, collect pictures and prepare a report.

A **Label the different layers of the atmosphere.**

B **Life Skills**

Water is a precious resource. Let us save every drop we can.

Turn off taps while brushing your teeth, soaping clothes and scrubbing vessels.

Fixing leaking taps does not take much, but it can save a significant amount of water.

Using a bucket instead of a shower to bathe can reduce your water consumption by 80 per cent!

Energy-star-rated dishwashers and washing machines use less water.

Low-flow showerheads and toilets with smaller flush tanks use less water.

To recycle water on your own, do simple things like using the water in which vegetables have been washed to water plants.

Write three other ways to save water.

1. ______________________________

2. ______________________________

3. ______________________________

2 Rocks and Minerals

Learning Checklist

- Types of rocks
- Minerals
- Uses of rocks and minerals

Let's Get Started

Look at the pictures given below and fill in the blanks with the given words.

Chalk Ruby Granite

__________ is used to make kitchen slabs.

__________ is used to write on blackboards.

__________ is used in making jewellery.

Rocks and minerals are of different shapes, sizes and colours. They are found everywhere on the Earth. Let us learn more about them.

TYPES OF ROCKS

Rocks can be divided into three groups based on how they are formed: igneous, sedimentary and metamorphic.

Igneous Rocks

We have learned in Chapter 9 that the core of the Earth is made of molten rock called **magma**. When magma comes out to the surface of the Earth through volcanic eruptions, it is called **lava**.

The lava cools down and hardens to form igneous rocks. Some of the minerals present in igneous rocks are mica, feldspar, magnesium and quartz. Igneous rocks derive their name from the Latin word *ignis* which means 'fiery'.

Granite, pumice and obsidian are examples of igneous rocks.

Igneous rocks

Granite is formed due to the slow cooling of lava. The three main minerals found in granite are mica, feldspar and quartz. The colour of granite varies from grey to pink based on the amount of feldspar present. Granite is used to make buildings, interiors of kitchens, floorings, etc.

Pumice is formed by the rapid cooling of lava. It is creamish or grey in colour. The release of gases from the lava forms the pores in the pumice rock.

Unlike other rocks, pumice is lightweight. It is used in making lightweight building materials, footscrubs, etc.

Obsidian is also formed due to the rapid cooling of lava. It is a dark or black-coloured rock. It is smooth and glassy; hence it is also called **volcanic glass**. It has very sharp edges. It is used in making jewellery.

Sedimentary Rocks

Sedimentary rocks are formed due to the deposition of small pieces of rock, soil, and plant and animal matter over thousands of years by the action of wind, rainwater and flowing river water.

Rivers flowing down a mountain wear away rocks. Wind and rainwater also wear away rocks. These small pieces of rocks are deposited at some other place. Layer over layer is deposited over a long period of time. This repeated deposition hardens the lower layers, leading to the formation of sedimentary rocks.

Conglomerate, sandstone, shale and limestone are examples of sedimentary rocks.

Conglomerate contains gravel, round pebbles and boulders held together by minerals. It has an uneven texture and is used as a building material.

Limestone contains the mineral calcium and tiny animal shells. Its grains are soft and fine. It is used to make lime, cement, paint, etc.

Sandstone is formed by the deposition of sand particles held together by minerals like silica. Famous Indian monuments like the Red Fort and the Qutub Minar are made of sandstone.

Shale contains solidified clay and mud piled up in layers. It is used to make construction materials like bricks, tiles and cement.

Sedimentary rocks

Metamorphic Rocks

Metamorphism means a gradual change in form. Igneous rocks and sedimentary rocks change into metamorphic rocks over time due to high pressure and temperature.

Slate, marble, quartzite and gneiss are examples of metamorphic rocks.

Slate is formed from the sedimentary rock shale. Slate mainly contains clay, mica and other minerals. It can be broken into thin layers. It is used to make slates for children, blackboards for classrooms and cement.

Marble is formed from the sedimentary rock limestone. It has been widely used for construction from ancient times. One of the best examples of this is the Taj Mahal in Agra, which is made of white marble. Marble is also used in making flooring material and statues.

Quartzite is formed from the sedimentary rock sandstone. It mainly contains iron, quartz and silica. These are hard rocks and are not easily broken. It is used in making floorings and stairs, and in the glass and ceramic industries.

Gneiss is formed from the igneous rock granite. It has light and dark bands of varying length and thickness. It is used as a building material.

Slate | Marble | Quartzite | Gneiss

Metamorphic rocks

Revise and recall

Match the following.

Column A	Column B
(a) Taj Mahal is made of	(1) Obsidian
(b) Molten rock inside the Earth's core	(2) Sandstone
(c) Lightweight rock with holes	(3) Marble
(d) The rock used in building Red Fort	(4) Magma
(e) Volcanic glass	(5) Pumice

MINERALS

Rocks are made up of substances called minerals. Minerals are formed inside the Earth.

There are two types of minerals: metallic and non-metallic.

Metallic Minerals: These minerals yield metals. Metal-yielding minerals are also called **ores**. A few examples of ores are bauxite, pyrite and hematite. These ores can be processed to obtain aluminium, copper and iron, respectively.

Metals are used in making machines, cars, ships, wires, etc. Gold, silver and platinum are precious metals that are used to make jewellery and ornaments.

Gold

Iron bars used in construction

Copper

Metals obtained from minerals

Non-metallic Minerals: Some important non-metallic minerals are coal, salt, gypsum, mica and feldspar.

Coal is used in the thermal power generation, for cooking and in other industries where a large amount of heat is required.

Coal

Emerald (a gemstone)

Non-metallic minerals

Gemstones are also obtained from minerals. Pieces of these minerals are cut and polished for using them to make jewellery. These gemstones are found in very attractive colours like red, green and yellow.

A few examples of gemstones are diamond, ruby, sapphire and emerald. These are also known as precious stones.

Science in Context

Diamond is the hardest mineral and can withstand very high temperatures.

USES OF ROCKS AND MINERALS

Rocks and minerals are being used by human beings from ancient times. Even to this day, we use products obtained from the rocks and minerals.

Following are some of the most common uses of rocks and minerals.

Construction: We use rocks and stones for building houses, offices, etc. Stones and jelly stones are used all through the building process. Even the cement used in construction of buildings is derived from minerals.

Tar is used to make roads, and marbles are used for flooring. Iron and steel are used in making pillars for the buildings.

Metals: Utensils are the basic requirements of a kitchen in a home. These are made from iron, copper, aluminium and steel. All these are made or obtained from the mineral ores.

Metals like gold, silver and platinum are used in making ornaments, decorative items and jewellery.

Gemstones: Gemstones like diamond, ruby, sapphire and emerald are used to make jewellery.

Fuels: Coal is used as a fuel to keep homes warm in colder regions and for cooking. Uranium is a rare mineral. It is used in nuclear reactors to produce large amount of energy.

Fertilizers: Minerals like sulphates and nitrates are constituents of fertilizers. Fertilizers are added to the soil to increase the fertility of soil, thereby increasing the yield of crops.

Food: We use rock salt (*kala namak*) in food. It is obtained from the rocks in the Earth.

Many other minerals like calcium, iron and potassium are required for the growth and development of our body. We get these from the vegetables and fruits we eat. Plants obtain these minerals from the soil.

The following table lists some minerals and their use in our daily lives.

Minerals	Used in
Quartz	Watches
Talc	Talcum or face powder
Graphite	Pencils
Diamond	Jewellery
Copper	Electrical wires
Mica	Welding rods, electronic goods

Let's Say Together!

Igneous	Sedimentary	Metamorphic
Magma	Ores	Minerals

Keywords

Crust: The outer surface of the Earth on which we live

Magma: Molten rock present inside the Earth

Lava: Magma flowing on the surface of the Earth after a volcanic eruption

Igneous rocks: These are the rocks formed as a result of cooling and solidification of molten rock

Sedimentary rocks: These are the rocks that are formed due to deposition of small pieces of rock, soil, and plant and animal matter carried by the wind or flowing water

Metamorphic rocks: Igneous rocks or sedimentary rocks undergo changes over a period of time to form these rocks

Ore: Metal-yielding minerals

Summary

1. There are three kinds of rocks: igneous, sedimentary and metamorphic.
2. Igneous rocks are formed due to the cooling and solidification of molten magma.
3. Sedimentary rocks are formed due to the formation of sediments due to wind and flowing water.
4. Metamorphic rocks are formed by the gradual changes that take place in the igneous and sedimentary rocks.
5. Rocks are made up of minerals. Minerals are found inside the Earth. There are two types of minerals: metallic and non-metallic.
6. Rocks and minerals are widely used by human beings.

EXERCISE

A Fill in the blanks with the correct words.

1. The molten rock present inside the Earth is called ________________. (magma/lava)
2. Pumice is a type of ________________ rock. (sedimentary/igneous)
3. Gneiss is formed from the igneous rock ________________. (granite/shale)
4. ________________ is used to make roads. (Tar/Marble)
5. ________________ is used in making jewellery. (Graphite/Diamond)
6. ________________ is used in food. (Talc/Rock salt)

B State whether the following statements are true (T) or false (F).

1. Granite is formed from limestone. ☐
2. Coal is a metallic mineral. ☐
3. Slate can be broken into thin layers. ☐
4. Shale is used in making bricks. ☐
5. Pumice is formed by the rapid cooling of lava. ☐
6. Minerals like sulphates and nitrates are the constituents of fertilisers. ☐

C Give one example for each of the following.

1. Igneous rock ____________
2. Sedimentary rock ____________
3. Metamorphic rock ____________
4. Mineral ____________
5. Gemstone ____________

D Match the following.

Column A	Column B
(a) Igneous	(1) Marble
(b) Sedimentary	(2) Feldspar
(c) Metamorphic	(3) Obsidian
(d) Non-metallic mineral	(4) Diamond
(e) Gemstone	(5) Conglomerate

E Answer the following questions in brief.

1. Which types of rocks are formed after a volcanic eruption? Give two examples.
2. Which rock is also called volcanic glass? Give one use of this rock.
3. What are the two things that help in the formation of sedimentary rocks?
4. What are the two constituents of sandstone? Name two monuments made of sandstone.
5. What are metamorphic rocks? Give two examples.
6. What are minerals? Name the two types of minerals.
7. What are gemstones? What are they used for?
8. What are ores? Give two examples.

F **Answer the following questions.**

1. Explain the formation of igneous rocks.
2. Write a note on the formation and uses of pumice.
3. Explain the formation of sedimentary rocks. Give two examples and explain their features.
4. Explain the features of the metamorphic rocks and their formation.
5. Describe the rock quartzite.
6. Give the various uses of rocks and minerals.

G **HOTS (Higher Order Thinking Skills)**

Romila says gold and silver are metals, but Lekha says they are minerals. Who is correct? Can both be correct? Why or why not?

H **Identify the rocks and write whether they are igneous, sedimentary or metamorphic.**

I **Project**

Collect stones of different colours and identify them with the help of your teacher. Keep them in egg trays and make an exhibit for your school science exhibition.

Write the name of the rock or mineral that is used for making the following products.

Slate

____

Pencil lead

____

Cement

____

Wristwatch

____

Kitchen slab

____

Talcum powder

____

3 Earth, Sun and Moon

Learning Checklist

- The solar system
- Sun
- Earth
- Moon
- Eclipses

Let's Get Started

Identify the objects shown in the pictures below that we normally see in the sky.

Objects seen in the sky are called **celestial objects**. The sun and the other celestial objects that revolve around it form the solar system.

Let us learn more about the solar system, the sun, the Earth and the moon.

THE SOLAR SYSTEM

The sun and the eight planets that revolve around the sun together form the **solar system**. Other than the planets, satellites[1] of various planets, comets and asteroids are also part of the solar system.

Word Web

[1]**Satellite**: a celestial object that moves around a planet

The sun is at the centre of the solar system. There are eight planets revolving around the sun. These planets are Mercury, Venus, Earth, Mars, Jupiter, Saturn, Uranus and Neptune. They revolve around the sun in fixed paths called **orbits**.

Mercury is the smallest planet and is also the closest planet to the sun. Venus is the hottest and brightest planet. Earth is also called the blue planet. It is the only planet where life is known to exist. Mars is also called the red planet. Jupiter is the largest planet of the solar system. Saturn is the second largest planet after Jupiter. It has rings around it. Saturn is so light that if there was a tub of water big enough to hold it, it would float in it. Uranus is the coldest planet of the solar system. Neptune is the planet farthest from the sun.

The solar system (not to scale)

SUN

The sun is a star that is situated at the centre of our solar system. It is a huge ball of burning gases. Its size is about 109 times that of the Earth. Its mass is about 330,000 times that of the Earth. It is almost 99.86% of the total mass of the solar system.

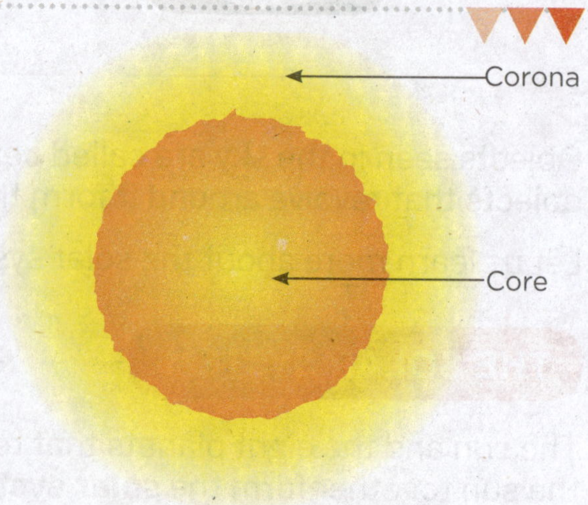

The Sun

Hydrogen and helium gases are the major constituents of the sun. The sun has a thin outer layer called the **corona** and a central part called the **core**.

In the core of the sun, hydrogen gas continuously gets converted into helium. A very large amount of heat and light energy is released during this process. Energy released by the sun is called the **solar energy**. The temperature on the surface of the sun is about 6000°C. All living things on the Earth ultimately depend on the solar energy for their existence.

EARTH

The Earth is the third planet from the sun. It is surrounded by an envelope of air known as the **atmosphere**. The atmosphere of the Earth protects us from the harmful radiations of the sun. The interior part of the Earth is divided into three main layers: crust, mantle and core.

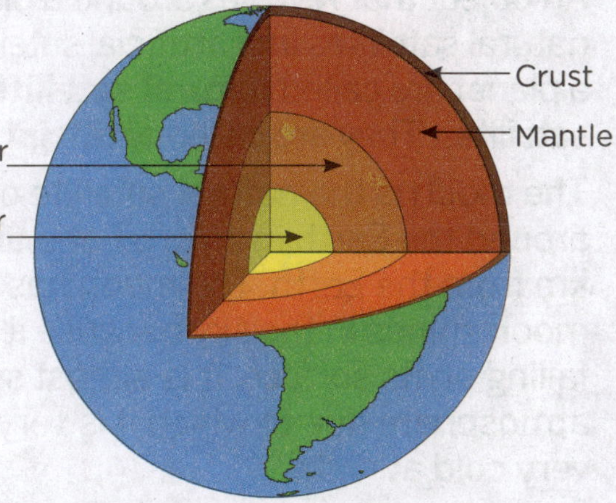

Internal structure of the Earth

Crust is the outermost layer of the Earth. Its thickness ranges from about 5 km below the ocean floor to about 70 km below the land. The continents and the oceans are on this layer. It is made up of rocks and contains all the things essential for life.

Mantle is the middle layer of the Earth lying between the crust and the core. The thickness of the mantle extends up to 2,890 km. The outer region of the mantle consists of solid rocks. The inner regions of the mantle consist of molten rocks. During volcanic eruptions, molten magma comes out from this layer to the surface of the Earth.

Core is the innermost layer of the Earth. It is mainly composed of iron and nickel. The outer core is in a molten liquid state. It extends to about 3,400 km. The inner core is a solid sphere of mostly iron situated about 1,220 km from the outer core.

Revise and recall

Fill in the blanks with the correct words.

1. The outer thin layer of the sun is called the ________________. (core/corona)
2. In the core of the sun, _________ gets converted into helium. (hydrogen/nitrogen)
3. The interior part of the Earth is divided into ________________ main layers. (three/five)
4. The middle layer of the Earth is called the ________________. (mantle/crust)
5. The major element in the inner core is ______________. (iron/gold)

MOON

An object that revolves around a planet is called a **satellite**. Satellites are of two types: natural satellites and artificial satellites. Naturally existing objects revolving around a planet are called **natural satellites**. Some satellites of the Earth are man-made satellites. They are called **artificial satellites**.

The moon is the natural satellite of the Earth. It revolves around the Earth in an orbit at a distance of about 384,400 km from the Earth. The moon has no light of its own. The moon shines in the sky because it reflects the sunlight falling on its surface. It is almost spherical in shape. It has no atmosphere due to which it is very hot during the day and very cold at night.

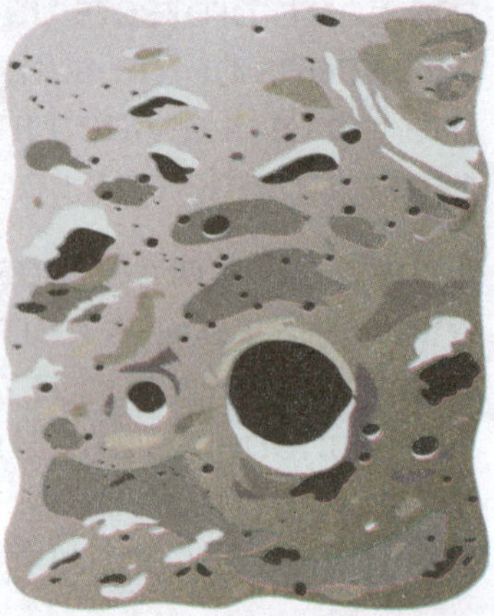
Surface of the moon

The surface of the moon has a lot of craters. These are formed when huge rocks called meteorites[1] hit its surface. There are also lots of mountains on the surface of the moon.

Landing on the moon: Neil Armstrong was the first man to land on the moon, followed minutes later by Edwin Aldrin and Michael Collins on 20th July 1969. They were the astronauts of the American space mission Apollo 11.

Word Web

[1]**Meteorites**: rocks from outer space

The rocks that they brought from the surface of the moon helped the scientists to obtain a lot of information about the moon.

There were some unmanned missions to the moon which obtained a lot of information about the surface of the moon through photographs.

Astronaut on the moon

Footprint on the moon

Chandrayaan Mission

Chandrayaan-1 was India's first unmanned mission to the moon. It was launched on 22 October 2008 from Satish Dhawan Space Centre, Sriharikota, Andhra Pradesh. The mission helped to obtain a lot of information about the moon.

Phases of the Moon

When we look at the moon, it appears to change its shape every night. Sometimes it is a round ball, sometimes C-shaped and sometimes it disappears completely. This happens because we see only that part of the moon that reflects the sun's light as it moves around the Earth in its orbit. These varied shapes of the moon are called the **phases of the moon**.

ECLIPSES

An **eclipse** is a natural phenomenon in which one celestial object (or a portion of it) becomes temporarily invisible as it is hidden by the shadow of another celestial object. It happens when three celestial objects are in a straight line.

The revolution of the Earth around the sun and the revolution of the moon around the Earth cause lunar and solar eclipses.

Lunar Eclipse

When the Earth comes between the sun and the moon, the shadow of the Earth falls on the moon. This causes the lunar eclipse.

Lunar eclipse can be **partial** in which a part of the moon may be visible or **total** in which the moon is not visible at all. The type and duration of a lunar eclipse depends on the position of the moon in the orbit.

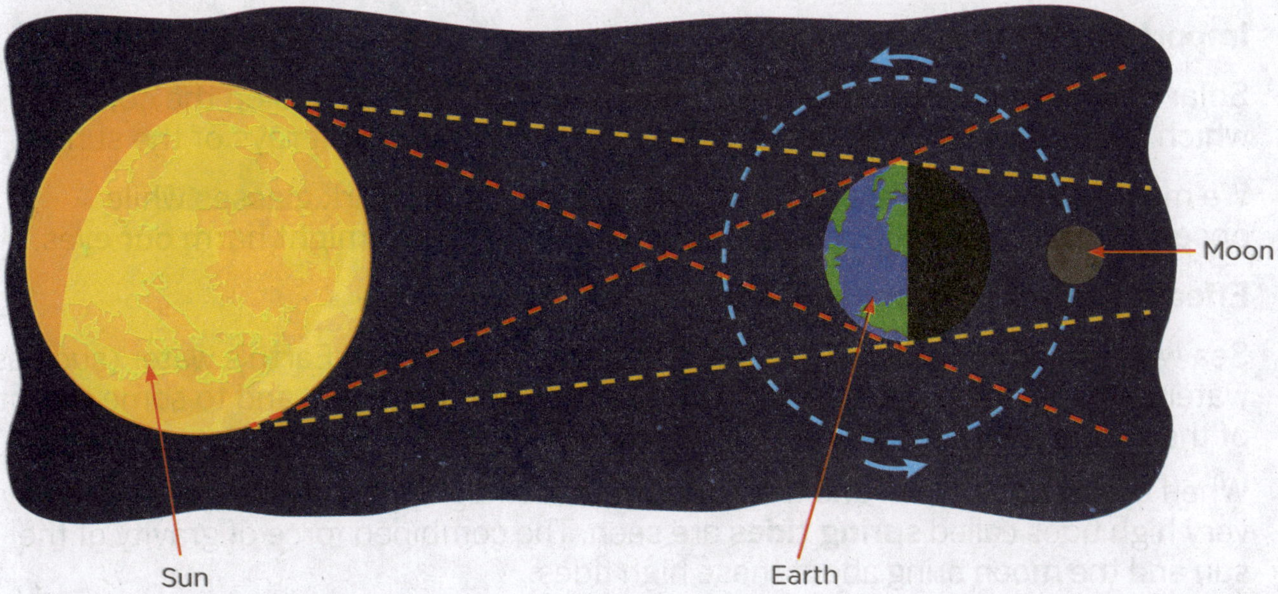

Lunar eclipse

Solar Eclipse

Solar eclipse occurs when the moon comes between the sun and the Earth, and the shadow of the moon falls on the Earth.

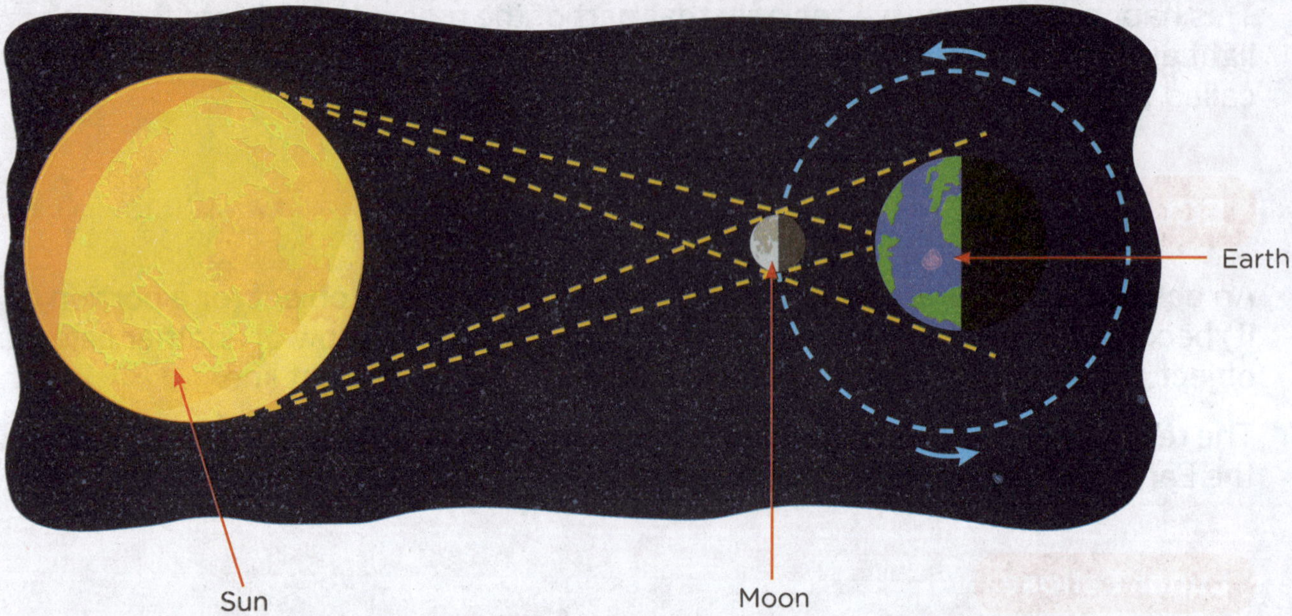

Solar eclipse

If we observe from an area on the Earth where the dark inner shadow of the moon falls, we can see a **total solar eclipse**. If we observe from an area on the Earth where the faint outer shadow of the moon falls, we can see a **partial solar eclipse**. If only a bright ring is seen around a central eclipsed area, then we see a ring-shaped eclipse or **annular eclipse**.

Importance of the solar eclipse

Solar eclipse enables us to study the outer layer of the sun called the corona, which is otherwise very difficult to observe due to the bright rays of the sun.

We must always remember to wear UV rays-protected dark glasses while observing the solar eclipse as the bright light of the sun might harm our eyes.

Effect of the eclipse on the Earth

Sea water rises and falls twice a day. The rise and fall of the Earth's water (such as water in the oceans) due to the gravitational pull of the moon, and to some extent of the sun, is called a **tide**.

When the sun, the moon and the Earth are in a straight line (during new moon days), very high tides called **spring tides** are seen. The combined force of gravity of the sun and the moon bring about these high tides.

When the sun and the moon are at a right angle to each other, we get very low tides called **neap tides**. They usually occur twice a month during the first and the third quarter of the moon.

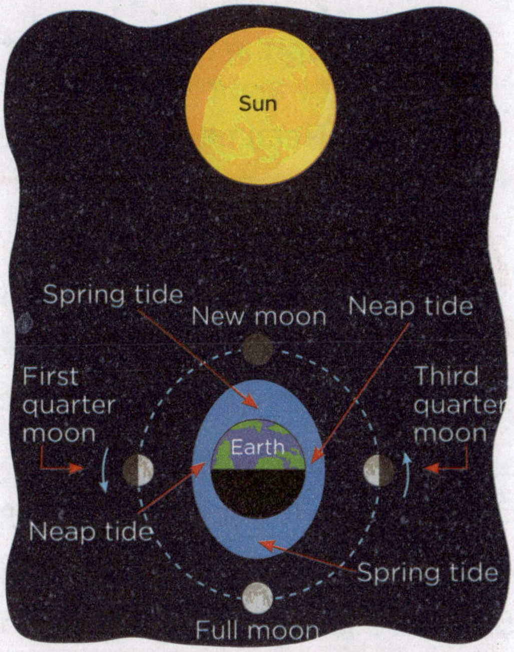

Spring and neap tides

Let's Say Together

Corona	Crust
Mantle	Satellite
Solar eclipse	Lunar eclipse
Spring tide	Neap tide

Keywords

Crust: The outermost layer of the Earth
Mantle: The middle layer of the Earth lying between the crust and the core
Core: The innermost layer of the Earth
Satellite: An object that revolves around a planet
Lunar eclipse: The phenomenon in which the moon is covered by the shadow of the Earth
Solar eclipse: The phenomenon that occurs when the moon comes between the sun and the Earth and the shadow of the moon falls on the Earth
Tides: The rise and fall of the Earth's water due to the gravitational pull of the moon and the sun

Summary

1. The sun and the eight planets revolving around the sun together form the solar system.
2. The Earth has three main layers known as the crust, the mantle and the core.
3. The sun is a star that is situated at the centre of the solar system and it is a huge ball of burning gases.
4. The moon is the natural satellite of the Earth.
5. Lunar eclipse occurs when the Earth comes between the sun and the moon.
6. Solar eclipse occurs when the moon passes between the sun and the Earth.

7. Spring tides occur when the sun, the moon and the Earth are in a straight line on new moon days.
8. Neap tides occur when the sun is at a right angle to the moon.

EXERCISE

A State whether the following statements are true (T) or false (F).

1. The inner core of the Earth is a solid sphere. ☐
2. In the core of the sun, hydrogen gets converted into helium. ☐
3. The moon produces its own light. ☐
4. The moon has a lot of craters on its surface. ☐
5. Total solar eclipse is visible from all parts of the Earth. ☐

B Fill in the blanks using the correct words.

1. The outermost layer of the Earth is called the __________. (crust/core)
2. During volcanic eruptions, molten magma comes out from the __________ of the Earth. (crust/mantle)
3. The moon is the __________ satellite of the Earth. (natural/artificial)
4. The __________ has no atmosphere. (Earth/moon)
5. Spring tides are seen on __________ days. (full moon/new moon)

C Answer the following questions briefly.

1. What is the solar system?
2. What are artificial satellites?
3. What is an eclipse? Name the two eclipses that are visible to us.
4. What is the difference between a total solar eclipse and a partial solar eclipse?
5. What is an annular eclipse?
6. What are tides? How are they formed?

D Answer the following questions.

1. Write a note on the features of the sun.
2. Explain the different layers of the Earth.
3. Explain the features of the surface of the moon.
4. How does a lunar eclipse occur?
5. How does a solar eclipse occur?

E HOTS (Higher Order Thinking Skills)

1. What is the special feature of the Earth compared to other planets in the solar system? (Hint: Think about the things that are found only on the Earth.)
2. A lunar eclipse occurs only on a full moon day. Why? (Hint: What is the position of the sun, the moon and the Earth during a lunar eclipse?)
3. Can we hear someone speak on the moon? (Hint: Sound waves cannot travel without a medium.)

F Label the different layers in the internal structure of the Earth.

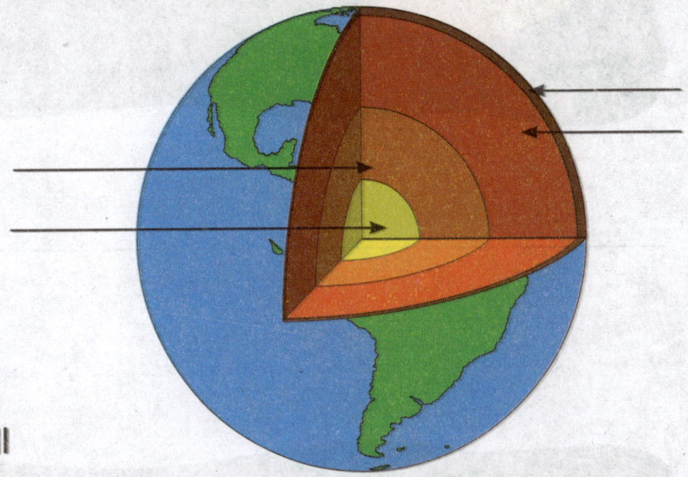

G Project

1. Using a torch, a big ball, a small ball and a screen, we can demonstrate the lunar eclipse. Place the torch and the screen on a table. Light the torch and place a big ball between the torch and the screen.

   Now, place the small ball at point A as shown in the diagram. You can see the shadows of both the balls on the screen. Move the small ball along the line from A to B. You cannot see the shadow of the small ball when it enters in the shadow of the big ball, and again as you move the ball further, the shadow appears.

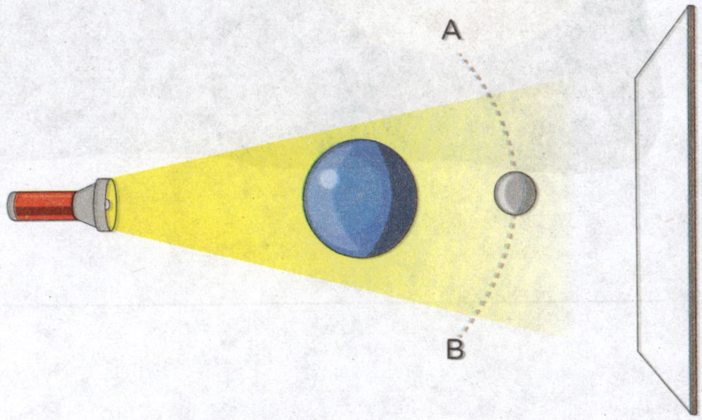

H Life Skills

The Earth is the only planet on which life is known to exist. It is at the right distance from the sun and has an atmosphere that protects it from the harmful rays of the sun. It also has green plants that produce oxygen during photosynthesis. Oxygen is essential for living things to survive.

Suppose the astronauts who land on the moon decide to stay there forever. Would they be able to survive there? Give reasons for your answer.

Label the diagrams given below and name the phenomena they represent.

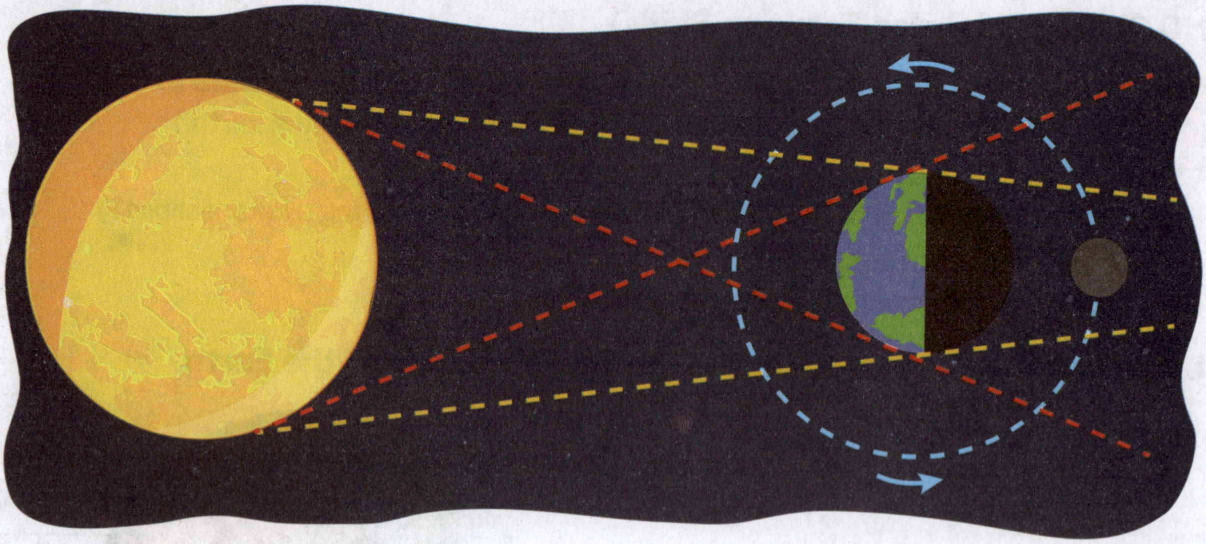

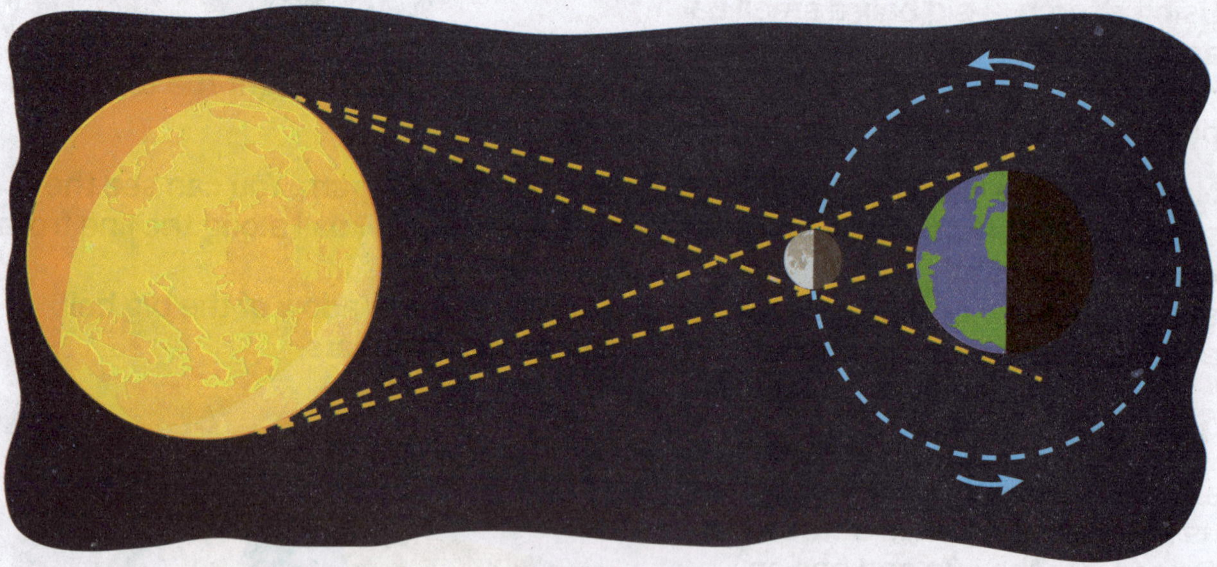

4 Our Environment

Learning Checklist

- Pollution of air, water, land and noise
- Saving the environment

Let's Get Started

Human beings have made their environment dirty in many ways. Look at the pictures given below and tick the ones that make the environment dirty.

☐

☐

☐

☐

ENVIRONMENT

The things around us form our environment.

Our environment contains both living things and non-living things. All living things, including us, depend on the non-living things. For example, we need air to breathe and water to drink. We get these from the environment around us.

The food we eat also comes from plants and animals. We get raw materials like soil, sand, stones, etc. from the Earth to build our homes and buildings.

A natural environment

POLLUTION

The addition of harmful substances to the environment which makes it dirty is called **pollution**.

The substances that cause pollution are called **pollutants**. Pollution has harmful effects on plants, animals and human beings.

AIR POLLUTION

Air in the cities contains a lot of impurities. Smoke from industries and vehicles is the main source of air pollution. In the villages, many houses still use firewood and coal for cooking. This gives out smoke causing air pollution in the rural areas. Smoke from firecrackers also contributes to air pollution. People who breathe in the polluted air suffer from respiratory diseases like asthma, breathing problems and lung cancer.

Bursting of firecrackers causes air pollution

Burning of wood causes air pollution

Smoke from factories and vehicles causes air pollution

Gases like carbon dioxide and methane trap the heat from the sun and do not allow it to escape from the Earth's atmosphere. This is called the **greenhouse effect**. Over the years, increase in the amount of carbon dioxide in the atmosphere due to air pollution has lead to a gradual rise in the Earth's temperature. This is called **global warming**. Global warming can cause the ice at the polar regions to melt, leading to a rise in the water level of the oceans, which results in floods.

WATER POLLUTION

The main sources of water pollution are the wastes from industries, and the sewage pipelines that come from homes and other buildings. In the villages, the lakes or rivers are polluted due to the various activities that are done in or near the water source. Villagers depend on the lake or river for washing clothes and bathing cattle. The dirt and soap from all this washing goes into the water and causes pollution. The solid wastes dumped in the water also causes water pollution.

Sewage let into the water source

The seas and oceans have a threat from oil spillage from ships that transport oil. The oil does not mix with the water, and harms the lives of the plants and animals living in these water bodies.

Various causes of water pollution

Pollution of water makes it unfit for human use. Sewage contains harmful germs that cause diseases like cholera, diarrhoea and typhoid. If these germs are present in drinking water, they can cause diseases.

Science in Context

The Exxon-Valdez oil spill in Alaska happened on 24 March 1989. A tanker was carrying 55 million US gallons of crude oil. The tanker met with an accident causing the spillage of oil into the seawater. This caused the loss of life of animals like sea otters, seals, bald eagles and seabirds. Fish population in the sea was disturbed and the decrease in fish population caused a loss to the people working in the fishing industry.

LAND POLLUTION

Dumping wastes like plastic bags, glass and metal containers causes land pollution. Overuse of chemicals such as fertilizers, insecticides and pesticides also causes land pollution.

Soil is held together by the roots of trees. Deforestation or cutting of trees makes the soil loose. This loose soil is easily carried away by the blowing wind. The rainwater also washes away the loose soil. The process of removal of the top layer of soil by wind and rainwater is called **soil erosion**.

Garbage dumped in the soil causing land pollution

Soil erosion

Revise and recall

Fill in the blanks with the correct words.

1. Smoke from automobiles causes __________ pollution. (land/air)
2. The wastes from industries and the sewage pipelines are the sources of ______________ pollution. (water/air)
3. Dumping wastes like plastic bags, glass and metal containers causes ______________ pollution. (air/land)
4. The roots of trees hold the ______________ together. (soil/water)

NOISE POLLUTION

Noise pollution is caused by the loud sounds that disturb the normal activities of human beings and animals.

Honking of vehicles, sound from the loud speakers, television, etc. cause noise pollution.

Noise from firecrackers, and construction of buildings and roads also cause noise pollution.

Noise pollution has many adverse health effects such as hypertension, hearing impairment, heart disease and sleep disturbance.

Noise pollution in a city

SAVING THE ENVIRONMENT

We should try to minimize pollution to save our environment. Some ways of reducing pollution are given below:

1. Reducing air pollution by using the vehicles only when needed, and walking or cycling to short distances.
2. The smoke and gases produced from the factories should be processed and made safe before letting out through chimneys.
3. Planting more trees to reduce air pollution to get pure air to breathe and to prevent soil erosion.
4. Treatment of waste from factories and sewage from homes before being let into water bodies.
5. Proper management and disposal of garbage.
6. Using environment-friendly manures and natural fertilizers in fields.
7. Using cloth bags instead of polythene bags and minimizing the use of plastics.
8. Construction of factories far away from the main city.
9. Use of solar energy should be encouraged as it does not cause pollution.

Let's Say Together!

Environment	Pollution	Smoke
Global warming	Sewage	Erosion

Keywords

Pollution: The addition of harmful substances to the environment which makes it dirty
Pollutants: The substances that cause pollution
Greenhouse effect: The trapping of heat by the gases in the atmosphere that leads to increase in the Earth's temperature
Global warming: A gradual rise in the Earth's temperature due to greenhouse effect

Summary

1. All the living and non-living things in our surroundings form our environment.
2. Smoke and gases from industries and automobiles, firecrackers, burning of firewood, etc. cause air pollution.
3. The main sources of water pollution are sewage and waste from the industries.
4. Disposal of garbage or waste and overuse of chemicals like insecticides, fertilizers and pesticides are the main causes of land pollution.
5. Building construction, honking of vehicles, sound from the loudspeakers, etc. cause noise pollution.
6. Planting more trees and safeguarding the forests reduce pollution.
7. Stopping water pollution by proper treatment and safe waste disposal can reduce water and land pollution.

EXERCISE

A Choose the correct option for each of the following.

1. Which of the following is a cause of air pollution?
   (a) Trees (b) Smoke (c) House (d) All of these
2. Which of the following is not a cause of soil erosion?
   (a) Wind (b) Rain (d) Trees (d) None of these
3. Air pollution can cause
   (a) asthma (b) obesity
   (c) hearing impairment (d) cholera

4. Which of these causes land pollution?

(a) Loudspeakers (b) Polythene bags

(c) Smoke (d) Sewage

5. Honking of vehicles and loud noise from television cause ________ pollution.

(a) land (b) water (c) air (d) noise

B Fill in the blanks using the correct words.

1. The substances that cause pollution are called ________. (pollutants/smoke)
2. Global warming is caused due to increase in the amount of ________. (carbon dioxide/oxygen)
3. The main cause of soil erosion is ________. (deforestation/afforestation)
4. Washing clothes and bathing animals near a water source cause ________ pollution. (water/air)
5. Noise pollution causes ________. (sleep disturbance/asthma)

C State whether the following statements are true (T) or false (F).

1. Burning firecrackers causes air pollution. ☐
2. Global warming can cause melting of ice in the polar regions. ☐
3. Oil spillage from ships cause water pollution. ☐
4. Sewage contains germs that cause cholera, diarrhoea, etc. ☐
5. Pollution of air, water, noise and land is beneficial for us. ☐

D Give two examples for each of the following.

1. Kinds of pollution ________ ________
2. Activities that cause water pollution ________ ________
3. Causes of soil erosion ________ ________
4. Wastes that cause land pollution ________ ________
5. Health effects of noise pollution ________ ________

E Answer the following questions briefly.

1. What is pollution?
2. What are pollutants?
3. Write the harmful effects of air pollution.
4. What is global warming?
5. What is soil erosion?

F Answer the following questions.

1. Write a note on air pollution.
2. What are the causes of water pollution in cities and villages?
3. Describe the sources of noise pollution.
4. Write any five ways to save our environment.

G HOTS (Higher Order Thinking Skills)

1. What does the sign given alongside signify? Where is this sign usually found? (Hint: Noise pollution)
2. If firecrackers are burst, they cause two types of pollution. What are they? (Hint: Firecrackers make loud sound and give out smoke.)
3. We must protect and conserve our environment. Justify the statement. (Hint: Effects of pollution)

H Tick the things that can be used to reduce pollution.

 ☐

 ☐

 ☐

 ☐

 ☐

I Project

Make posters on the four types of pollution you have studied in this chapter and ways to prevent them. Write catchy slogans to create awareness.

J Life Skills

1. Where would you throw the empty plastic juice bottles?

   (a) Dustbin (b) River water (c) Soil

2. When should you use the bell on your cycle?

   (a) When you want to alert people crossing the road

   (b) To have fun (c) Near the hospital

3. To reduce air pollution and to get fresh air, you should

   (a) plant trees (b) burst firecrackers (c) use cars for travel

Identify the type of pollution shown in the following pictures and write in the space provided.

_______________ _______________

_______________ _______________

5 Natural Disasters

Learning Checklist

- Earthquake
- Volcanoes
- Tidal waves and tsunami
- Floods
- Drought

Let's Get Started

Look at the pictures shown below. Can you identify the given phenomena? Choose the words from the help box.

Earthquake	Drought	Thunderstorm	Volcanic eruption

____

____

____

____

A **disaster** is defined as an unexpected event resulting in great damage, loss and destruction to life and property. Natural events occurring on the Earth that cause great damage or loss of life are called **natural disasters**.

In this chapter, we will learn more about natural disasters.

EARTHQUAKE

The sudden movement of a part of the Earth's surface is called an **earthquake**. These movements are caused by shifting of layers of rocks deep under the Earth's crust. The actual point deep inside the Earth where an earthquake begins is called the **focus** and the point on the Earth's surface directly above the focus is called the **epicentre**. The maximum effect of the earthquake is felt at the epicentre and the effect reduces as we move away from the epicentre.

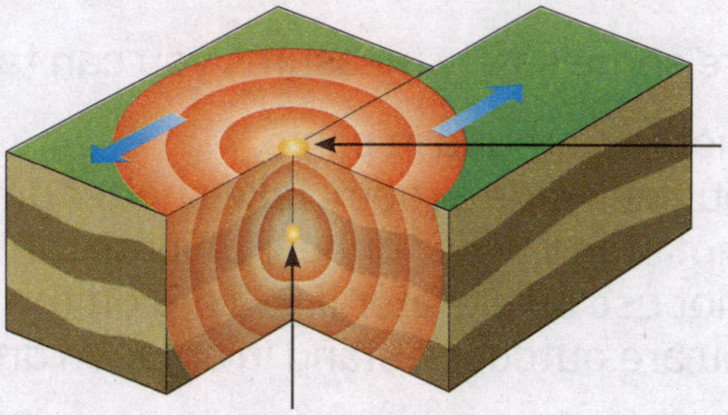

After-effects of Earthquakes

1. Destruction of buildings, trees, roads and vehicles
2. Huge loss of life (humans and animals)
3. Spread of diseases

Destruction caused by earthquakes

Measuring Earthquakes and Their Effects

The effects of earthquakes depend on the force with which they occur. Some earthquakes are so weak that they just shake materials kept on a shelf, while some are so strong that they cause buildings to fall down and lead to deaths of numerous people.

The intensity and duration of an earthquake can be measured using an instrument called the **seismograph**. **Richter scale** is a standard scale used to find out the magnitude[1] of earthquakes on a scale of 1 to 10. Earthquakes measuring 1 to 2 on the scale will hardly be felt. Earthquakes measuring 3, 4 and 5 on the scale can cause damage to property. Earthquakes measuring 6 and above on the scale can result in widespread damage to property and also cause death.

Word Web

[1]**Magnitude**: relative size or extent

Modern seismograph

Know the Fact!

Zhang Heng of China's Han dynasty was the first person to build an instrument to detect earthquakes.

Safety Measures During an Earthquake

Here are some safety measures you can take to be safe during an earthquake:

- Do not run around in panic.
- If you are inside a room, take shelter under a table or a bed.
- Do not stand under or near objects that can fall and hurt you.
- Do not use an elevator if you are on the upper floors. Always use the staircase.
- If you are outdoors, stand in an open area away from any buildings and trees.

VOLCANOES

The core of the Earth is made up of molten rock called **magma**. A crack or vent on the Earth's surface that allows hot magma from below the surface to come out is called a **volcano**.

A **vent** is the region where the Earth's crust is weak and develops a crack. Once hot magma comes out of the Earth's surface, it is called **lava**. After a volcanic eruption occurs, a crater is formed at the region of vent.

Volcanoes are of three types depending on how frequently they erupt: active, dormant and extinct.

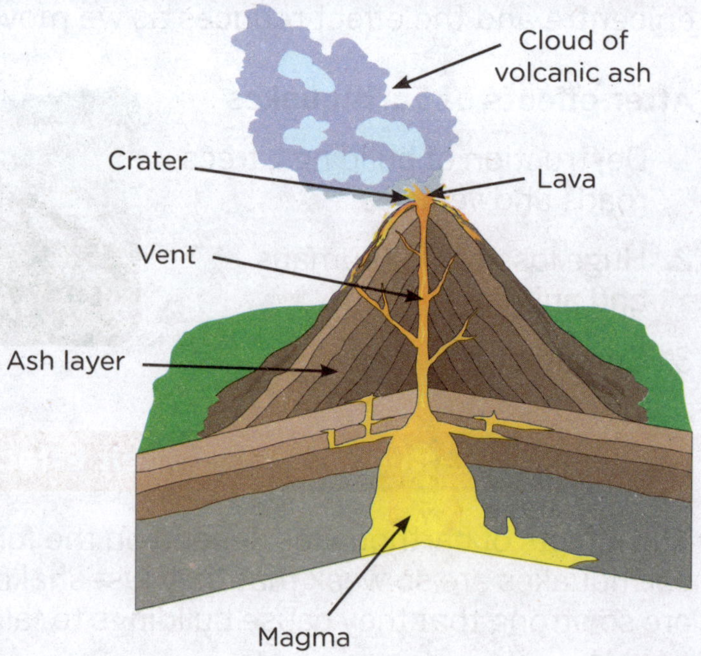

A volcano

Active volcanoes: These are considered to be highly dangerous. They may erupt at any time or have erupted in recent years. Some of the most active volcanoes are Mount St. Helens in the United States, Mount Mayon in the Philippines and Mount Lassen in the United States.

Dormant volcanoes: Volcanoes that have not erupted for a long period but may erupt in the future are called dormant volcanoes. Some of the dormant volcanoes are Mauna Kea in Hawaii, Mount Edziza in Canada and Narcondam in Andaman Islands of India.

Extinct volcanoes: Volcanoes that are not expected to erupt in the future are called extinct volcanoes. Some of the extinct volcanoes are Mount Ashitaka in Japan, Shiprock in the United States and Zuidwal in the Netherlands.

After-effects of Volcanic Eruptions

1. Destruction of farmlands and roads, damage to property and loss of life.
2. Volcanic dust blocks sunlight for a long period, which leads to change in the weather pattern.
3. Spread of diseases

Know the Fact

A region in the Pacific ocean that consists of 452 volcanoes is called **the ring of fire**.

Advantages of Volcanic Eruptions

1. After a volcanic eruption, the soil becomes very fertile and good for farming.
2. Some of the volcanic locations can be used to generate geothermal energy[1].

Word Web

[1]**Geothermal energy**: energy obtained from the Earth

TIDAL WAVES AND TSUNAMIS

Tides are the cyclic rise and fall of sea levels caused due to the gravitational pull of the sun and the moon. At times the waves on the sea are high and some times they are low. Tides reach the maximum height when the sun, the moon and the Earth are in a straight line.

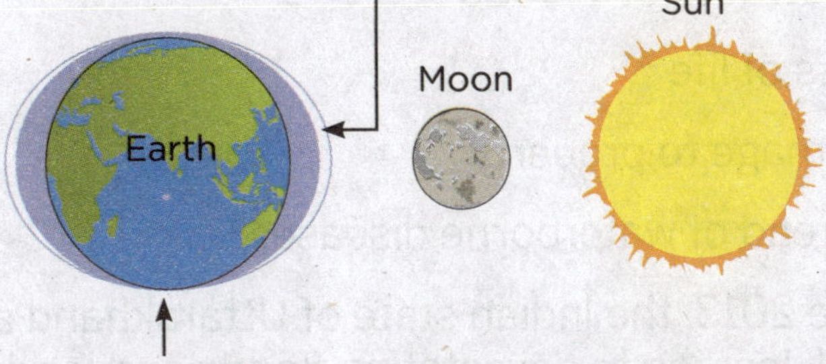

Rise of large amount of water in the form of huge waves from oceans due to underwater earthquakes, volcanic eruptions, etc. is called **tsunami**. When there is a disturbance in the layers of rocks in the Earth's crust under water bodies, a large amount of energy is released, which leads to the formation of huge waves. Large tsunami waves lead to the loss of life and property. It is advisable to stay at high altitude regions during a tsunami threat.

Tsunami waves

On 26 December 2004, a tsunami occurred in the Indian Ocean, causing a major loss of life and property in the coastal regions of Tamil Nadu and Kerala. The Andaman and Nicobar islands were among the worst hit areas in India.

FLOODS

Approximately 75% of the Earth's surface is covered by water. When water bodies like the oceans, rivers, lakes and ponds have excess water, they overflow leading to floods.

Flood

Floods occur due to the following natural factors:

- Heavy rainfall
- Low-pressure region formed in the ocean
- Excess melting of snow in the mountains and glaciers

Floods can be prevented by taking the following measures:

- Constructing proper streams or channels for the excess water to flow through
- Planting enough trees to slow down the force with which water flows
- Constructing proper embankments[1] that control the level of water flowing into the rivers

Word Web

[1]**Embankment**: a wall made of mud and stone to keep water back

After-effects of Floods

- Loss of life
- Damage to property
- Spread of waterborne diseases

In June 2013, the Indian state of Uttarakhand and nearby places received heavy rainfall, leading to devastating floods and landslides. It caused heavy damage to life and property.

Safety Measures During Floods

Some safety measures you can take to be safe during a flood are given below:

- Do not panic. Always listen to flood warnings given on radios and news channels.
- Leave the area where the flood water is bound to flow.
- Shift to higher locations where the flood water cannot reach.
- Keep medicines, food supplies and clean drinking water in plenty.
- Follow instructions given by rescue team workers.

DROUGHT

Drought is a condition or state of severe shortage of water supply (both surface and underground). Some droughts are of shorter duration, whereas some continue for years.

Drought

Droughts occur due to lack of or insufficient rainfall along with excessive usage of existing water resources.

Effects of drought

Some effects of droughts are as follows:

- Destruction of crops
- Malnutrition and death of humans and animals
- Mass movement of people from one place to another

The effects of drought can be controlled by taking the following steps:

- Making judicious[1] usage of available water resources
- Adapting to rainwater harvesting
- Recycling of water
- Cultivating crops that require less water

Word Web

[1]**Judicious**: careful and sensible

Major drought-prone regions in India are Southern and Eastern Maharashtra, Northern Karnataka, Andhra Pradesh, Odisha, Gujarat and Rajasthan.

In 2012, the Indian state of Karnataka faced severe drought.

Science in Context

Drip irrigation is a modern irrigation technique that saves water. It is done using narrow tubes that allow very small quantity of water to drip into the roots of plants.

Keywords

Earthquake: The sudden movement of a part of the Earth's surface

Volcano: A crack or vent on the Earth's surface that allows hot magma from below the surface to come out

Tide: The cyclic rise and fall of sea levels caused by the gravitational pull of the sun and the moon

Tsunami: Rise of large amount of water in the form of huge waves from oceans due to underwater earthquakes, volcanic eruptions, etc.

Drought: A state of severe shortage of water supply (both surface and underground)

Flood: A natural disaster caused by the overflow of oceans, rivers, etc., due to excess water

Summary

1. Natural events occurring on the Earth that cause great damage to life and property are called natural disasters.
2. The actual point deep inside the Earth where an earthquake begins is called the focus and the point on the Earth's surface directly above the focus is called the epicentre.
3. Intensity and duration of an earthquake can be measured using an instrument called seismograph.
4. Volcanoes are of three types: active, dormant and extinct.
5. Tides reach the maximum height when the sun, the moon and the Earth are in a straight line.
6. Disturbance in the layers of rocks in the Earth's crust under water bodies leads to generation of huge waves called tsunami.
7. When the water bodies like oceans, rivers, lakes and ponds have excess water, they overflow, leading to floods.
8. Drought occurs due to lack of or insufficient rainfall along with excessive usage of existing water resources.

EXERCISE

A Choose the correct option for each of the following.

1. Which of the following natural disasters is caused by disturbances in the Earth's crust?

   (a) Earthquake (b) Flood (c) Tide (d) Drought

2. The actual point deep in the Earth's crust where an earthquake begins is called

   (a) Mantle (b) Core (c) Focus (d) Epicentre

3. Which volcanoes are capable of erupting?

   (a) Dormant and active (b) Active and extinct

   (c) Extinct and dormant (d) Active, dormant and extinct

4. Which of the following natural disasters is caused by shortage of water?

   (a) Drought (b) Tsunami (c) Earthquake (d) Volcanic eruption

5. Heavy rainfall can cause

   (a) Earthquake (b) Drought (c) Volcanic eruption (d) Flood

B State whether the following statements are true (T) or false (F).

1. Tides are formed due to the gravitational pull of the sun and the moon. ☐
2. Drought occurs when water bodies overflow due to excess water. ☐
3. The effect of an earthquake is felt more at the epicentre. ☐
4. Tides and tsunami are one and the same. ☐
5. When magma comes out of the Earth's surface, it is called lava. ☐

C Fill in the blanks using the correct words.

1. The innermost layer of the Earth is called ___________. (core/mantle)
2. The magnitude of an earthquake is measured using ___________. (seismograph/ Richter scale)
3. Volcanoes that erupt frequently are called ___________ volcanoes. (active/extinct)
4. Floods occur due to ___________ water. (excess/lack of)
5. Earthquake measuring ___________ on the Richter scale is considered to be highly dangerous. (3/8)

D Name the following.

1. The actual point inside the Earth where an earthquake begins ___________
2. Huge waves formed due to an earthquake occurring underwater ___________
3. The instrument used to measure the intensity and duration of earthquakes ___________
4. The region where the Earth's crust is weak and develops a crack ___________
5. The natural disaster that occurs due the lack of rainfall ___________

E Answer the following questions briefly.

1. What is an earthquake?
2. What is an epicentre?
3. What is a dormant volcano?
4. What causes tides?
5. What is a tsunami?

F Answer the following questions.

1. What are the after-effects of an earthquake? Give three safety measures to be followed during earthquakes.
2. What is a volcano? Explain different types of volcanoes with one example each.

3. Write two after-effects and two advantages of volcanic eruption.
4. When do floods occur? What are the after-effects of flood?
5. Give the measures that can be taken to prevent or reduce the effects of drought.

G HOTS (Higher Order thinking Skills)

1. Amit is on the first floor of a building. If an earthquake occurs suddenly, which method is better for him to come out of the building: using the stairs or the elevator? Why? (Hint: Recall the safety measures during an earthquake.)
2. Can an earthquake cause a tsunami? Explain. (Hint: What is a tsunami?)

H Label the parts of the volcano shown below.

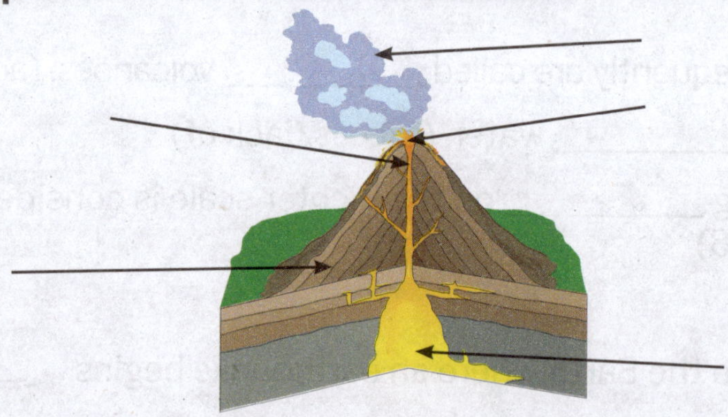

I Project

Search the Internet or newspapers with the help of an elder and make a report on natural disasters. Cover the following points:

(a) Name of the disaster
(b) The date on which it occured
(c) Places affected by the disaster
(d) Details of damage or loss of life caused, if available

J Life Skill

Suppose you are inside your house and you experience a slight shake. Suddenly you realize that it is an earthquake. Read the following points to know what you should do to save yourself.

- Drop down; take shelter under a bed or a table and hold on.
- Stay indoors until the shaking stops and you are sure it is safe to exit.
- Stay away from bookcases or furniture that can fall on you.
- Stay away from windows. In a high-rise building, expect the fire alarms and sprinklers to go off during a quake.
- If you are on bed, hold on and stay there, protecting your head with a pillow.
- If you are outdoors, find a clear spot away from buildings, trees and power lines. Drop down to the ground.

WORKSHEET

Identify the natural disasters shown below. Write a few sentences on the after-effects of each.

6 Light and Shadow

Learning Checklist

- Transparent, translucent and opaque materials
- Shadows

Let's Get Started

We have learned in earlier classes that objects that produce light are called **luminous objects**. They help us to see the non-luminous objects, which do not produce light.

In the picture given below, put a tick mark (☒) against luminous objects and a cross mark (☒) against non-luminous objects in the boxes provided.

Non-luminous objects are made from different materials. Materials can be grouped on the basis of the amount of light they allow to pass through them. Let us understand this with the help of an activity.

Activity 1

Aim: To identify different types of materials

Materials required: A clear (see-through) plastic cover, a sheet of butter paper and an A4 size chart paper

Procedure:

1. Take a clear plastic cover, a butter paper and an A4 size chart paper.
2. Ask your friend to stand in front of you.
3. Now, try to see your friend through each—the plastic cover, the butter paper and the chart paper.

Conclusion: You will be able to see your friend clearly through the clear plastic cover, partially through the butter paper and not at all through the chart paper.

TRANSPARENT, TRANSLUCENT AND OPAQUE MATERIALS

Materials that allow light to pass through them completely are called **transparent materials**. Examples of transparent materials are clear glass, clear water and clear plastic sheet.

Materials that allow light to pass through them partially (not completely) are called **translucent materials**. Examples of translucent materials are butter paper, frosted glass and coloured glass.

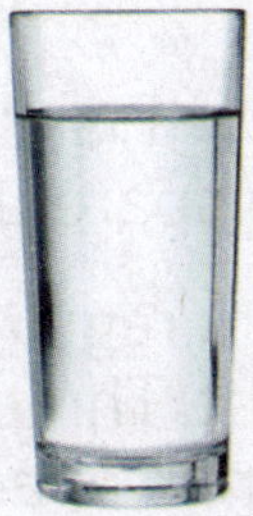

Clear water (transparent)

Frosted glass (translucent)

Know the Fact

Is mirror a transparent object? It is not because we cannot see objects on the other side of a mirror, though we can see our own image clearly.

Materials that block light or do not allow light to pass through them are called **opaque materials**. Examples of opaque materials are wood, bag and books.

Bag (opaque)

Book (opaque)

SHADOWS

We know that a shadow is formed when an object is placed in front of a source of light. Let us perform an activity to understand the formation of shadows by transparent, translucent and opaque objects.

Activity 2

Aim: To understand the formation of shadows by transparent, translucent and opaque materials

Materials required: A transparent plastic sheet (A4 size), a translucent tracing sheet (A4 size), a cardboard sheet (A4 size), a torch and a screen

Procedure:

1. Take the plastic sheet, the tracing sheet, the cardboard sheet and the torch.
2. Hold the objects one by one in front of the screen and project the light from the torch onto each object from the opposite side. What do you observe?

Observation:

1. You will see that the opaque cardboard sheet blocks the light completely and hence forms a clear and dark shadow on the screen.
2. The translucent tracing sheet partially blocks the light and thus forms a lighter shadow on the screen.
3. The transparent glass does not block the light from passing through it and hence does not form any shadow.

From the above activity, it is clear that opaque and translucent objects form shadows, whereas transparent objects do not form shadows.

Thus, a **shadow** is a dark region formed by a translucent or an opaque object when it blocks the path of light. Three things are required for a shadow to form: a light source, a translucent or an opaque object and a screen (a surface on which the shadow can form).

Features of a Shadow

Following are some features of a shadow.

(a) A shadow is always formed on the opposite side of the light source.

(b) A shadow shows only the outline of the shape of the object, and not any other details.

(c) The colour of a shadow does not depend on the colour of the object. Shadows are always dark.

(d) The size of a shadow depends on the distance of the light source from the object and also on the distance of the screen from the object.

When the light source is close to the object or the screen is away from the object, the size of the shadow increases. When the light source is away from the object or the screen is close to the object, the size of the shadow decreases.

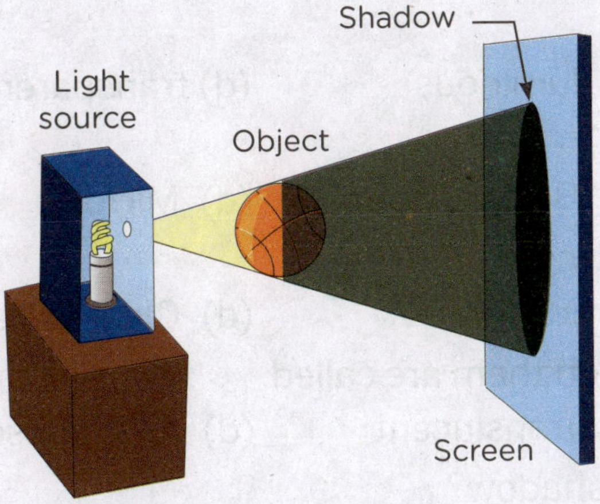

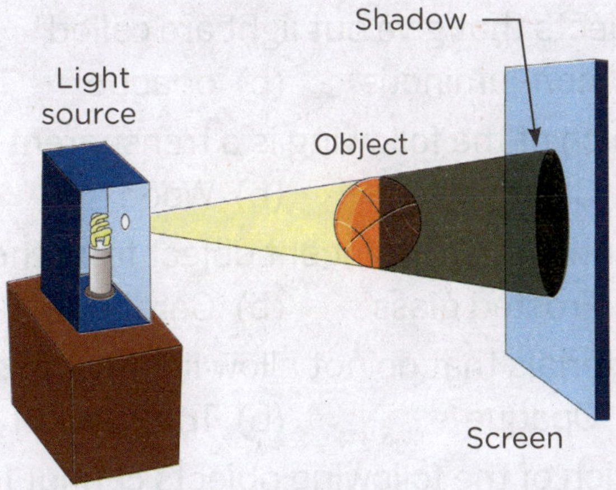

Science in Context

The shadow of an object is the longest in the morning and evening, and the shortest at noon. This is because the rays of the sun are slanting in the morning and evening, and straight above the head at noon.

Let's Say Together

Transparent Translucent Opaque Shadow Screen

Keywords

Transparent materials: Materials that allow light to pass through them completely
Translucent materials: Materials that allow light to pass through them partially
Opaque materials: Materials that do not allow light to pass through them
Shadow: The dark region formed by a translucent or an opaque object when it blocks the path of light

Summary

1. Materials can be classified as transparent, translucent and opaque based on the amount of light they allow to pass through them.
2. Only opaque and translucent objects form shadows.
3. Shadows are always dark.
4. Shadows are formed on the opposite side of the light source.

EXERCISE

A **Choose the correct option for each of the following.**

1. Objects that give out light are called
   (a) non-luminous (b) opaque (c) luminous (d) transparent
2. Which of the following is a transparent object?
   (a) Clear glass (b) Wood (c) Butter paper (d) Mirror
3. Identify the translucent object from the following.
   (a) Frosted glass (b) Cardboard (c) Mirror (d) Clear water
4. Materials that do not allow light to pass through them are called
   (a) Opaque (b) Transparent (c) Translucent (d) All of these
5. Which of the following objects cannot form a shadow?
   (a) Pencil (b) Clear glass (c) Bag (d) Notebook

B **State whether the following statements are true (T) or false (F).**

1. Translucent materials allow light to pass through them completely. ☐
2. Shadows are always dark. ☐
3. Only transparent materials can form shadows. ☐
4. Shadows can be formed without a light source. ☐
5. The size of the shadow of an object is always the same. ☐

C **Fill in the blanks using the correct words.**

1. A shadow is always formed on the __________ side of the object. (same/opposite)
2. Butter paper is an example of __________ material. (transparent/translucent)
3. Shadows are formed by __________ materials. (transparent/opaque)
4. The size of a shadow depends on the distance of the __________ from the light source. (object/shadow)
5. The colour of a shadow is always __________. (white/dark)

D **Write two examples for each of the following.**

1. Transparent materials __________ __________
2. Translucent materials __________ __________
3. Opaque materials __________ __________
4. Things required to form a shadow __________ __________

E Answer the following question briefly.

1. What is the difference between transparent and translucent materials?
2. Why do transparent materials not form shadows?
3. Which material would form a darker shadow: translucent or opaque? Why?
4. State two factors on which the size of a shadow depends.

F Answer the following questions.

1. Define transparent, translucent and opaque materials. Give two examples of each.
2. What is a shadow? What are the features of a shadow?
3. Why is it that only translucent and opaque materials form shadows?

G HOTS (Higher Order Thinking Skills)

You and your mother went to the market to buy new containers for her kitchen. What kind of containers would you suggest her to buy: opaque, transparent or translucent? Give reasons for your answer. (Hint: Think of the features of these materials.)

H Write transparent, translucent or opaque for each of the following.

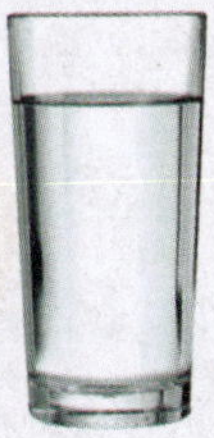

Clear water

____

Bag

____

Frosted glass

____

Apple

____

I Project

Change a transparent object into translucent and opaque objects. Also, change an opaque object into a translucent object.

Materials to be used: A4 size transparent sheet of plastic, A4 size tracing paper (2 sheets), A4 size white opaque sheet (2 sheets), small bottle of hair oil, glue

Procedure:

1. Take a transparent plastic sheet. Stick tracing papers on both sides. (Apply glue only on the edges.) Now, the transparent plastic sheet becomes translucent. Paste one of the opaque white sheets on it. Can you see through it now?
2. Take an A4 size opaque white sheet. Place two drops of coconut oil on the sheet and gently spread it across the sheet. You will find that the opaque sheet has become translucent.

A **Draw the shadows of the tree given below for three different positions of the sun during the day.**

B Life Skills

You are given the task of setting up your study room. Make a list of the materials you would need. Classify those materials as transparent, translucent and opaque. Justify their purpose and usage. Include two materials from each category.

7

Force and Energy

Learning Checklist

- Effects of force
- Types of force
- Energy
- Simple machines

Let's Get Started

Force and energy are the terms that we often use in our daily lives. To find out how much we know about force and energy, let us do this short exercise.

Look at the picture given below. Fill in the blanks using the correct options.

In a volleyball game, the ball hit by the players initially goes up, but always comes down due to ______________ (frictional/gravitational) force.

The referee on the side uses ______________ (sound/heat) energy from his whistle to control the game.

Since the game is mostly played indoors, the stadium needs to be sufficiently lit. The floodlights produce a lot of ______________ (light/sound) energy.

You have learned in Class 3 that **push** or **pull** are the actions that make objects move, for example, a bullock pulling a cart, a man pushing a bike, a boy lifting his school bag and a girl kicking a ball. In all these cases, what makes the objects move? It is the push or pull applied on the objects.

Force is defined as a push or a pull applied on an object. Let us learn about the effects that force can produce.

EFFECTS OF FORCE

Force can make an object move

A force acting on a stationary object can make it move. Also, a force acting on a moving object can make it move faster, if the force is applied in the same direction in which the object is moving. For example, a football player kicks a ball to make it move. A boy pushes a cart to make it move forward.

Force can move a cart

Force can stop a moving object

A force acting on a moving object can slow it down or stop it completely, if it is applied in the direction opposite to the direction of motion.

For example, a goalkeeper uses his hands to stop a football from rolling into the net.

Force can stop a moving football

Force can change the direction of a moving object

A force acting on a moving object from an angle can change the direction in which the object is moving.

For example, in cricket, a batsman hits a moving ball with such force that it changes its direction.

Force can change the direction of a moving ball

Force can change the shape of an object

A force acting on an object can change its shape.

Have you ever kneaded dough or made chapatis? Notice how a rolling pin makes a ball of dough flat and round when you apply force.

Another example is to squeeze a sponge and see how its shape changes.

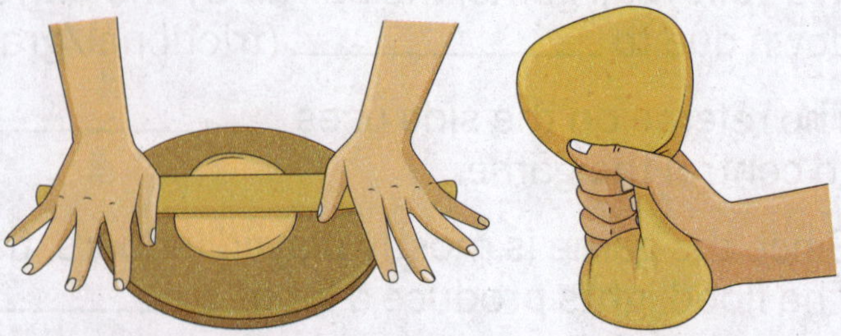

Force can change the shape of objects

TYPES OF FORCE

Various types of forces exist in nature. Some of them are given below.

Gravitational Force

Gravitational force or gravity is the force with which all objects in the universe attract each other. The gravitational force of the Earth pulls objects towards its centre. Any object that is thrown upwards always comes down because of the Earth's gravity. Gravitational force always acts in the opposite direction when an object moves away from the Earth; it acts along the direction of motion of the object when it moves towards the Earth.

Electrostatic Force

The attractive or repulsive force that acts due to the presence of 'charges' is called **electrostatic force**. Let us perform an activity to understand this better.

Activity 1

Aim: To understand electrostatic force

Materials required: Plastic ruler and bits of paper

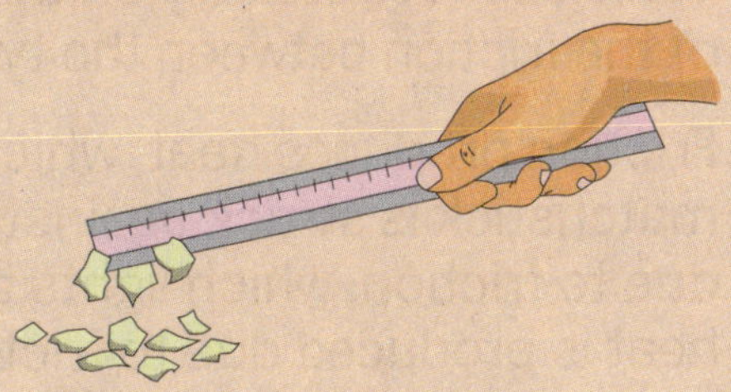

Procedure:

1. Place bits of papers on a table.
2. Take the plastic ruler and rub it against your hair. Ensure that your hair is dry.
3. Bring the plastic ruler near the bits of paper and observe what happens.

Observation: You will find that the bits of paper move towards the plastic ruler.

Conclusion: The plastic ruler gets charged due to rubbing against hair and the bits of paper get attracted towards it when brought closer.

You will learn more about electrostatic force in higher classes.

Magnetic Force

Magnets are substances that attract certain materials towards them. The force with which a magnet attracts certain materials is called **magnetic force**. The materials that get attracted towards a magnet are called **magnetic materials**.

Magnet attracts magnetic materials

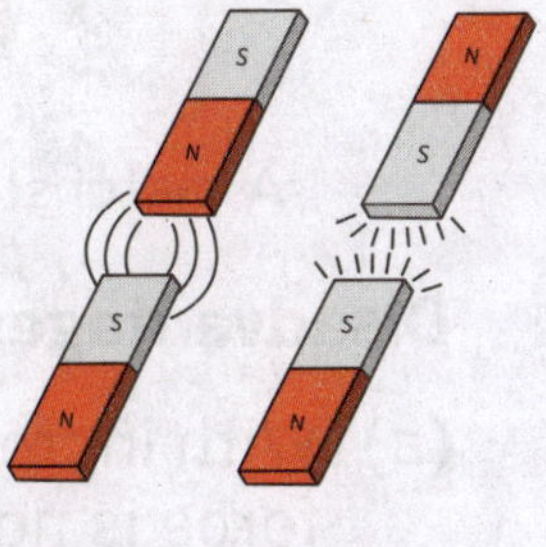

Unlike poles attract and like poles repel

Magnetic force

Magnets also apply force on each other. Every magnet has two poles known as the **north pole** and the **south pole**. When two like poles are brought near each other, they repel or oppose each other, whereas unlike poles attract each other.

Frictional Force

Frictional force or **friction** acts on two objects that are in contact and at least one of them is in motion. It always acts opposite to the direction of motion. Hence, it slows down the motion of an object or stops it from moving completely.

The force of friction produced depends on the nature of objects in contact. Rough surfaces offer more friction than smooth surfaces. Let us learn about some advantages and disadvantages of friction.

Advantages of Friction

(a) Friction allows steady motion of objects. For example, we are able to walk steadily due to the friction between the ground and our shoes. The grooves on the sole of our shoes provide enough friction to prevent us from falling. Vehicles move steadily on the road because of the friction between the tyres and the road.

Friction helps us to walk

(b) Friction produces heat, which we use for different purposes. For example, a matchstick is struck against the rough surface of a matchbox, heat is produced due to friction, which lights the matchstick. When we rub our hands together, heat is produced due to friction, which keep our hands warm.

A matchstick is rubbed against a matchbox

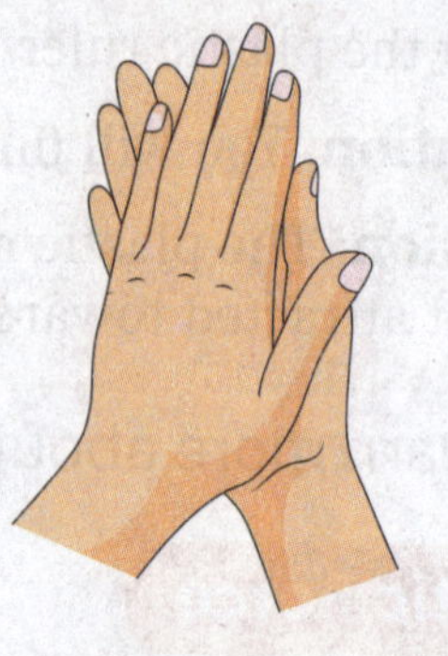

Rubbing hands produces heat

Disadvantages of Friction

(a) With increase in friction, it becomes difficult to move an object as more force is needed to overcome friction. For example, moving heavy objects on a rough surface is difficult.

(b) Friction causes the surface of an object to wear out. For example, soles of shoes and surface of tyres wear out because of friction.

ENERGY

The ability to do work is called **energy**. Energy is present around us in many forms and we get it from different sources. For example, during the day, the sun gives out light and heat energy. At night, street lights use electrical energy to light the roads. The food we eat gives us the energy to work and play.

Let us now learn about the different forms of energy.

Heat Energy

Heat is a form of energy. Heat energy is obtained from the sun, and also by burning fuels like coal, petrol and kerosene. We use heat energy for cooking food and keeping us warm.

Heat energy

Light Energy

Light energy helps us to see things around us. The sun is a natural source of light. Some artificial sources of light are electric bulb, candle, tubelight, lamp, etc. Plants also use light energy from the sun to prepare food.

Light energy

Mechanical Energy

The energy that an object has due to its position or its motion is called **mechanical energy**.

Mechanical energy is of two types: potential energy and kinetic energy. The energy that an object has due to its position with respect to the ground is called **potential energy**. For example, water stored in a dam or overhead tank.

The energy that an object has due to its motion is called **kinetic energy**. All moving objects have kinetic energy. For example, a moving car and a bullet fired from a gun.

A moving car has mechanical energy

Electrical Energy

The most common and useful form of energy nowadays is electrical energy. This form can be easily converted to other forms of energy. Sources of electrical energy are cells and generators. Most of the common household appliances such as fans, mobiles, watches, televisions and computers run on electrical energy.

Electrical energy

Sound Energy

Sound is a form of energy that is produced by vibration of objects. Some sources of sound energy are radio, loudspeakers and musical instruments.

Speaker

Wind Energy

The energy obtained from the moving wind is called wind energy. Windmills help in converting wind energy into electrical energy.

Windmill

SIMPLE MACHINES

Machines are tools that make our work easier by reducing the amount of force (effort) needed to do the work. Machines can be simple or complex.

Tools such as scissors, screws, tongs and knives that help us in doing work efficiently and easily are called **simple machines**. There are six basic types of simple machines: lever, pulley, inclined plane, screw, wedge, and wheel and axle.

Complex machines are made of two or more simple machines. For example, a bicycle is a complex machine made up of lever, screw, and wheel and axle.

Let us learn more about simple machines.

Lever

A lever is a rigid rod made to rest on and move around a fixed support. It consists of three parts:

Fulcrum: It is the fixed point or support on which the rod moves freely.

Effort: It is the force that is applied on the free end of the rod to enable the other end to perform work.

Load: It is the object on which work has to be done.

Depending on the position of these parts, levers are classified into three types: first-class, second-class and third-class.

First-class levers: In this type of levers, the fulcrum is between the load and the effort. Some examples are scissors, crowbars, see-saw and claw hammers.

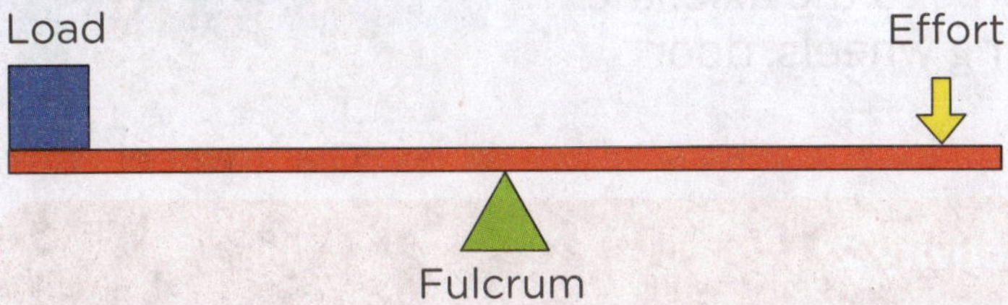

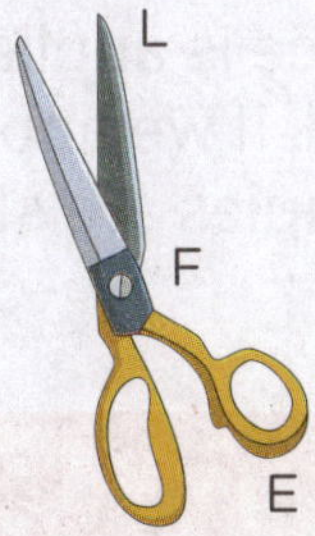

Scissors

See-saw

Second-class levers: In this type of levers, the load is between the effort and the fulcrum. Some examples are wheelbarrows, bottle openers and lemon squeezers.

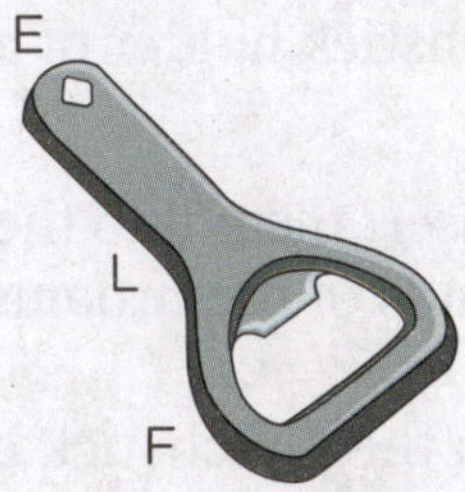

Bottle opener

Wheelbarrow

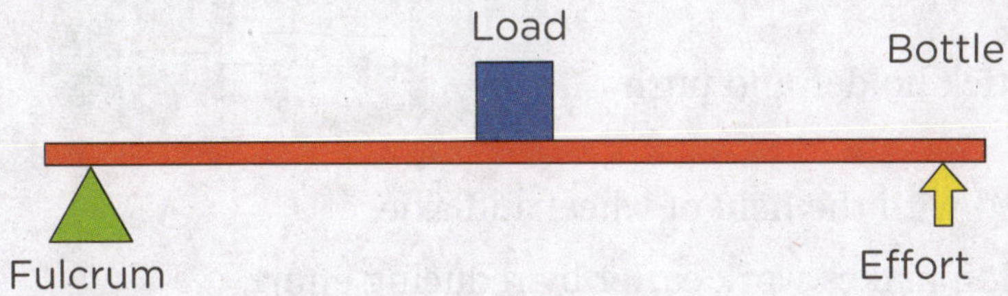

Third-class levers: In this type of levers, the effort is between the fulcrum and the load. Some examples are a pair of tongs, a stapler, a fishing rod and tweezers.

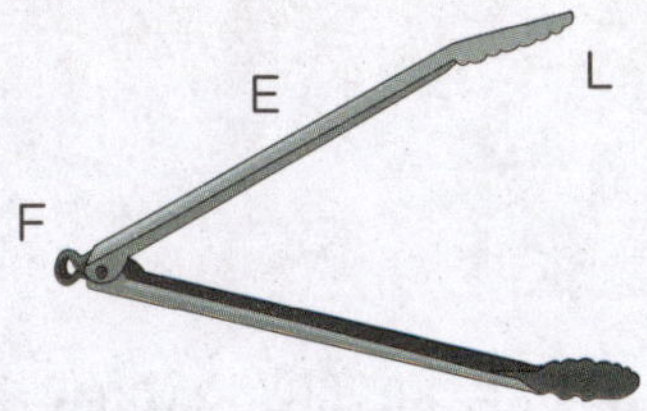

Tongs

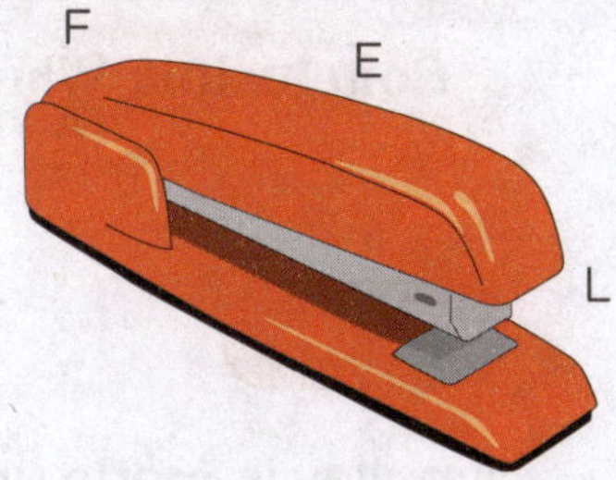

Stapler

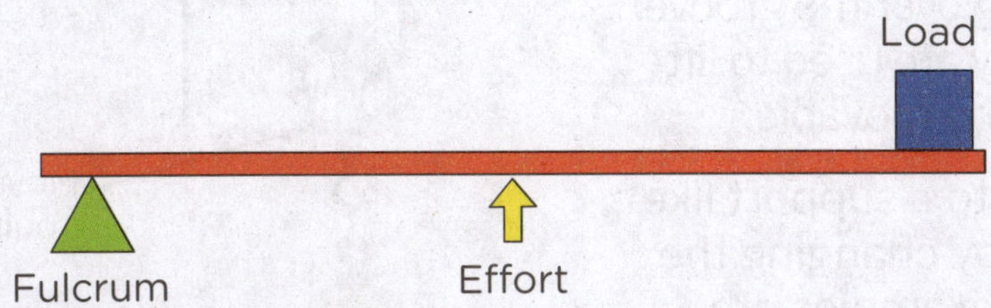

Science in Context

When attempting to lift a load, the human hand acts as a third-class lever.

Wheel and Axle

Giant wheel

Wheel and axle is a simple machine in which a wheel is attached to a rod called the axle. The wheel and the axle work together. When force is applied to the wheel, the axle turns. On the other hand, if we apply force to the axle, the wheel turns. Some examples are steering wheels, door knobs and giant wheels.

Activity 2

Aim: To study the wheel and axle combination

Materials required: Four bottle caps, two pieces of thick broomstick (6 cm length), two straws (4 cm length), the matchstick holder of a matchbox and glue

Procedure:

1. Take the broomsticks and insert them into the straws.
2. Fix the bottle caps to the ends of the broomsticks to look like a wheel and axle.
3. Insert the broomsticks into the matchstick holder as shown in the image given alongside.
4. Place a weight on top of the matchstick holder and push the set-up from behind.

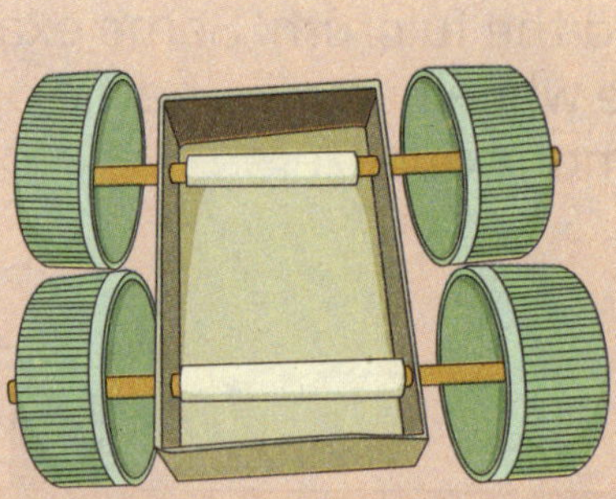

Observation: The set-up moves forward with the help of wheel and axle.

Conclusion: Wheel and axle combination makes work easier by reducing effort.

Pulley

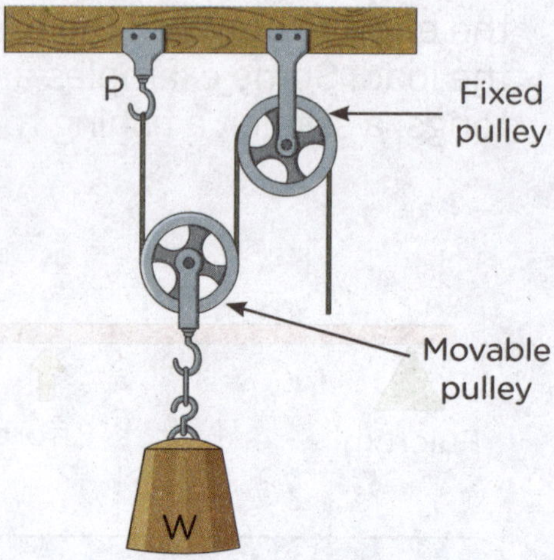

A pulley

A pulley is made up of a small wheel with a groove on its outer edge and a rope or chain running over the groove. The wheel rotates around an axle. They are used to lift weights. They are of two types: fixed and movable.

In a fixed pulley, the axle is attached to a support like a hook or wall. It makes work easier by changing the direction of the force applied. Some examples are pulleys used in wells and on flagpoles.

In a movable pulley, the axle is not attached to any support and is free to move along with the load. Movable pulleys are used along with fixed pulleys to reduce the effort. An example is cranes used in construction sites to lift heavy loads with less effort.

Inclined Plane

An inclined plane is a slope or a ramp or any slanting surface that helps to carry loads. It requires less force to move an object up an inclined plane than it does to lift the object vertically. Some examples are a slide in the park, ramps in hospitals to push wheelchairs up and down, and ramps for loading and unloading goods on trucks and aeroplanes.

A slide

Ramp for loading goods

Wedge

A wedge is a simple machine made by placing two surfaces at least one of which is an inclined plane back to back to form a sharp cutting surface. Some examples are cutting edges of knives, needles and axes.

Knife

Axe

Screw

A screw is an inclined plane wrapped around a central cylinder. It is used to hold things tightly together. It can be turned using a screwdriver. Screws are useful in fixing door hinges and handles. Nuts and bolts, a dentist's chair, a bottle or toothpaste cap and a screw jack (big screws used to lift cars and other heavy objects) are all examples of screws.

Screw

Bottle cap

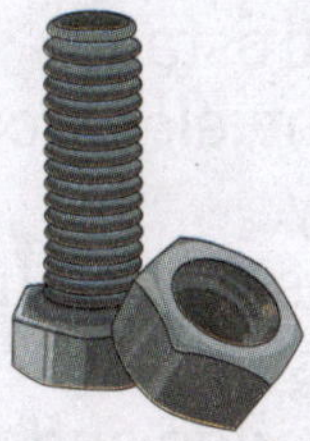

Nut and bolt

Activity 3

Aim: To make a screw from an inclined plane

Materials required: A pencil, a sketch pen and a triangular sheet of paper

Procedure: Colour the inclined surface of the triangular paper. Now, wrap this paper around the pencil so that the coloured surface faces outside.

Observation: The coloured surface resembles a winding road or a staircase. We have thus made screw out of an inclined plane.

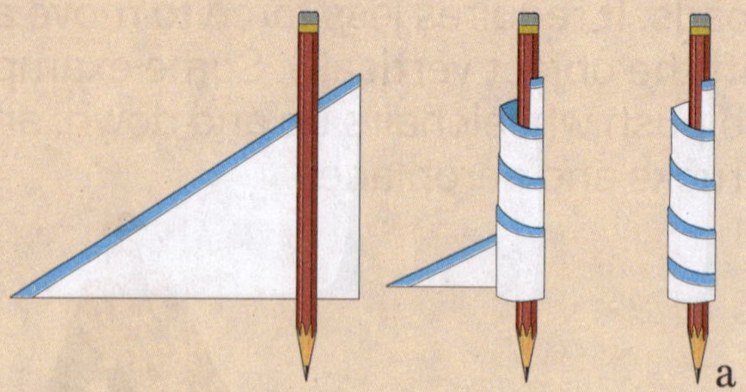

a

Let's Say Together

Electrostatic Friction Potential energy Kinetic energy

Keywords

Magnetic force: The force with which a magnet attracts certain materials

Frictional force: A force that acts on two objects that are in contact and at least one of them is in motion

Heat energy: Energy obtained by burning fuels like oil and gas

Mechanical energy: Energy that an object has due to its position or motion

Sound energy: Energy produced by the vibration of objects

Simple machine: A tool or a device that makes work easier by reducing the effort

Summary

1. Force is a push or a pull applied on an object.
2. Force can start or stop the motion of an object or change the speed and direction of motion or set an object in motion at rest.
3. Force can change the shape of an object.
4. The different types of forces are gravitational, frictional, magnetic and electrostatic.
5. Heat, light, electrical, mechanical, wind and sound are different forms of energy.
6. Machines make our work easier.
7. Six types of simple machines are lever, wheel and axle, inclined plane, pulley, wedge and screw.

EXERCISE

A State whether the following statements are true (T) or false (F).

1. Force can change the direction of motion of an object. ☐
2. Energy and force are one and the same. ☐
3. Sun is a source of only heat energy. ☐
4. Simple machines reduce the effort required to do work. ☐
5. Pulley does not change the direction of the force applied. ☐

B Choose the odd one out.

1. Scissors, crowbar, see-saw, bottle opener
2. Stapler, wheelbarrow, tweezers, tongs
3. Ramp, flyover, slide, see-saw
4. Screw, bottle cap, ramp, nut and bolt
5. Knife, needle, flagpole, axe

C Fill in the blanks using the correct option.

1. Friction always acts ______________ the direction of motion. (opposite to/along)
2. A fan uses ______________ energy to work. (electrical/light)
3. A light bulb gives ______________ energy. (light/sound)
4. A wheelbarrow is an example of a ______________ lever. (second-class/third-class)
5. A simple machine used to draw water from a well is ______________ . (lever/pulley)

D Answer the following questions briefly.

1. Mention the effects of force on objects.
2. What is friction?
3. What is energy?
4. What is a simple machine?
5. Name the six types of simple machines.
6. What is fulcrum?
7. What is a wedge?

E Answer the following questions.

1. Define friction. What are its advantages and disadvantages?
2. What is a lever? Explain the types of levers with one example of each.

F HOTS (Higher Order Thinking Skills)

1. When you stand out in the sun, which energies would you be affected by?
2. How are nails different from screws? Which one will you use to hold things tightly?
3. How are a screw, a wedge and an inclined plane interrelated?

G Identify the energy represented in each of the images given below.

____

____

H Project

1. Look at a bicycle and try to identify the simple machines that are used to make it function. Write them in the table given below.

Name of the cycle part	Simple machine represented

2. Identify the simple machines used in your house and make a list of them.

Identify the six simple machines shown in the picture given below. Write the name and the type of each in the space provided.

1. ______________________________

2. ______________________________

3. ______________________________

4. ______________________________

5. ______________________________

6. ______________________________

A **Identify the energy represented in each of the images given below.**

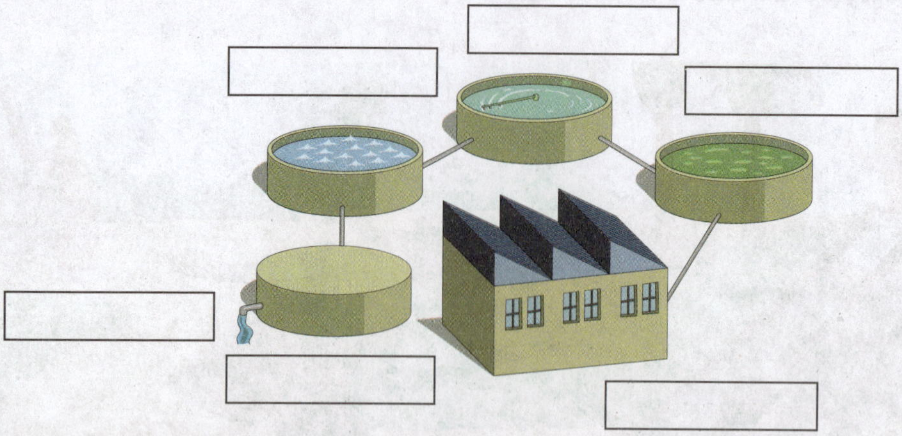

B **Solve the crossword puzzle using the given clues.**

1				2					3					
							4							
		5												
								6						

ACROSS

1. The ore from which aluminium is obtained
4. The rock used for flooring
5. Qutub Minar is made of
6. A gemstone used in jewellary

DOWN

2. The metal bars used to make bars for construction purpose
3. The mineral used in nuclear reactors

C **Label the image given below to represent the formation of spring and neap tides.**

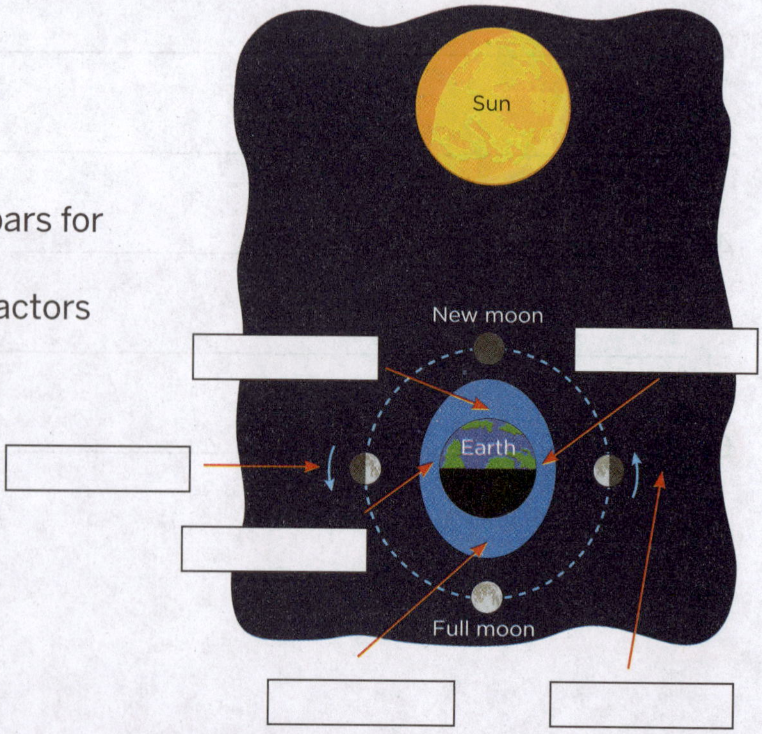

D **Find the names of objects that cause pollution in the word grid using the word help given below.**

U T P E S T I C I D E S
L O U D S P E A K E R S
S S O W H J Q Z R C A C
E F E R T I L I Z E R S
W O I L S P I L L S F G
A H E K G A R B A G E Y
G F W S M O K E A D K R
E L Y L G S A A Y K Q B

Fertilizers
Oil
spills
Sewage
Garbage
Smoke
Loudspeakers
Pesticides

E **Label the diagram (Fig. A) and name the instrument (Fig B).**

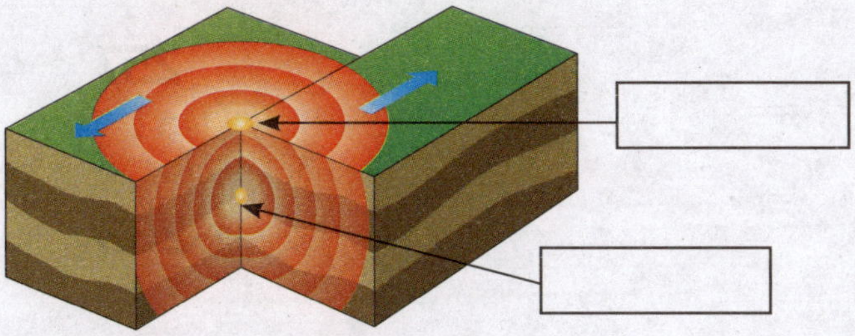

Fig. A

Fig. B

F **Give reason for the difference in size of the shadows.**

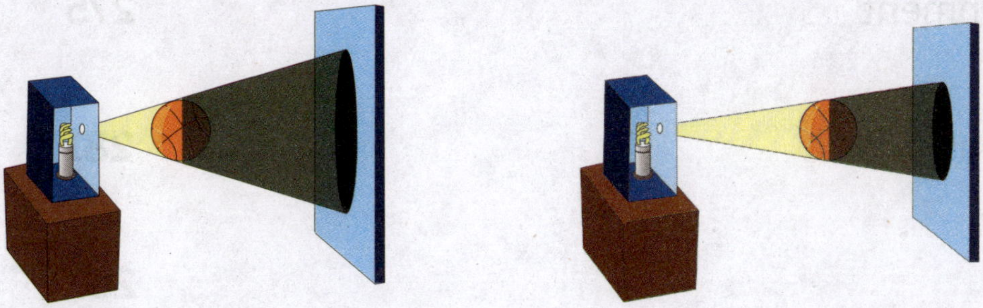

Reason: ____________________

____

G **Mark the position of load, effort and fulcrum for the class of levers below.**

a. First-class lever

b. Second-class lever

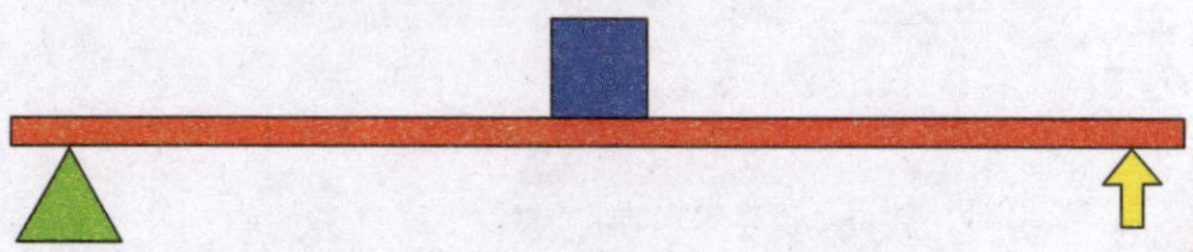

SOCIAL STUDIES

1. Environmental Pollution 241
2. Evolution of Transport 246
3. Evolution of Communication 252
4. British Period in India 257
5. Attaining Freedom 263
6. The Great Indians 269
7. Indian Government 275
8. United Nations 281

Assessment 287

1 Environmental Pollution

Observe and Reflect

- What are the people doing?
- Is the water clean?
- Do you think doing this is good for the rivers?

Our natural environment is made up of living and non-living things. We get air, water, food, shelter and clothing from the Earth. However, sometimes we carelessly use the things that we get from the Earth without any concern for our surroundings. Overuse and misuse of our natural resources causes **pollution**. Pollution is the process by which air, soil, water and other natural resources become dirty. Human activity is the main cause of the pollution of environment. The **increasing population**, **urbanization** and **industrialization** make the air polluted as harmful smoke is released from factories and cars into the air. Disposal of waste in the water sources and land area causes pollution.

The major types of pollution are air pollution, noise pollution, water pollution and soil pollution. We will now learn about the various types of pollution, their causes and harmful effects.

Air Pollution

Air is made up of the different types of gases that are vital for the survival of living things. Harmful gases and smoke cause air pollution. Polluted air is harmful for health. There are two ways in which the air gets polluted—**natural** and **human-made**.

Volcanoes, forest fires, sandstorms and pollen from plants are the natural sources of air pollution which harm the living things on the Earth.

Volcanic eruption

The main causes of air pollution are human-made. Smoke and poisonous gases that are **emitted** from cars and factories cause air pollution. Have you noticed how smoky the sky becomes a day or two after Diwali? This is because firecrackers give out smoke and pollute the air. Burning of wood, dry leaves, coal and kerosene releases harmful substances into the air, thus causing air pollution. Another cause of air pollution is **deforestation**. Deforestation is the process of cutting down of trees and clearing forests to build roads and buildings. Rapid urbanization and industrialization has led to widespread deforestation resulting in air pollution.

Find Out

Which countries get acid rain on a regular basis?

Effects of Air Pollution

Air pollution is very harmful for the health of living things as people develop breathing problems. Animals and plants also fall sick when the air is polluted. Air pollution can give rise to **climate change** and **global warming**. When harmful substances and gases increase in a particular place, the temperature of that place rises, affecting the climate. One of the major effects of air pollution is **acid rain**. This takes place when the harmful substances are released while burning **fossil fuels** combine with water particles in the air. When they fall down as either snow or rain, they cause damage to forests, water bodies, soil and buildings. Air pollution depletes the **ozone layer** that protects us from the harmful ultraviolet (UV) rays of the Sun.

Water Pollution

Water is necessary for all living beings, however the water that we drink is getting polluted. Throwing waste into water bodies causes water pollution. This affects the lives of the water plants and animals. Water also becomes unfit for drinking, cooking, bathing and even washing clothes.

Pollution in the river Ganga

Factories dump chemicals, oils and various other toxic wastes containing poisonous chemicals into water bodies, which cause harm to the fish and other aquatic plants and animals. Often agricultural waste is dumped into the sea and this too **endangers** the marine life in the oceans. Fertilizers and pesticides used in agriculture often seep through the soil into the groundwater, polluting it. Water also gets polluted when oil from the tankers carrying petroleum leaks into the ocean water, causing harm to the marine ecosystem.

Effects of Water Pollution

Drinking and swimming in polluted water can lead to a number of diseases like cancer, skin diseases and stomach diseases like cholera, dysentery and typhoid.

Do It Yourself

Collect old kettles and pots and grow plants in them.

When rivers become polluted, fish and other marine animals die. Seas and oceans have a variety of plant life that are also at risk when exposed to water pollution.

Soil Pollution

Soil is an important natural resource which plants and crops require to grow and live. Soil pollution occurs when the soil becomes dirty due to the use of harmful chemicals like fertilizers and pesticides, from the improper disposal of waste in landfills and from practices like mining.

Non-biodegradable waste like plastic, glass, cans and metal scraps cannot be broken down by the bacteria present in the soil. It also prevents the organisms living in the soil from getting the oxygen that they need to breathe. Other non-biodegradable wastes are metal scraps, glass remains, bottles and aluminium cans. **Biodegradable** wastes such as vegetable peels and food waste do not harm the soil.

Eco Zone

All biodegradable waste should be thrown in a compost pit. Non-biodegradable wastes should be recycled.

If the soil gets polluted, it has an adverse effect on the crops and creatures living in it and plants are not able to survive.

Soil pollution

Noise Pollution

When the sound levels in the environment become unpleasant and go beyond what we can handle, it is known as sound or noise pollution. We should keep the environment, water and soil clean and not make too much noise. The main sources of noise pollution are the excessive honking of buses and cars, firecrackers and loud music. During festivals, the excessive bursting of firecrackers causes air as well as noise pollution. Noise pollution causes stress, irritation and at times, even loss of hearing. We should keep the environment, water and soil clean and not make too much noise.

Fact Zone

In ancient Rome, people were not allowed to drive chariots at night to prevent sleep disturbance and commotion.

Remember

» Pollution is the process by which air, soil, water and other natural resources become dirty.

» Different types of pollution are air pollution, water pollution, soil pollution and noise pollution.

» More trees should be planted to absorb the excess carbon dioxide in the atmosphere.

» We should keep the environment, water and soil clean and should not make too much noise.

Review Zone

A Fill in the blanks with correct answers.

1. Air pollution can happen because of ....
   a. sandstorms b. snowstorms c. sleet
2. When people throw .... in the water, it causes water pollution..
   a. garbage b. food c. clothes
3. Excessive usage of pesticides can lead to .... pollution.
   a. soil b. noise c. air
4. Fertilizers and pesticides used in agriculture often seep through the soil into the ....
   a. rivers b. groundwater c. seas and oceans

B Name the following.

1. The layer of the atmosphere that protects us from the harmful ultraviolet (UV) rays of the Sun: ....
2. An occasion during which firecrackers are burned: ....
3. The process of cutting down of trees: ....
4. Waste that cannot be broken down by the bacteria present in the soil: ....

C Write T for True and F for False.

1. Excessive usage of natural resources can lead to pollution. ☐
2. Humans are not responsible for pollution. ☐
3. Water is necessary for all living beings. ☐
4. Factories play no role in causing pollution. ☐

5. Loud music can be regarded as a source of pollution. ☐

D **Answer these questions in brief.**

1. What is air pollution?
2. What are the effects of water pollution?
3. What is non-biodegradable waste?
4. How does non-biodegradable waste affect the soil?
5. What is noise pollution?

E **Answer these questions in detail.**

1. Discuss the causes for air and water pollution in the environment.
2. Describe how human beings and plant life are affected by polluted air and water.
3. What happens when the soil is polluted?
4. Enumerate two ways by which we can try to reduce noise pollution.

Think Zone

A Human action is primarily responsible for environmental pollution. However, only human action can save the day. Find out various steps that you can take to prevent environmental pollution.

B **Look at the picture and answer the questions.**

1. What type of pollution is being shown here?
2. How can this type of pollution be prevented?

Life Skills Zone

Cattle in India die when they eat plastic bags dumpedon the roadsides. List two ways in which this can be prevented.

Value Zone

Planting more trees around the house keeps the air fresh and clean. It also adds to the beauty of the surroundings.

Activity Zone

Create groups in your class. Every day a group should devote one hour and collect all the garbage in school and throw it in a bin. Your effort will spread the message among other people that we should keep our environment clean.

2 Evolution of Transport

Observe and Reflect

- What do you see in the picture?
- How does it travel?
- What does it run on?

We have already learnt that early humans travelled from one place to another on foot. But how did they travel long distances? Early humans invented the wheel, which helped them to cover long distances. This reduced their travelling time and made their work easier.

The invention of the wheel brought a **revolutionary** change in the way early humans travelled. Wheels were attached to carts, and animals like bullocks and horses were made to pull them. It made travelling faster, more comfortable and safer. Since then, wheels have **evolved** and today they are used in all types of vehicles. The wheel is also used for pottery, milling and irrigation. Rafts and dug-out canoes were the other means of transport during that time. Thus, humans used carriages and boats to move from place to place.

The next turning point in the history of transportation was the invention of the steam engine by James Watt. Steam power was used to pull carriages, and is now used to run trains and huge cargo ships across the oceans. Humans also use engines powered by diesel, petroleum and even electricity.

Over the years, advancements in science and technology have led to easier and faster means of transportation. The invention of aeroplanes and bullet trains has made it easier for humans to conquer huge distances in the blink of an eye. Let us learn about the different ways in which people travel and how important each mode of travelling is.

Roads

In the beginning, people travelled on tracks, which were naturally carved into the ground by humans and animals as they walked along the same path regularly. Later, these tracks widened as vehicles like chariots and carts began to be used. The Romans were the first to build paved roads built with stone and soil. With advances in the means of road transport, better and more durable roads were required. Today, broad metalled roads known as **highways**, **expressways** and **freeways** connect different cities within a country. International highways connect one country to another. For example, the **Grand Trunk Road** connects Kolkata in India to Peshawar in Pakistan. India's network of roads, both *kuchcha* and *pucca*, make up one of the largest road networks in the world.

Highway

Nowadays, the traffic on roads has increased and this has led to greater levels of pollution. Air is getting polluted because of the smoke and dust released from vehicles. There are more road accidents as well. In order to reduce the number of road accidents, various countries have come up with strict rules to ensure safe driving.

Find Out

When was the Grand Trunk Road built and by what name was it previously known?

Railways

The invention of the steam engine led to the setting up of the railways. Today, railways are the most important means of transport. Railways connect different countries in Europe and North America. The **Grand Orient Express** connects Paris in France to Istanbul in Turkey. In North America, the USA has the longest railway network in the world. The railways of India are the fourth-longest network in the world. Countries like Japan, Germany, France and China have some of the fastest trains in the world. They can travel at the minimum speed of 400 km per hour. The bullet trains or **Shinkansen** of Japan, **TGV** of France and **Maglevs** of China are famous for their speed. In India, the **Rajdhani** and **Shatabdi** trains connect many states of India. Rapid transit is usually

Bullet train, Japan

Fact Zone

The **Trans-Siberian Railway** travels through Asia and Europe. It starts at St Petersburg in the European part of Russia and ends at Vladivostok in the Asian stretch of Russia. It travels for a week and covers a distance of 8000 km.

built on the ground or underground through tunnels. The **Seikan Tunnel** in Japan is the longest and deepest in the world.

Find Out

Find out why the North Atlantic Route—located between Western Europe and Eastern North America—is the busiest sea route in the world.

Waterways

We know that early humans used rafts and boats to cross rivers and travel through water. As humans learnt trade, they carried goods over a far greater distance on early rafts and crude boats. New boats that ran on steam power were built at the same time as **steam-powered** railways. These huge boats were called ships and they could move a lot faster and carry huge amounts of goods. In modern times, ships no longer run on steam engines, they run on diesel. They are by far the cheapest means of travel.

Countries are connected through port cities, where ships are docked, and import and export items are moved. Both river ports and sea ports harbour ships. Special ships called **oil tankers** are used in order to transport oil. **Refrigerated ships** are used to transport vegetables, fruits, meat and dairy products. **Luxury cruise ships** are used to ferry passengers around the world.

Across the world, rivers, lakes and canals are used as waterways. The **Yangtze Kiang** and **Hwang Ho** rivers in China, the **Rhine** and **Danube** rivers in Europe, the **Nile** and **Congo** rivers in Africa, the **Amazon** river in South America and the **Great Lakes** in North America are some of the important inland waterways in the world. The **Suez Canal** connects the **Red Sea** to the **Mediterranean Sea** and the **Panama Canal** connects the **Pacific Ocean** to the **Atlantic Ocean**.

Panama Canal

Do It Yourself

List five major ports of the world and name the countries where they are located.

Port					
Country					
River/sea					

Eco Zone

Oil spills are a major threat to marine life and ecosystems.

Airways

Airways are the fastest means of transport. But they are also the costliest means of travelling. The first successful model of the aeroplane was built in 1903 by the Wright brothers. Since then, there have been many improvements and better aeroplanes have been invented. Aeroplanes have become faster and capable of carrying huge amounts of cargo and as many as 500 people at a time. This is why, despite being expensive, air transport is popular.

Today, there is a wide array of air networks that cover almost the entire world. North America and Western Europe see the maximum air traffic. Cities like London, Paris, New York, Moscow, Tokyo, Rome and Jeddah have huge airports with various modern facilities.

While travelling **satellites** help tremendously. They help in navigation by picking up messages instantly and sending it to the receiver. The GPS system that we use today while travelling anywhere in the world is assisted by artificial satellites. They can pick up the location of a place and help in reaching the destination by following the correct route. Weather satellites help in forecasting weather conditions thus, enabling us to know what type of weather condition will prevail at any place. They also help the authorities to know if any natural disaster is about to occur, thus enabling them to send out an alert to save the lives of people.

Remember

» Early humans covered distances and travelled from one place to another on foot.

» Today, people travel on road, through waterways or by air to go from one place to another.

Review Zone

A Fill in the blanks with the correct answers.

1. The biggest railway network in the world can be found in ....

   a. USA b. Egypt c. China

2. The steam engine was invented by ....

   a. Wright brothers b. Johannes Gutenberg c. James Watt

3. The .... Canal connects the Pacific Ocean to the Atlantic Ocean.
   a. Suez b. Pacific c. Panama
4. The Grand Trunk Road connects Kolkata in India to Peshawar in ....
   a. Pakistan b. Afghanistan c. Bangladesh

B Name the following.

1. Cheapest means of transport: ....
2. Ships used to transport vegetables, fruits, meat and dairy products: ....
3. A river in South America: ....
4. The fastest and costliest means of transport: ....

C Write T for True and F for False.

1. The Wright brothers invented the first aeroplane in 1903. ☐
2. Ships are the costliest means of travel. ☐
3. The invention of the wheel made travel difficult. ☐
4. International highways connect different countries. ☐

D Answer these questions in brief.

1. Name two rivers in China.
2. Who invented the steam engine?
3. List any five things for which a wheel is used.
4. Name the two trains in India that connect various states.

E Answer these questions in detail.

1. What do you know about railways?
2. Write a short note on waterways.
3. How have airways helped in travelling?
4. How have roadways improved?

Think Zone

A The transport system of a country depends upon its geographical features. It is easier to build roads and railway tracks over plains than in deserts or mountainous regions. Explain why.

B **Look at the picture and answer the questions.**

1. Identify the means of transport shown here.
2. What is the purpose of this type of transport?

Life Skills Zone

Early humans did not have aeroplanes or cars. What difficulties did they face while travelling? Discuss in class.

Value Zone

If you travelled by car to school on a rainy day and you saw your neighbour walking to school, what would you do?

Activity Zone

Find out the oldest road in India. Trace its history over the years. Prepare a chart on it and present it in class.

3 Evolution of Communication

Observe and Reflect

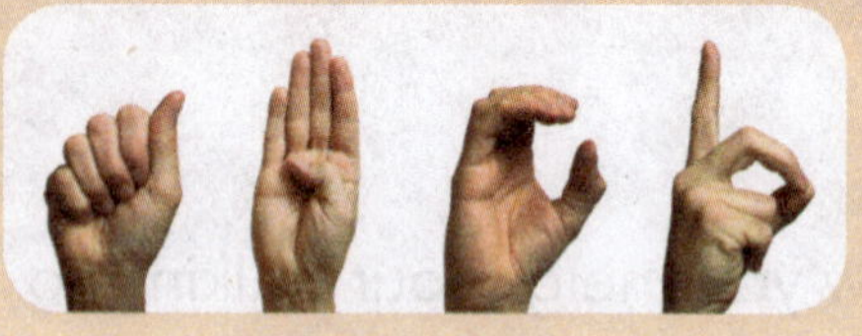

- What do you see in this picture?
- Do you think it is beneficial to have this type of communication in media?

Communication Systems

Early humans first began to communicate with each other through signs and hand **gestures**. Later, they began to draw pictures on the walls of the places where they lived like caves. Soon, humans learnt to speak, leading to the evolution of languages. The next turning point was the development of the written speech.

Hieroglyph

Human beings learnt to write approximately 5000 years ago, and started to put down their ideas and thoughts in the form of symbols that stood for sounds and words. Soon, letters evolved from these **pictorial** symbols. This is how the alphabet came into being.

Humans started writing on clay **tablets**, skins of animals and leaves. Soon, they moved on to **papyrus** sheets, palm leaves and paper. They used sharp tools made from bamboo or wood and bird feathers as pens.

Till 1443, people wrote using their hands. They also copied books by hand. However, it was a time-consuming process and it was also very costly to produce these books. In 1443, the printing press was invented by Johannes Gutenberg. With this invention, the printing of books was initiated. This enabled the production of more number of books

Fact Zone

In ancient Egypt, a system of writing using symbols and pictures was used. This system is called hieroglyphics.

Eco Zone

Millions of trees are cut to produce paper on which the books are printed. We should plant more trees.

at a lesser cost. Today, printing technology has improved tremendously with millions of books being printed every year. This has made books, newspapers and magazines much more affordable.

Means of Communication

Communication can be categorized into two types:

> **Find Out**
>
> How do artificial satellites act as a means of communication?

- **Personal communication** normally takes place between two people—the receiver and the sender. Letters, telegraph, telephone, fax and e-mail are a few examples of personal communication.
- **Mass communication** takes place when something is communicated to a large number of people. This is done through newspapers, magazines, radio, television, Internet, cinema and advertisements.

Earlier, communication was carried out through letters and messages. These however took a long time to be delivered and were often lost on the way. Now, with the evolution of communication, those days are long gone. Let us take a look at some of the ways in which people communicate today.

Personal Communication

The **postal system** helps to deliver letters, parcels, aerogrammes and postcards. While letters take a long time to be delivered, telegrams were used to send urgent messages. Telegrams are sent through Morse Code with the help of a telegraph machine, which was invented by Samuel Morse.

The **telephone** was invented by Alexander Graham Bell in 1876 and its invention revolutionized the ways of communication. It is by far the fastest means of communication. Nowadays, wireless mobile or cellular phones are used to send messages and speak to people all around the world.

The **fax machine** is used to send an exact copy of a printed or handwritten document to another place through telephone lines.

The **Internet** has made communication faster and easier. The **electronic mail** or e-mail is very popular. Letters and messages are sent instantly.

Mass Communication

We read **newspapers** and **magazines** or journals to gain knowledge about the different events occurring around the world. Newspapers and magazines are published in different languages to make them accessible to a large number of people. The **radio** was invented by Marconi in 1886. It provides news, relays information and entertains people. It is an auditory medium.

John Logie Baird invented the **television** in 1926. Today, television is one of the most popular means of mass communication. It is an audio-visual medium through which news, sports, entertainment and a variety of recorded programmes can be viewed.

Film or **cinema** is another audio-visual means of mass communication. It is possible to educate and entertain people through cinema. Short films and documentaries are educational and informative, while feature films are entertaining.

The **Internet** is a vast source of knowledge and information. There are millions of websites on the Internet that supply a wide range of information. Nowadays, people don't need to step out of their houses for shopping or banking. They can do all these tasks through the Internet.

Do It Yourself

Take a look at the pictures provided below. State the type of communication they may be categorized into.

Remember

- Humans first began to communicate with each other through signs and hand gestures.
- Humans started writing in the form of pictorial signs and symbols which later evolved into the alphabet.
- The invention of the printing press made books easily accessible to the people.
- There are two forms of communication—personal and mass communication.

Review Zone

A Fill in the blanks with the correct answers.

1. Personal communication takes place between a receiver and a ....
   a. transmitter   b. transformer   c. sender
2. Paper is made from ....
   a. papyrus   b. shrubs   c. wood lice
3. The printing press was invented by ....
   a. Johannes Gutenberg   b. the Egyptians   c. the Chinese
4. The television was invented by .... in 1926.
   a. Johannes Gutenberg   b. John Logie Baird   c. Samuel Morse

B Name the following.

1. Marconi invented this means of mass communication: ....
2. This machine can be used to send an exact copy of a printed or handwritten document to another place through telephone lines: ....
3. He is credited with inventing the telephone: ....
4. An audio-visual means of communication: ....

C Write T for True and F for False.

1. Papyrus was once used to print newspapers. ☐
2. Earlier, letters would often get lost. ☐
3. We use the Internet to send e-mails. ☐
4. We can send parcels through the Internet. ☐

D Answer these questions in brief.

1. What is mass communication?
2. Which is the fastest means of communication?
3. What was the system of writing used in ancient Egypt?
4. Name some activities that can be done using the Internet.

E Answer these questions in detail.

1. How has communication evolved?
2. Differentiate between mass communication and personal communication.

3. Write about the different modes of mass communication.
4. How has the invention of the printing press affected communication?

Think Zone

A According to you, which is the most important way of communication? Why?

B **Look at the picture and answer the questions.**

1. What do you see in the picture?
2. Does it need an envelope?
3. Does it need a stamp?

Life Skills Zone

Stamps carry important information about the location where the stamp is issued, the time when it was issued and whether the stamp has been used or not. Look at the picture of the stamp below and read the descriptions given. Draw a line connecting the description to where this information is being displayed in the stamp.

1. Name of the country where the stamp is issued
2. The cost of the stamp issue
3. A mark showing that the stamp has been used

Value Zone

When you receive a letter, always remember to send a response. Remember, someone took the time to write you a letter by hand, so you should return the gesture.

Activity Zone

Write a letter to a friend telling him or her about what do you enjoy learning the most in school. Then, writing your friend's address send it to him or her. Don't forget to paste stamps!

4 British Period in India

Observe and Reflect

- What do you see in this picture?
- How did the British reach India?
- Why do you think the British came to India?

India was famous for its spices, gold, pearls and silk from ancient times. The discovery of the sea route to India via the Cape of Good Hope by Vasco da Gama, a Portuguese explorer, in 1498 opened up new doors for merchants and traders in India and Europe. Trade between India and European countries like the Netherlands, France and Great Britain flourished and each country established a company in India.

All the **colonial** powers that came to India from Europe set up their own East India Company. The company set up by the English was known as the British East India Company. As trade flourished, **rivalry** broke out between these nations as each was looking to gain more profit and wanted to control the trade. Among them, the British emerged **victorious**. They went on to control most of the trade in India and finally established a colonial empire in the Indian subcontinent.

Do It Yourself

You know four colonial powers made their base in India. Find out more about them and complete the table given below.

Country	Great Britain	France	Portugal	The Netherlands
Company name				
Base Place				

Battle of Plassey and Battle of Buxar

The British first landed at Surat in Gujarat and started trading in cloth and spices. Slowly, they established trading centres in Bombay (now Mumbai) and Madras (now Chennai), and got permission from the Mughal rulers to conduct trade in Bengal too. In order to gain more control over the subcontinent, they began to maintain an army in the rich state of Bengal. As no permission was taken from Siraj-ud-Daulah, the then Nawab of Bengal, the **Battle of Plassey** took place in 1757 between the Nawab's army and the British. The British became victorious and gained control over Bengal.

Discontented with the misuse of power by the British, the combined armies of the Nawabs of Bengal and Awadh, and the Mughal emperor faced the British forces in 1764 at the **Battle of Buxar**. The British won and gained the right to collect revenue in Bengal. This laid the foundation of British rule in India.

Discontent against British Rule

As soon as the British East India Company gained control over India, they started **exploiting** the people. They forced farmers to grow cash crops like indigo and cotton in place of food crops. They bought these crops at really low prices and sent them to be used as raw materials in the British factories. Indians were not permitted to open mills and factories, and were forced to buy the British-made goods. As a result, Indian weavers and craftsmen were unable to sell their handicrafts. The British made huge profits, while Indian farmers made little or no profit at all. As British gained control over India, they began to tax the people heavily and enacted laws to **wield** greater control. Thus, discontent began to grow among the people of India.

The Revolt of 1857

As a result of their growing discontent, the people of India decided to revolt against the British. This rebellion is called the **Revolt of 1857**.

The revolt was started by the Indian soldiers serving in the British Army at Meerut. The soldiers were asked to use a new rifle named **Enfield** by biting off the edge of its cartridge. The edges were rumoured to be coated with the fat of pigs and cows. This angered the Hindu and Muslim soldiers as this was against their religion. Thus, they rose in revolt against the British. This revolt soon spread to other parts of the country. The Indian leaders who took part in the revolt were Rani Lakshmibai of Jhansi, Nana Saheb and Tantia Tope in Kanpur, Begum Hazrat Mahal in Awadh, Maulavi Ahmadullah, Rao Tula Ram and Kunwar Singh. Within a year, the British succeeded in crushing the revolt.

The revolt brought about several changes. The British government took control over the country, bringing an end to the rule of the East India Company. Queen Victoria became the Empress of India and she appointed a viceroy to rule over India on her behalf. The freedom that remained was just in name because the Indian princes now had to report to the Viceroy of India.

Find Out

What caused all the kings from different parts of the country to come together and revolt against the British?

Spread of New Ideas and Social Reforms

The news of the revolt spread to all corners of the country. This was made possible by the introduction of modern education. The English-educated Indians were influenced by modern thoughts and ideas, which were spread through articles in various English and regional newspapers. The growth of railways helped to bring the people of the country closer. Feelings of **nationalism** and **patriotism** arose amongst the Indians. The educated Indians worked towards social reforms. Reformers like Raja Rammohan Roy, Ishwar Chandra Vidyasagar, Maharshi Debendranath Tagore and Dayanand Saraswati all raised their voices against various social evils like child marriage, caste system, female infanticide and *sati*. They also encouraged education for women and were in favour of widow remarriage.

Eco Zone

With increasing urbanization in India, many forests were cleared and trees were cut. Steps should be taken to ensure that forests are preserved.

Raja Rammohan Roy

Formation of the Indian National Congress

The British exploited India and as a result, due to the exploitation by the British, India was becoming poor. At this point, the people understood that the British were not interested in developing the nation but in accumulating riches for themselves. Many reformers spread their ideas through **vernacular** and English newspapers to make the common people aware of the political

Dadabhai Naoroji

issues and the real nature of British rule in India. In 1885, AO Hume founded the Indian National Congress (INC). It aimed at involving the educated Indians in the country's administration. Dadabhai Naoroji, Badruddin Tyabji, Pherozeshah Mehta, Surendranath Banerjea and Gopal Krishna Gokhale were some prominent members of the INC.

At the onset, the INC did not demand independence. It tried to shift the attention of the British towards the problems faced by Indians. However, the British ignored their demands. This soon gave rise to **radicals** who believed that the British should be forced out of the country. Leaders like Bal Gangadhar Tilak and Lala Lajpat Rai were some of the radicals who fought for freedom during that period. This organization soon became an important political party that shaped the future of India.

Remember

- Vasco da Gama discovered the sea route to India.
- The British established their rule in India by winning two consecutive wars—the Battle of Plassey and the Battle of Buxar.
- The British forced the Indian farmers to cultivate cash crops, such as cotton and indigo, rather than growing food crops.
- Feelings of nationalism and patriotism arose amongst the Indian people after the 1857 revolt.
- In 1885, AO Hume founded the Indian National Congress to involve the educated Indians in the country's administration.

Review Zone

A Fill in the blanks with the correct answers.

1. Vasco da Gama came to India in ....

   a. 1498 b. 1499 c. 1500

2. At the time of Battle of Plassey, the Nawab of Bengal was ....

   a. Siraj-ud-Daulah b. Mir Zafar c. Mir Kasim

3. The Revolt of 1857 started in ....

   a. Meerut b. Kanpur c. Agra

4. Farmers were forced to grow ....

   a. rice b. wheat c. indigo

5. The Indian National Congress was founded by ....

a. Annie Besant   b. AO Hume   c. Dadabhai Naoroji

B Name the following.

1. The first British Empress of India: ....
2. A woman leader who took part in the Revolt of 1857: ....
3. The organization founded in 1885: ....
4. A famous social reformer: ....

C Write T for True and F for False.

1. India was well known for its spices, gold, pearls and silk. ☐
2. The British were the only ones to establish a company in India. ☐
3. The British East India Company exploited the Indians. ☐
4. The Revolt of 1857 took place 110 years after the Battle of Plassey. ☐
5. The spread of modern education helped to bring about social reforms. ☐

D Answer these questions in brief.

1. Name the Portuguese explorer who discovered a sea route to India.
2. Who fought against the British in the Battle of Plassey?
3. Apart from the British, which other European countries traded with India?
4. Why were Indians discontented with the British rule in India?
5. Why was the Indian National Congress established?

E Answer these questions in detail.

1. How did the East India Company establish its rule in India?
2. Why were the Indian people not satisfied with British rule?
3. Describe the Revolt of 1857 and the events that followed.
4. Write a short note on the formation of the Indian National Congress.

Think Zone

A If Indian farmers were made to grow cash crops instead of food crops, who would be affected the most?

B **Look at the picture and answer the questions.**

1. What does the picture depict?
2. What happened to this product once British goods began to be sold?

Life Skills Zone

The British contributed to the spread of western education in India and the development of railways. How did these two contributions help the Indians attain independence?

Value Zone

We should love and respect our country and all that it stands for.

Activity Zone

Organize a debate in the class on the topic 'It is more profitable to cultivate cash crops than food crops'. Speak either in favour of the topic or against it. Give proper reasons to support your view and ask all your classmates to participate.

5 Attaining Freedom

Observe and Reflect

- Identify the person in the image.
- Why is he an important figure in Indian history?

We have already learned that the formation of Indian National Congress led to feelings of nationalism and patriotism amongst the people. By this time, the Indian National Congress had become a very important party. This worried the British. So, they passed strict laws to **curb** the Indians from organizing and revolting against the British.

Towards Freedom

The British feared the unity of the people and decided to create a divide among them. They created a partition between the Hindu-dominant and the Muslim-dominant areas of Bengal into two separate states with the hope of causing a rift between the two communities. The **Partition of Bengal** came about in 1905.

Mahatma Gandhi

Bal Gangadhar Tilak, Lala Lajpat Rai and Bipin Chandra Pal encouraged the people to protest against the partition. People took part in several strikes and protests, boycotting goods made by the British and even burning them. This movement was called the **Boycott** or **Swadeshi Movement**. The partition was removed in 1911 but people continued with the movement even after that. The British tried to **suppress** the movement but by that time it had spread to all parts of the country.

Gandhian Period—Non-Violence and Satyagraha

Mohandas Karamchand Gandhi, also known as the Father of the Nation, was born on 2 October 1869 in Gujarat. He was one of India's greatest freedom fighters. He taught people that independence could be achieved by non-violent and peaceful means.

Gandhi had initially spent a few years in South Africa and there he contributed in the struggle against **apartheid** using **non-violence** and **Satyagraha**. When he came back to India, he was shocked to see extensive poverty in India. He decided to use the same methods he used in South Africa to help India gain independence. This marked the beginning of the Satyagraha movement. He **protested** against several social and religious **malpractices** in India and also asked people not to obey the laws that were unjust. Peaceful protests and marches were held all around the country even though the protestors were often badly beaten.

Fact Zone

Rabindranath Tagore gave back his knighthood title, which the British had conferred upon him, as a protest against the Jallianwala Bagh massacre.

Non-cooperation Movement

On 13 April 1919, thousands of people gathered at the Jallianwala Bagh in Amritsar for a peaceful protest. However, the British blocked the exit and opened fire on the gathering, killing about 400 people and injuring about 1200. This was one of the most **crucial** events in India's fight for freedom. Outraged by the **indiscriminate** killing, Gandhi along with other **prominent** leaders demanded complete independence from the British. This led to the launch of the **Non-cooperation Movement** in 1920. Gandhi encouraged people to show complete disobedience and non-cooperation with the British. Famous leaders like Sardar Vallabhbhai Patel, Deshbandhu Chittaranjan Das, Maulana Abdul Kalam Azad, Rajendra Prasad, Motilal Nehru, Sarojini Naidu and Jawaharlal Nehru actively participated in the movement. Although it was a non-violent movement, things took an ugly turn in Chauri Chaura, Uttar Pradesh, when people set fire to a police station, killing 22 policemen. This brought an end to the movement.

Freedom struggle

The Simon Commission

The increasing success of the independence movement worried the British. The **Simon Commission** was created in 1927 to work towards reforms. It was headed by Sir John Simon and comprised seven members. However, these efforts were not appreciated by the Indians as the commission had no Indian representative. The commission was boycotted by the Indian National Congress and the famous slogan 'Simon go back!' was used to protest against the commission.

Civil Disobedience Movement

By December 1929, Congress had started demanding *poorna swaraj*, which means total independence. The **Civil Disobedience Movement** was launched in 1930 after the British introduced a salt tax on the production of salt in order to control salt trade in the country. Gandhiji urged people to produce salt without paying any tax. He led a march of hundreds of people from Sabarmati Ashram in Ahmedabad to Dandi in Surat, where he made salt in **defiance** of the British law that bars Indians from producing salt. This was called the Salt Satyagraha March or more famously known as the Dandi March.

Find Out

Name the leaders that were imprisoned by the British during the Quit India movement?

Quit India Movement

Soon afterwards, the efforts to free India increased and Gandhiji told the British to quit India in August 1942. This led to the **Quit India Movement**. He coined the slogan 'do or die' as an appeal to the people to continue fighting till the British left the country. All the key leaders of the Indian National Congress including Gandhi, Nehru and Patel were imprisoned by the British government and the protesting Indians were subject to severe beatings in the jails.

Eco Zone

The British hunted wild animals as a sport during their rule in India. Today efforts are being made to prevent hunting of wild animals.

Do It Yourself

The INA established by Subhash Chandra Bose was the second one. Find out when and who established the first one.

Indian National Army

Subhash Chandra Bose, one of India's popular freedom fighters, believed that India could become independent only by waging war against the British. He created the Indian National Army (INA) in 1941. The army saw people from different religions coming together to fight the British.

India Wins Independence

Once the Second World War ended, the British were forced to grant independence to India. India became free on 15 August 1947. India was, however, divided into two separate nations—India and Pakistan. Dr Rajendra Prasad was the first president of India and Jawaharlal Nehru was elected as the first prime minister of India.

Fact Zone

Pakistan gained independence a day earlier than India on 14 August 1947.

Remember

- Bengal was partitioned because the British feared the unity of people and they divided the Hindu-dominant and the Muslim-dominant areas of Bengal into two separate states.
- The Partition of Bengal led to the Swadeshi Movement in which British goods were boycotted.
- Gandhiji practised non-violence and Satyagraha to gain independence.
- The Jallianwala Bagh massacre led to the launch of the Non-cooperation Movement leading to the Chauri Chaura incident.
- The Civil Disobedience Movement was started to protest against the salt tax and led to the Dandi March.
- The Quit India Movement was a call for complete independence.
- Subhash Chandra Bose formed the Indian National Army.
- India finally attained freedom on 15 August 1947.

Review Zone

A Fill in the blanks with the correct answers.

1. Gandhiji started the Dandi March from the .... ashram in Ahmedabad.

   a. Sabarmati b. Gomti c. Ganga

2. Gandhiji ended the Non-cooperation Movement after the ....

a. Chauri Chaura incident b. Dandi March

c. Jallianwala Bagh massacre

3. The slogan 'do or die' was coined by ....

a. Gandhi b. Subhash Chandra Bose c. Jawaharlal Nehru

4. .... was the first prime minister of India.

a. Dr Rajendra Prasad b. MK Gandhi c. Jawaharlal Nehru

B Name the following.

1. The policy of bias and discrimination followed by the South African government: ....

2. The violent incident that led to suspension of the Non-cooperation Movement: ....

3. Gandhiji broke the salt law here after a long march: ....

4. The first president of India: ....

C Write T for True and F for False.

1. The Indian National Army was established by Subhash Chandra Bose. ☐

2. Dr Rajendra Prasad was the first prime minister of India. ☐

3. Gandhiji practised non-violence and satyagraha. ☐

4. Jallianwala Bagh is located in Lahore. ☐

5. People died during the Civil Disobedience Movement. ☐

D Answer these questions in brief.

1. Who established the Indian National Army?
2. Write a short note on India's independence.
3. Why did the British partition Bengal?
4. What was the Non-cooperation Movement? Why did the Indians oppose the Simon Commission?
5. What happened during the Civil Disobedience and Quit India movements?

Think Zone

A India and Pakistan are two separate nations today. What do you think would have been the situation if India was not divided into two nations?

B **Look at the picture and answer the questions.**

1. What is happening in the picture?
2. When did it take place and why?

Life Skills Zone

Do you think that Gandhiji's policy of non-violence was appropriate for the purpose of attaining independence?
Why do you think it was better than the policy of violence? Give reasons to support your answer.

Value Zone

Gandhi's views on non-violence are accepted and appreciated worldwide.

Activity Zone

Make an Indian flag

You will need kidney beans, rice, green, orange and blue paint, glue, a sheet of paper.

1. On a sheet of paper, draw the outline of the Indian flag.
2. Paste the rice along the portion where the flag is supposed to be and the kidney beans in a line for the post.
3. Once it dries, paint the rice with the national colours. Don't forget to paint the circle at the centre!

6 The Great Indians

Observe and Reflect

- Identify the person shown in the picture. He was a famous mathematician and astronomer of ancient India.
- What was his contribution in the field of mathematics?
- Find out the name of one of the books he wrote.

India has a rich heritage of scientists, poets, artists, mathematicians and freedom fighters known for their bravery, courage and self-sacrifice. In this chapter, we will learn about some Indians who have made significant contributions in various fields.

Rani Lakshmibai

Rani Lakshmibai was one of the bravest women in Indian history. Born in 1835, the young queen of Jhansi refused to bow down to the British and became a prominent figure in the Revolt of 1857. Her childhood name was Manikarnika and after marriage to the ruler of Jhansi she was called Lakshmibai. Married at a young age to the ruler of Jhansi, Maharaja Gangadhar Rao, Rani Lakshmibai took over as the head of the state after his death. When the British army tried to conquer Jhansi, Rani led her army against them and fought bravely. Along with Tatya Tope of Bithur, she became an important leader of the Revolt of 1857. She died in Gwalior while fighting against the British army in 1858.

Rani of Jhansi

Bal Gangadhar Tilak

Also known as Lokmanya Tilak, Bal Gangadhar Tilak was born in Maharashtra in 1856. He was one of the first Indians to demand self-rule or *swaraj* from the

Find Out

Who were collectively known as 'Bal-Pal-Lal' during the freedom struggle?

British. Tilak gave the slogan '*Swaraj* is my birthright and I shall have it.' Along with leaders like Lala Lajpat Rai and Bipin Chandra Pal, Tilak opposed the British **vigorously** during the Swadeshi and Boycott movements between 1905 and 1907.

Tilak established the Deccan Education Society in 1884, which established the Fergusson College in Pune. He also started the Marathi paper *Kesari* and an English paper *Mahratta* in Pune.

He established the Home Rule League with Annie Besant and Mohammad Ali Jinnah in 1916. He breathed his last in 1920.

Do It Yourself

Find out about one famous Indian personality you know who has contributed a lot to the development of the nation. List his or her accomplishments and write how this person has helped the nation.

Birsa Munda

Birsa Munda was born in 1875 in Jharkhand. He belonged to the Munda tribe and grazed sheep in the forests when he was young. In the 1870s, the British encouraged big farmers and landlords to acquire the tribal lands. As a result, many tribesmen from the Munda and Oraon tribes lost their rights to their own property and became farm labourers. Birsa led a movement in the tribal area around Chhota Nagpur plateau, forcing the colonial government to pass laws to protect the land rights of the tribesmen. He became a popular leader of the tribal movement.

Fact Zone

Birsa Munda is the only leader whose portrait can be seen in the Indian Parliament's Central Hall.

Jawaharlal Nehru

Jawaharlal Nehru was the first prime minister of India. His term lasted from 1947 to 1964. Also known as Pandit Nehru, he was born on 14 November 1869 at Allahabad in Uttar Pradesh. Jawaharlal Nehru participated in India's freedom movement under Mahatma Gandhi's leadership. He was appointed the president of the **Indian National Congress** in 1929. He participated in the Quit India Movement and was imprisoned.

Find Out

Why was Subhash Chandra Bose called Neta*ji*? Who gave him this name?

Known as the creator of modern India, Nehru led India on the path of planned development. Nehru started the Non-aligned Movement, which brought every country in Asia and Africa together so that they could be heard as a single entity on global issues. He was called Chacha Nehru or Uncle Nehru by children.

Jawaharlal Nehru

Sarojini Naidu

Sarojini Naidu, born in 1879 in Hyderabad, was one of the foremost women leaders in India's struggle for freedom. She joined the Indian freedom struggle in 1905 during the Swadeshi and Boycott movements. Being an excellent poetess and orator, she used these skills to work for the masses, especially for women. She campaigned extensively for the women **suffrage**. After Annie Besant, she became the second woman president of the Indian National Congress during the Kanpur session in 1925.

> **Fact Zone**
>
> Sarojini Naidu is also known by the name 'Nightingale of India'.

Sarojini Naidu

She was inspired by Mahatma Gandhi's Satyagraha movement. She actively participated in the Non-cooperation Movement in 1920 and Civil Disobedience Movement in 1930. Sarojini Naidu became the first woman governor of independent India when she took charge of the state of Uttar Pradesh.

BR Ambedkar

Bhimrao Ramji Ambedkar or BR Ambedkar was born on 14 April 1891 in Madhya Pradesh. Popularly known as Babasaheb, Ambedkar fought for the rights of the untouchables in India. He overcame several struggles and obstacles in his early life to become one of the well-known jurists of India. BR Ambedkar was a great leader and a top scholar with several doctorates and a law degree. He was appointed Chairman of the Constitution Drafting Committee while framing the Constitution of India. He started publishing a newspaper called *Mooknayak* in 1920 to highlight the plight of the Dalits and campaigned for their rights to enter temples and gain access to taps and common wells. Ambedkar died in 1956. His birthday is now commemorated as Ambedkar Jayanti.

> **Fact Zone**
>
> BR Ambedkar was the first law minister of India.

APJ Abdul Kalam

Dr APJ Abdul Kalam was a multi-talented personality —a professor, an aerospace scientist and an author. Born in Rameswaram in 1931, he was also known as the 'Missile Man of India' because of his contribution towards the development of missile technology in India. He studied physics and aerospace engineering, and became a scientist and administrator at the Defence Research and Development Organisation (DRDO) and the Indian Space Research Organisation (ISRO). Kalam played a key role in the nuclear test, which was conducted in Pokhranin 1998.

Fact Zone

UNESCO has announced that 15 October, the birthday of Dr APJ Kalam, will be celebrated as World Students' Day from 2015 onwards.

^ **Dr APJ Abdul Kalam**

He served as the eleventh president of India from 2002 to 2007. He received several prestigious awards throughout his lifetime, including the Bharat Ratna.

He is an inspirational figure for students and his humility touched everyone. He passed away on 27 July 2015 in Shillong.

Remember

- Born in 1835, Rani Lakshmibai of Jhansi refused to bow down to the British and became a prominent figure in the Revolt of 1857.
- Also known as Lokmanya Tilak, Bal Gangadhar Tilak was born in Maharashtra in 1856.
- Birsa led the tribal movement in the tribal area around Chhota Nagpur plateau.
- Jawaharlal Nehru participated in India's freedom movement under Mahatma Gandhi's leadership.
- Sarojini Naidu, born in 1879 in Hyderabad, was one of the foremost women leaders in India's struggle for freedom.
- BR Ambedkar was a top scholar and a great leader. He was appointed as the Chairman of the Constitution Drafting Committee while framing the Constitution of India.

Review Zone

A Fill in the blanks with the correct answers.

1. Rani Lakshmibai was the ruler of ....

   a. Hansi   b. Jhansi   c. Malwa

2. Bal Gangadhar Tilak demanded .... from the British.

   a. *swarn*   b. *swadeshi*   c. *swaraj*

3. Birsa, the tribal leader, belonged to the .... tribe.

   a. Munda   b. Oraon   c. Santhal

4. Farmers were forced to grow ....

   a. rice   b. wheat   c. indigo

B Name the following.

1. The only tribal leader whose portrait can be seen in the Indian Parliament's Central Hall: ....
2. The second woman president of the Congress: ....
3. The chairman of the Constitution Drafting Committee: ....
4. The Missile Man of India: ....

C Write T for True and F for False.

1. BR Ambedkar worked towards uplifting Dalits. ☐
2. Rani Lakshmibai was the ruler of Jhansi. ☐
3. Only Bal Gangadhar Tilak started the Home Rule League. ☐
4. Birsa Munda was born in Jharkhand. ☐
5. Sarojini Naidu never became president of the Congress. ☐

D Answer these questions in brief.

1. What do you know about Jawaharlal Nehru?
2. What do you know about Bal Gangadhar Tilak?
3. Who was Birsa Munda?

E Answer these questions in detail.

1. Write a short note on Sarojini Naidu.
2. What were the contributions made by BR Ambedkar?
3. Describe the life of Rani of Jhansi.

Think Zone

A Which particular section of India's Constitution reflects the cause for which BR Ambedkar always fought for?

B **Look at the picture and answer the questions.**

1. Identify the person in the picture.
2. What contributions did this person make to the nation?

Value Zone

We must respect and be thankful for the people who have worked towards the development and enrichment of the country.

Life Skills Zone

Which historic figure described in the chapter is the most important in your opinion?

Activity Zone

Complete the table with a famous short slogan given by these great Indians.

Leader	Slogan
Mahatma Gandhi	
Bhagat Singh	
Netaji Subhash Chandra Bose	
Lal Bahadur Shastri	
Jawaharlal Nehru	

7 Indian Government

Observe and Reflect

- Who was the first president of India?
- When did he become the president of India?
- Who was the prime minister during that time?

We have already learnt in the previous class that every country has a set of rules. The Constitution includes the rules and laws that govern every citizen of a country. India has a written constitution. India is divided into 28 states and eight union territories. Since India is such a vast country, one government is not enough to administer it. Therefore, the Constitution of India provides for one central government and state governments for each state.

The **central government** looks after the entire country. It makes the laws that are **applicable** to everyone in the country. It is also responsible for defending the country and it deals with issues that concern the entire nation. The central government also looks after the union territories.

The **state governments** maintain the law and order in their respective states. The central government helps the state government when required.

Do It Yourself

Write six rules that you think make you a good student.

Do you think these are applicable even outside school?

The government includes the branches of legislature, executive and judiciary. The parliament or legislature makes laws, the executive that is, the president and his appointed officers implement the laws and the judiciary ensures that laws are not violated or misused.

Central Government

The central government makes laws for the entire country through the Parliament. The Parliament comprises two houses—**Lok Sabha** and **Rajya Sabha**.

Eco Zone

The government is making efforts to conserve our natural environment both at the national as well as state level.

Lok Sabha

The Lok Sabha is also called the House of the People since it comprises members who have been directly elected by the common people of India. It is also known as the Lower House. It is **presided** by the Speaker who is elected by the members of the House. The Indian Constitution states that the Lok Sabha can have a maximum of 552 members. Any Indian citizen can contest for election in the Lok Sabha if he or she is more than 25 years old. If successful, he or she will become a **Member of Parliament** (MP). The MPs elect a person from amongst themselves as the Speaker of the Lok Sabha.

Fact Zone

The first ever elections to Lok Sabha were held in 1952.

Find Out

Currently, who are the people that have been nominated in the Rajya Sabha by the president?

Rajya Sabha

The Rajya Sabha is the Upper House of the Parliament. The members of the Rajya Sabha are chosen by members of the state legislative assemblies. The president also **nominates** 12 members in the Rajya Sabha. They are generally famous people like intellectuals, artists, authors, scientists, prominent names from the world of social sciences or sportspersons. The vice president of India acts as the chairman of the Rajya Sabha. The members of the Rajya Sabha are elected for a period of six years. After every two years, one-third of its members retire and new members are elected.

Parliament

The President

The **president** is the head of the country. He is also the supreme commander of the armed forces. He or she is elected by the members of both the Houses of the Parliament as well as the state legislative assemblies. He serves a term of five years.

The Prime Minister

The **political party** that wins the majority of votes gains the power to form the government. The party then chooses a leader and the president invites him or her to form the government. This leader becomes the **prime minister** of the country. He or she then selects the members to form the council of ministers.

Fact Zone

Narendra Modi is the only prime minister of India who was born after independence.

State Governments

The elections are organized in all the 28 states of India in order to elect members of the state legislative assemblies. The state legislative assembly is also known as the **Vidhan Sabha**. The legislative assembly makes laws for the state. The members of these assemblies are called the members of legislative assembly (MLAs). They are elected for a term of five years.

Find Out

Which states in India have bicameral legislatures?

The political party that wins the election in a state is invited to create the state's government. The leader of this party is chosen as the chief minister, who in turn appoints a council of ministers to assist him or her. The head of a state is a governor. The president of India appoints the governors of the states.

Judiciary

The **judiciary** is also a part of the government. It ensures that all the citizens obey the laws. It provides justice and punishes those who have violated the laws of the country. It is made up of the different courts spread across the country. The members of the judiciary are called judges. All the states have a series of courts right from the lower courts to the high courts. The high court is the highest judicial authority in a state or a union territory. The districts in the state also have their own courts. The **Supreme Court** is the highest judicial body in India. It has the final say in all legal matters. The president of India appoints the judges of the High Courts and the Supreme Court.

Supreme Court

Remember

- The Constitution of India provides the rules to govern the country.
- The central government makes laws through the Parliament. The Parliament comprises two houses— Rajya Sabha and Lok Sabha.
- The elections are organized in all the states of India in order to elect members of the state legislative assemblies.
- The judiciary is the part of the government which makes sure that the laws are obeyed by everyone.

Review Zone

A Fill in the blanks with the correct answers.

1. The Rajya Sabha is the .... House.
   a. Upper b. Lower c. People's
2. The .... looks into the affairs of the state.
   a. judiciary b. central government c. state government
3. The Lok Sabha can have .... members.
   a. 552 b. 553 c. 554
4. An Indian citizen can contest for elections in the Lok Sabha if he or she is more than .... years old.
   a. 25 b. 26 c. 27
5. The Lok Sabha can remain in force for .... years.
   a. five b. six c. seven

B Name the following.

1. A government that looks after the administration of the entire country: ....
2. A government formed by many political parties and not one majority party: ....
3. The person who presides over Lok Sabha meetings: ....
4. The supreme commander of the armed forces: ....

C **Write T for True and F for False.**

1. State governments maintain law and order in states. ☐
2. The Parliament has three houses. ☐
3. The prime minister is the head of the central government. ☐
4. State legislative assemblies are also called Vidhan Parishad. ☐
5. High Courts are the highest judicial authority in a state. ☐

D **Answer these questions in brief.**

1. What is the constitution?
2. How many states are there in India?
3. Which is the highest judicial body in India?
4. Name the houses of the parliament.
5. Who heads the union territories in India?

E **Answer these questions in detail.**

1. What are the responsibilities of the central government?
2. Write a short note on the responsibilities of the president.
3. What do you know about the state governments of India?
4. Explain the judicial system of India.

Think Zone

A What happens if no political party wins a majority to form the government?

B **Look at the picture and answer the questions.**

1. Whose office can you see in the picture?
2. What is the role of this official in the running of the government in India?

Life Skills Zone

Read each sentence carefully and write which government body is responsible for it.

1. Providing an adequate number of schools in a state ....
2. Making laws for the country ....

3. Filing a case against someone ....

4. Providing an adequate number of hospitals in union territories ....

Value Zone

We must always stand when the national anthem is being played. This shows that we love and respect our country.

Activity Zone

Conduct an election in your class for the position of the class monitor. The students who are interested in leading the class can stand as candidates. Make a ballot box and distribute chits to everyone in the class with the names of the candidates written on them. Each voter is allowed to vote only once.

8 United Nations

Observe and Reflect

- Which organization does this logo represent?
- What does this organization do?

Do you always get along with your family? You speak the same language, live in the same house and eat the same food but do you always agree with them? There are more than 7 billion people in this world and they speak different languages and have different beliefs. So, it is not surprising that conflict between nations arises.

Formation of the United Nations

There have already been two **disastrous** world wars—the **First World War** and the **Second World War**—where millions of people were killed. Can you imagine the suffering that these wars caused to the people all over the world? This is why the **United Nations** was created. The United Nations was created to help bring peace and to prevent wars in future. On 24 October 1945, representatives from 51 countries met in San Francisco, USA, and signed the **UN Charter**. Today, there are nearly 200 member states that form this organization. The membership to the UN is open to all 'peace-loving states' that are willing to accept the terms given in the charter.

Headquarters of the UN

Find Out

Which countries are not members of the UN?

Fact Zone

The UN has six official languages—Arabic, English, French, Mandarin, Russian and Spanish.

The UN adopted its own flag and logo in 1946. The blue flag with white logo stands for peace and unity.

Objectives of the United Nations

The main objectives of the UN are:

- To maintain peace in the world
- To maintain friendly relations between the nations
- To work together to help the poor, to fight hunger, **illiteracy** and disease, and to have respect for each other's rights and freedom
- To act as the centre that helps nations achieve their goals

Bodies of the UN

The work of the UN is carried out by six main organs. They are the General Assembly, Security Council, Economic and Social Council, Trusteeship Council, International Court of Justice and the Secretariat.

Fact Zone

Oliver Lincoln Lundquist led the design team, which created the UN logo and flag.

The **General Assembly** is the main body of the UN. It deals with important **global** issues, prepares budgets and collects reports. It is like the parliament of the UN. All the member countries of the UN have one vote in the General Assembly. The headquarters of the General Assembly is in New York. This body meets once a year in November to discuss important issues concerning world peace. The members of the General Assembly elect one person as their leader. This person leads the General Assembly and heads all the important matters.

The UN Security Council

The **Security Council** maintains global peace and security. It has 15 members. UK, China, France, Russia and USA are its permanent members and the remaining are non-permanent members who are chosen for a term of two years. If there are misunderstandings, conflicts, international disputes or any other problems amongst the member countries, the Security Council suggests peaceful ways to resolve them. The decisions made by the Security Council have to be followed by all the countries.

The **Economic and Social Council** looks after the economic, **humanitarian**, social and cultural activities that the UN undertakes. It has 54 member countries, which are elected to serve a term of 3 years. It has a chain of agencies spread across the world, which work on different social crises, human rights issues and many more.

When the United Nations was created, there were 11 nations that required supervision. The **Trusteeship Council** was created to look after these nations. Today, this council is not functional anymore.

Eco Zone

The United Nations Environment Programme (UNEP) works on the issues concerning the environment.

The **International Court of Justice** is the legal court of the UN. It is located at The Hague in Netherlands. It deals with international legal issues and advises countries on international legal matters. This court comprises 15 judges. These judges are elected by the members of the General Assembly and the Security Council.

The **Secretariat** deals with the daily activities of the UN. The Secretary General of the UN heads the Secretariat. He is the most powerful official of the UN.

Fact Zone

Trygve Lie was the first Secretary General of the UN. He was from Norway.

Special Agencies of the UN

The UN also has some special agencies where it employs experts from the various fields of life in order to help its member nations. Some of them are listed below:

- **United Nations Educational, Scientific and Cultural Organization** (UNESCO) encourages cooperation amongst countries and enables the exchange of information in the fields of education, science, culture and communication.
- **United Nations Children's Fund** (UNICEF) defends, promotes and protects children's rights.
- **World Health Organization** (WHO) manages international health work and conducts research on the cure, prevention and elimination of diseases.

WHO response team vehicle sticker

- **Food and Agricultural Organization** (FAO) works to eliminate hunger and malnutrition, and to raise the levels of nutrition.
- **International Labour Organization** (ILO) formulates policies that ensure basic human rights for workers, improve their working as well as living conditions, and create more employment opportunities.

Do It Yourself

UNESCO has drawn up a list of sites from around the world and has classified them as World Heritage Sites. Find out the names of the sites declared as heritage sites by UNESCO in India. In your notebook, write in detail about any two of these sites.

India's Relation with the UN

India became a member of the UN on 30 October 1945. As one of the founding members, India strongly supports the purposes and programmes of the UN. It has made significant contributions in the United Nations peacekeeping missions by sending troops, reinforcements and conducting relief operations in war-struck areas and areas hit by calamities. In addition to all this, India is also one of the top contributors to the UN's regular budget. India, currently seeking permanent membership, has been elected as member of the UN Security Council for seven terms.

Remember

- After the Second World War ended, the United Nations was created to help bring peace and to prevent wars in future.
- The UN's main function is to find solutions to the problems and issues arising between the countries, which are its members.
- There are six main bodies of the UN—General Assembly, Security Council, Economic and Social Council, Trusteeship Council, the International Court of Justice and Secretariat.
- The UN also has some special agencies where it employs experts from the various fields of life in order to help its member nations.
- India is one of the founder members of the UN.

Review Zone

A Fill in the blanks with the correct answers.

1. The .... is the legal court of the UN.

   a. WHO b. Trusteeship Council c. International Court of Justice

2. Membership to the UN is open to all .... states.

a. wealthy b. poor c. peace-loving

3. The .... maintains global peace and security.

a. UNESCO b. Security Council c. ILO

4. The UN Charter was signed in ....

a. The Hague b. New York c. San Francisco

B Name the following.

1. The agency that manages health work internationally: ....
2. This is the parliament of the UN: ....
3. The most powerful official of the UN: ....

C Write T for True and F for False.

1. The International Labour Organization looks after the welfare of workers. ☐
2. The WHO looks into the education and welfare of children. ☐
3. The UN's main aim is to ensure world peace. ☐
4. India has been a member of the Security Council eight times. ☐

D Answer these questions in brief.

1. Why was the UN formed?
2. What are the objectives of the UN?
3. Which agency looks after the welfare of children?
4. What is the main responsibility of the International Court of Justice?

E Answer these questions in detail.

1. Write a short note on the bodies and special agencies of the UN.
2. Describe the relation between India and the UN.
3. How does the UN function, arbitrarily or by getting consent from member nations?
4. Name the agencies of the UN and write what they do.

Think Zone

A If there was no United Nations, would there have been the Third World War? What contributions has the UN made towards securing world peace?

B **Look at the picture and answer the questions.**

1. Who is being shown in the picture?
2. Which country is this person from?

Life Skills Zone

Write the name of the agency that would be responsible for handling the cases given below. Give reasons for your answers.

1. Girls stop going to school at an early age ....
2. Workers not being paid enough by their employers ....
3. People being denied access to clean water ....
4. Children being forced to work at low wages ....

Value Zone

UN peacekeeping troops monitor and resolve conflicts in different areas of the world.

Activity Zone

What is your idea of world peace? Draw a picture that demonstrates your idea of world peace and display it in class.

ASSESSMENT

Assessment

Maximum marks: 50

A Put a tick (✓) near the correct option. **(1 × 10 = 10)**

1. Which of the following is a cause of water pollution?
   a. Fertilizers ☐ b. Metal scraps ☐ c. Loud horns ☐
2. Which canal connects the Red sea to the Mediterranean Sea?
   a. Panama Canal ☐ b. Suez Canal ☐
   c. Canals of Venice ☐
3. Which is the largest ocean in the world?
   a. Atlantic Ocean ☐ b. Indian Ocean ☐ c. Pacific Ocean ☐
4. Which road connects Kolkata in India to Peshawar in Pakistan?
   a. Grand Orient Express ☐ b. Grand Trunk Road ☐
   c. Golden Quadrilateral Expressway ☐
5. Cinema is a form of ....
   a. mass communication ☐ b. personal communication ☐
   c. private communication ☐
6. Which freedom fighter was also known as Lokmanya?
   a. Bal Gangadhar Tilak ☐ b. Lala Lajpat Rai ☐
   c. Bipin Chandra Pal ☐
7. The British indifference to the demands of Congress gave rise to the ....
   a. moderates ☐ b. radicals ☐ c. conservatives ☐
8. When was INA formed?
   a. 1941 ☐ b. 1939 ☐ c. 1925 ☐
9. What is the tenure of the president?
   a. Six years ☐ b. Five years ☐ c. Four years ☐
10. Which newspaper was started by BR Ambedkar?
    a. *Mahratta* ☐ b. *Mooknayak* ☐ c. *Kesari* ☐

B State True or False. **(1 x 5 = 5)**

1. The natural resources on the Earth are exhaustible.
2. Birsa Munda was born in Jharkhand.
3. We can send parcels through the Internet.
4. BR Ambedkar was also known as Babasaheb.
5. The spread of modern education helped to bring about social reforms.

C Find an odd one in each line and write the reason why it is odd. **(1 x 5 = 5)**

1. Horns Loudspeakers Microphone Smoke from factories
   Reason: ....
2. Sarojini Naidu BR Ambedkar Jawaharlal Nehru APJ Abdul Kalam
   Reason: ....
3. Highways Waterways Expressways Freeways
   Reason: ....
4. Tilak Gandhi Gokhale Hume
   Reason: ....
5. President Rajya Sabha Lok Sabha Vidhan Sabha
   Reason: ....

D Answer in one word. **(1 x 5 = 5)**

1. An audio-visual means of communication: ....
2. The act of using natural resources carefully so that they last for a longer time: ....
3. Known as the creator of Modern India: ....
4. Wastes that do not harm the soil: ....
5. A famous social reformer: ....

E Answer these questions. **(3 x 5 = 15)**

1. Why were Indians discontented with the British rule in India?
2. Write a short note on Sarojini Naidu.
3. Explain the judicial system of India.
4. What are the causes of air pollution?
5. Write a note on the relationship between India and the UN.

GENERAL KNOWLEDGE

1. Let Us Compare 290
2. Great Sports People 291
3. Hill Stations of India 292
4. Road Signs 293
5. Earth Extremes 294
6. Animals Adapt 295
7. New Year in India 296
8. World Sobriquets 297
9. Natural Disasters 298
10. Northeast of India 299
11. Disposing Waste 300
12. Different Boats 301
13. Traditional Music Instruments 302
14. Word Search 303
15. Internet Country Codes 304
16. A Flock of Birds 305

Assessment 306

VALUE EDUCATION

1. It's Grandmother's Birthday! 307
2. Birthday Gift 312

1 Let Us Compare

Sometimes we give comparisons to express something while speaking. For example, 'a horse is to stable as man is to a home.' Complete the following expressions.

1. Bird is to fly as fish is to __________.
2. Parrot is to feathers as bear is to __________.
3. Zebra is to stripes as giraffe is to __________.
4. Canary is to yellow as polar bear is to __________.
5. Prime Minister is to country as __________ is to state
6. __________ is to Thames as Delhi is to Yamuna
7. Kitten is to cat as puppy is to __________.
8. The Nile is to Africa as Mount Everest is to __________.
9. Spectacles are to eyes as gloves are to __________.
10. Polar bears are to Antarctica as camels are to __________.
11. Goose is to flock as fish is to __________.
12. Bison is to walk as kangaroo is to __________.
13. Cat is to mouse as spider is to __________.
14. Gloves are to hands as socks are to __________.
15. Wings are to birds as fins are to __________.

Fact Zone

Bill Gates is to Microsoft as Steve Jobs is to Apple.

2 Great Sports People

Match the great sports people around the world with the sports they excelled in

1. 
Don Bradman

2. 
Tiger Woods

3. 
Mohammad Ali

4. 
Michael Phelps

5. 
Nadia Comaneci

a. Golf

b. Boxing

c. Cricket

d. Gymnastics

e. Swimming

f. Athletics

g. Tennis

h. Hockey

i. Basketball

j. Football

6. 
Michael Jordan

7. 
Pele

8. 
Jesse Owens

9. 
Dhyan Chand

10. 
Martina Navratilova

Fact Zone

Sachin Tendulkar scored hundred centuries in international cricket.

3 Hill Stations of India

Look at the jumbled names of some famous hill stations in India. The names of the states and union territories are given in the help box. Write the names of the hill stations in India and the states or union territories they are located in. One has been done for you.

Jumbled name	Correct name	State name
1. NILATANI	Nainital	Uttarakhand
2. TOYO		
3. OMUTN BUA		
4. ATMHRAEN		
5. IAMNLA		
6. ULGARMG		
7. APSATAUR		
8. SHLIL MRNOI		
9. DMAIKREI		
10. UMNARN		
11. APCMHAHRI		
12. ADREEJLNGI		

Gujarat, Tamil Nadu, Kerala, Maharashtra, Uttarakhand, Himachal Pradesh, Haryana, Rajasthan, Jammu and Kashmir, Karnataka, Madhya Pradesh, West Bengal

Fact Zone

Shimla, one of India's best known hill stations, was the summer capital of India from 1864 to 1939 during British rule.

4 Road Signs

Tick the correct road sign which matches with the description.

1\.
a.  ✓
b. 
slippery road

2\.
a. 
b. 
speed breaker ahead

3\.
a. 
b. 
dual carriageway ends

4\.
a. 
b. 
level crossing

5\.
a. 
b. 
falling rocks

6\.
a. 
b. 
T-junction

7\.
a. 
b. 
hairpin bend

8\.
a. 
b. 
road widens

Fact Zone

At first there were only two colours used as traffic signals-red and green. In 1920, a Detroit police officer added the yellow colour to warn drivers to slow down.

5 Earth Extremes

Match the extremes on planet Earth with the place.

Column A	Column B
1. Largest lake	a. Asia
2. Deepest point	b. Amazon
3. Hottest natural place	c. Death Valley
4. Largest river in volume	d. Mariana Trench
5. Largest continent	e. Caspian Sea
6. Coldest place	f. Angel Falls
7. Wettest place	g. Greenland
8. Longest river	h. Nile
9. Highest waterfall	i. Mawsynram
10. Remotest place	j. Antarctica

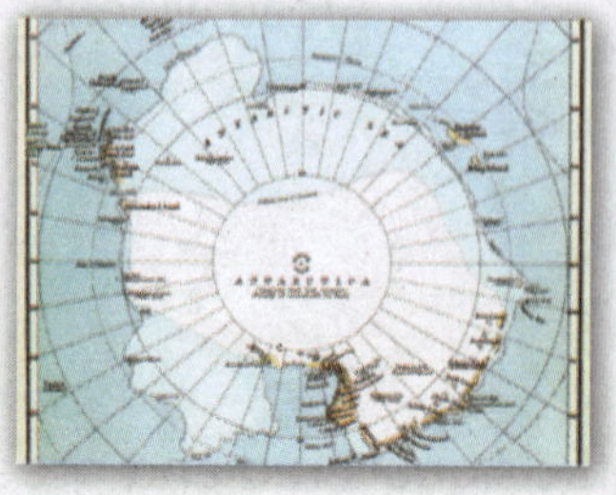

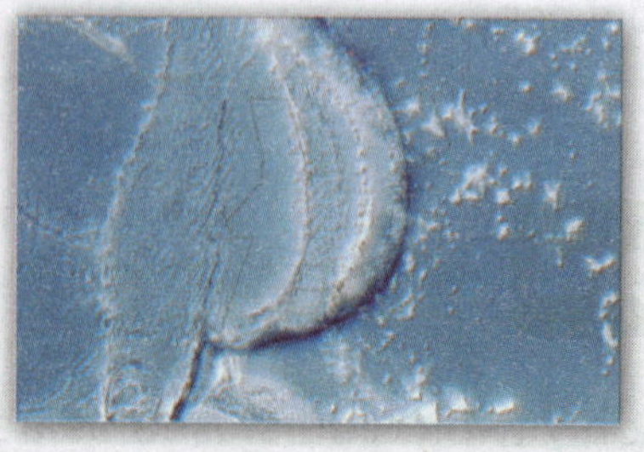

6 Animals Adapt

All animals adapt to their habitat. Use the clues in the sentences to fill in the blanks. Refer to the pictures for help.

dolphin

penguin

seal

octopus

1. An ____________ is a sea creature with a soft round body and eight long arms. It does not have any bones and can squeeze through tiny holes.
2. A ____________ is a bird that cannot fly but uses its wings for swimming. It looks like it is wearing a tuxedo.
3. A ____________ is a sea creature with a body like jelly and long thin parts called tentacles that can give a sharp sting.
4. The ____________ is huge, but a thick layer of fat under its skin helps it to keep its head above water and float.
5. A ____________ is a large deer with long antlers that lives in cold places. Its hooves are wide preventing it from sinking in the snow.
6. A ____________ looks like a large fish with a pointed nose. It breathes through a hole on the top of its head.
7. A ____________ can live on both land and water. It has flippers and that help it to swim.
8. A ____________ is a flat sea creature which has five arms and looks like a star.

hippopotamus

jellyfish

starfish

reindeer

Fact Zone

A reindeer's nose is specially designed to warm the air that it breathes before it gets into the lungs.

7 New Year in India

New Year is known by different names in different places in India. Locate these names in the word search. The state or region is given as a clue along with the starting letters.

1. Punjab

   B _ _ _ _ _ _ _

2. Maharashtra

   G _ _ _ P _ _ _ _

3. West Bengal

   N _ _ _ B _ _ _ _ _

4. Kashmir

   N _ _ _ _ _

5. Karnataka

   U _ _ _ _

6. Kerala

   V _ _ _ _

7. Marwar

   T _ _ _ _ _

A	C	E	V	O	B	M	G	T	U
G	U	D	I	P	A	D	W	A	P
A	P	I	S	N	I	Y	E	S	P
G	P	S	H	O	S	B	S	T	E
A	T	T	U	G	A	D	I	Y	R
M	H	R	X	Z	K	E	T	T	E
N	A	V	R	E	H	S	E	N	S
E	P	I	E	R	I	T	U	W	T
O	N	C	S	T	N	O	P	Q	O
N	A	B	A	B	A	R	S	H	A

Fact Zone

One-third of the world's population celebrate Chinese New Year.

8 World Sobriquets

Look at the picture clues and write the sobriquet of the country.

1. Japan is known as the Land of the ______________________.

2. Switzerland is known as the ______________________ of Europe.

3. Cuba is known as the ______________________ of the World.

4. Netherlands is known as the Land ______________________.

5. Bhutan is known as the Land of ______________________.

6. Thailand is known as the Land of the ______________________.

7. Canada is known as the Land of the ______________________.

8. South Africa is known as the ______________________ Nation.

9. Egypt is known as the ______________________ of the Nile.

10. New Zealand is known as the Land of the ______________________.

Fact Zone

Italians call their country Lo Stivale, which means 'the boot' because of its shape.

9 Natural Disasters

Read the clues and name the natural disaster to complete the crossword.

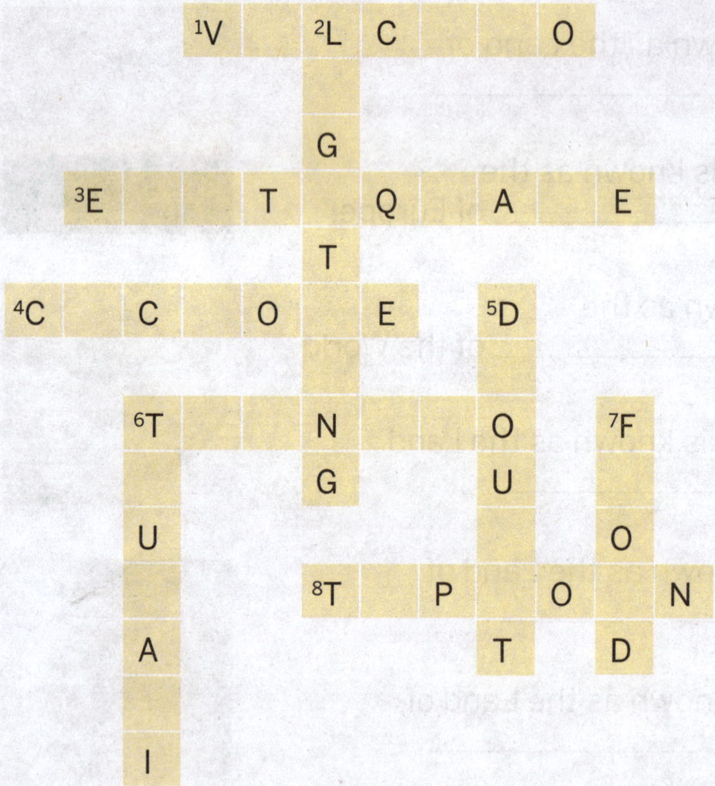

Clues

Across

1. A mountain with a large opening at the top through which gases and lava are forced out into the air
3. A sudden, violent shaking of the earth's surface
4. A violent tropical storm that occurs in the ocean in which strong winds move in a circle
6. A violent storm with very strong winds which move in a circle, sometimes called a twister. There is often also a long cloud which is narrower at the bottom than the top
8. A violent tropical storm with very strong winds occurring in the northwest Pacific Ocean

Down

2. A flash, or several flashes, of very bright light in the sky caused by electricity
5. A long period of time when there is little or no rain
6. An extremely large wave in the sea caused, for example, by an earthquake
7. A large amount of water covering an area that is usually dry caused by overflow of water from rivers, lakes or excess rainfall.

Fact Zone

In 2010, the earthquake in Haiti was the deadliest earthquake in almost 500 years, killing over 316,000 people.

10 Northeast of India

Look at the clues and complete the facts about north eastern states of India.

Clues

1. The name of this state means 'land of the dawn-lit mountains.'

2. This state is sometimes called Kangleipak or Sanaleibak. The Loktak Lake is in this state.

3. The Kaziranga Wildlife Sanctuary and Manas National Park are located in this state.

4. The name of the state came from the king whose name was Tripur and who ruled the region.

5. The name of this state in Tibetan language is known as Denjong. The Kitam Bird Sanctuary is located here.

6. The name of this state means 'abode of the clouds'. The cleanest village in Asia is located in this state.

7. The name of this state means the 'land of the hill people.' This state is known for the Cheraw Bamboo Dance.

8. The Hornbill Festival is the biggest festival of this state.

Fact Zone

Assam, in northeast India, is the largest tea-growing state in the world.

11 Disposing Waste

Sort these different kinds of waste into the three bins by writing the letters of the types of waste along the bins.

a. newspapers
b. old wires
c. nut shells
d. vegetable peels
e. computer parts
f. sweet wrappers
g. polythene covers
h. batteries
i. bulbs
j. egg shells
k. old crayons
l. dry leaves
m. fruit peels
n. clothes
o. broken toys
p. old medicine bottles

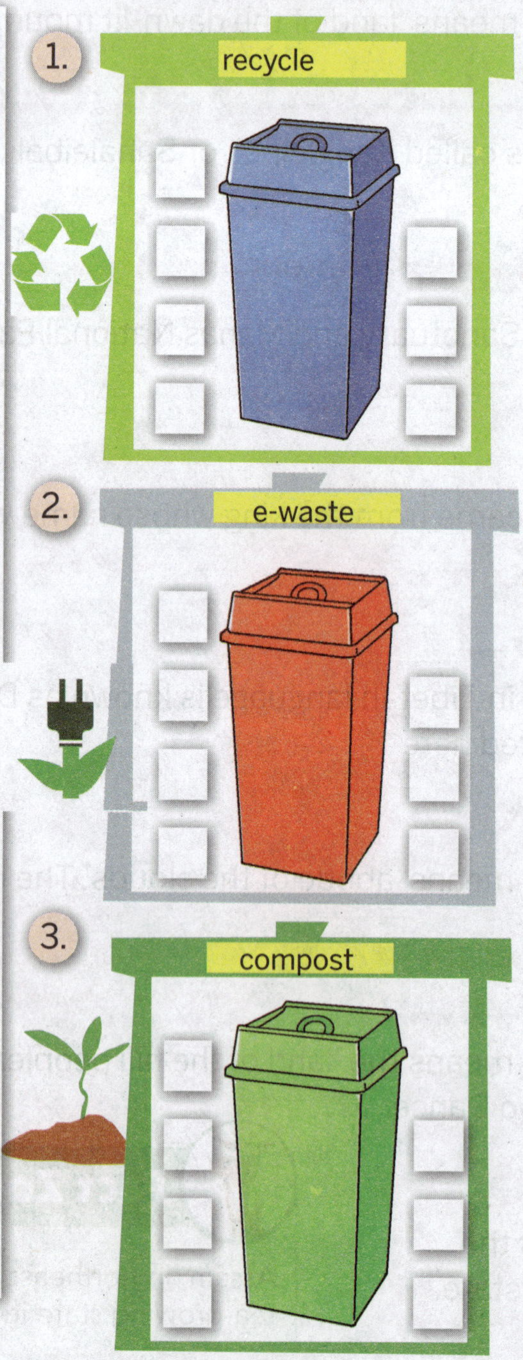

Fact Zone

Electronic waste contains poisonous chemicals and must be handled with great care.

12 Different Boats

Match the descriptions of different kinds of boats with the pictures.

1. A boat with a motor that can travel very fast

2. A ship that can travel underwater

3. A small powerful boat for pulling ships, especially into a harbour or up a river

4. A large sailing boat, often also with an engine and a place to sleep on board, used for pleasure trips and racing

5. A fast-sailing boat that moves with two hulls

catamaran

submarine

speedboat

tugboat

yacht

Fact Zone

Vallam Kali is a traditional boat race in Kerala. It is carried out during the season of the harvest festival Onam.

13 Traditional Music Instruments

Read the descriptions of these musical instruments and match them to their pictures.

1. A bowed, short-necked string instrument from India which is used in Hindustani classical music.
2. This is a bugle-like instrument, traditionally used for making or announcing the arrival of kings or lords or for motivating soldiers on the battlefield.
3. This is a traditional percussion instrument which consists of a pair of small hand cymbals.
4. This musical instrument has a pair of kettle drumsof different size and sound. One is made of copper and buffalo skin while the other is made of steel and camel skin.
5. This traditional musical instrument is made of wood and gourd that has three pipes but only one of them has holes for creating the various notes.

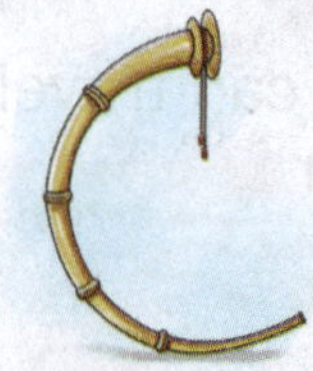

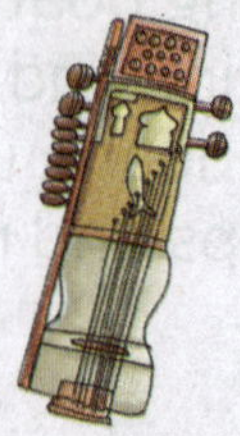

Fact Zone

The ancient Hindu system divided instruments into four categories—stretched, covered, hollow and solid. This system lead to the Western system of instrument classification which renames these groups—chordophones, membranophones, aerophones, and idiophones.

14 Word Search

Find all the words in the word search.

Car Parts

B	R	I	G	H	T	S	T	I	R
U	E	L	O	I	D	A	R	S	E
M	P	D	R	S	P	E	E	D	L
H	E	A	O	N	E	D	O	O	E
R	E	P	O	G	I	N	O	M	E
T	W	I	F	I	W	E	R	E	H
R	U	N	K	N	D	O	W	T	W
L	I	C	E	N	S	E	P	E	G
S	E	A	T	E	T	A	L	R	N
T	L	E	B	S	T	E	E	R	I

Find all the words from the word list (ignore spaces and dashes):

BUMPER	SEAT BELT
DOOR	SPEEDOMETER
ENGINE	STEERING WHEEL
HEADLIGHTS	TIRES
LICENSE PLATE	TRUNK
RADIO	WINDOW
ROOF	WIPER

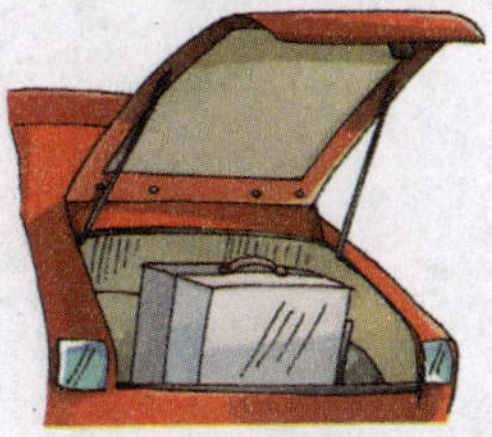

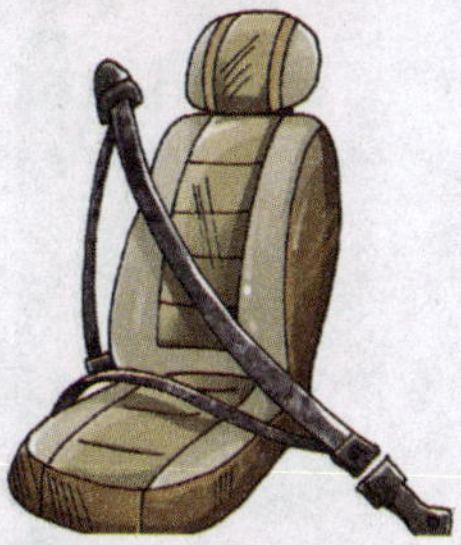

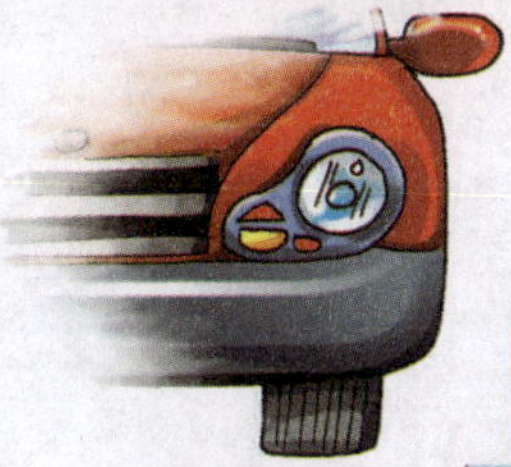

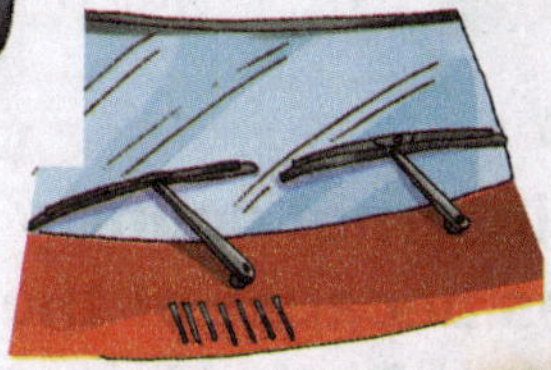

Fact Zone

A convertible is a car that has either a soft roof (made of canvas or cloth) or a hard roof (made of steel or another metal), which can be folded, slid open or shut.

15 Internet Country Codes

All official websites in India have the country domain name .in. Other well-known country specific domain names are .us, .uk, etc.

A Identify and write the country names from these easy domain names.

1. .cn ____________
2. .jp ____________
3. .fr ____________
4. .it ____________
5. .ru ____________
6. .br ____________
7. .ca ____________
8. .au ____________
9. .nz ____________
10. .pk ____________

B Some internet country codes are used for business, personal and other reasons because of their unique names. Match these cool codes with the countries. But watch out! There are four answers that do not match with any domain name.

Djibouti	Mauritius	Dominica	Tuvalu
Turkey	Montenegro	Federated States of Micronesia	
Macedonia	Denmark	Democratic Republic of the Congo	

1. .cd ________ 2. .tv ________ 3. .fm ________

4. .dj ________ 5. .me ________ 6. .mu ________

Fact Zone

Some common countries have domain names that look difficult, but simply match their names in the local language. These include .de for Germany (Deutschland), .ch for Switzerland (Confoederatio Helvetica), .es for Spain (España), .za for South Africa (Zuid Afrika) and .is for Iceland (Island).

16 A Flock of Birds

Groups of birds have very interesting and unusual names. Use the picture clue to guess the group name for different birds. One has been done for you.

1.

a parliament of owls

2.

a ____________ of swans

3.

a ____________ of penguins

4.

a ____________ of pigeons

5.

a ____________ of poultry

6.

a ____________ of ducks

7.

a ____________ of pheasants

8.

a ____________ of hawks

9.

a ____________ of rooks

10.

a ____________ of nightingales

11.

a ____________ of herons

12.
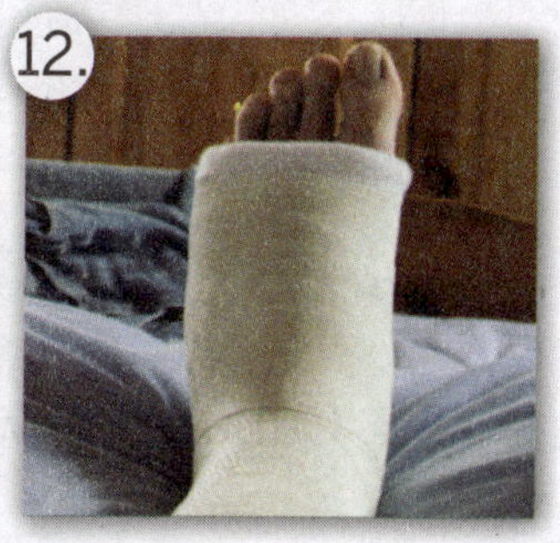

a ____________ of falcons

Fact Zone

Here are three more interesting names. Find more for fun!

- a murder of crows
- a screech of gulls
- a riot of robins

ASSESSMENT

A Identify the pictures.

1.

____

3.

____

2.

____

4.

____

B Fill in the blanks.

1. A ____________ is a sea creature that looks like a star.
2. A ____________ Is a flash of bright light in the sky.
3. A ____________ is a ship that can travel under water.
4. The state of ____________ Hosts the Hornbill festival annually.
5. Cuba is known as the land of the ____________ .
6. ____________ has a pair of kettle drums of different size and sound.
7. A ____________ can live both on land and on water.

1 It's Grandmother's Birthday!

Discuss

Look at the pictures. Talk about them in the class.

Read along

'Hey Sheenu, I have an idea!' cried Shampa as she ran towards her sister.

Sheenu asked, 'What is it?'

Shampa put her arms around Sheenu and said, 'You know that Grandmother's 90th birthday is approaching. Let's plan a party for her. We'll discuss with Mother, Father and all our cousins. I am sure that they will help us in whatever way we want.'

'That's great! Let us ask all our cousins to perform a dance routine for her. That will be really exciting!' said Shampa gleefully.

Sheenu and Shampa reached home and went straight to their mother. 'Mother, we want to plan a party for Grandmother's 90th birthday. We want to have all Grandmother's favourite things like chips, cutlets, *halwa*, *pav bhaji* and a huge cake,' said Sheenu.

'And we want to call all Grandmother's friends too,' added Shampa.

'That's a nice idea. We should start work on it immediately,' Mother smiled and encouraged the sisters.

The sisters then talked to their father and their cousins. Everybody was happy to contribute in whatever way they could to make the party a huge success.

Soon, it was Grandmother's birthday. What a surprise she got when she saw all her friends in the house. People did not stop pouring in. Her friends and all other family members came laden with gifts for her. She could not believe her eyes!

Sheenu's and Shampa's cousins presented a dance routine for her. At the end, Grandmother also joined in. After that, she cut the cake to loud cheers from the family. She was so happy.

When she asked who had planned the party, the cousins pushed Sheenu and Shampa to the front of the group. They smiled, put their arms around all their cousins and said, 'All of us planned your birthday together, Grandmother.'

Think and Say

Your sister has been studying really hard for her examinations. You know that it is time for her evening snack, but she has not come to the table. What would you do?

Figure out

A. Tick (✓) the correct option.

1. Should Sheenu and Shampa have waited for someone else to plan Grandmother's birthday party?
   a. No. They could easily plan it themselves. ☐
   b. Yes, after all, it was not as if it was their own birthdays. ☐
2. What did Sheenu want to surprise her grandmother with?
   a. A birthday gift ☐
   b. A surprise birthday party, attended by all her friends and family. ☐
3. Whom do Sheenu and Shampa ask to prepare a dance routine?
   a. Their cousins ☐
   b. Grandmother's friends ☐

4. Everybody contributed happily to Grandmother's party because
   a. they had no choice and had to contribute to the party.
   b. they wanted the party to be a success.
5. Who got the idea of celebrating Grandmother's birthday?
   a. Sheenu and Shampa
   b. Everybody in the family

B. Answer the questions orally.

1. Why did Sheenu and Shampa plan a party for Grandmother's birthday?
2. What did Sheenu and Shampa tell Mother they wanted for Grandmother's birthday party?
3. Why was Grandmother surprised on her birthday?

Relate

Choose the best option. Draw a smiley ☺ against it.

1. You come across a wonderful idea to have a small library in your class. What would you do?
   a. I would not tell my teacher or classmates about my idea because there is already a library in the school.
   b. I would talk to my teacher about it and collect old books from my classmates. This way, everyone in the class could exchange books and read them.
2. You see that your little sister has slept without keeping her toys back in the cupboard. What would you do?
   a. I would put her toys back in the cupboard and tidy up her play area.
   b. I would ignore the strewn toys and go to sleep too.
3. Your sister has wanted to watch a particular movie for a long time. As you are scrolling through the TV schedule, you notice that it is finally being aired the next day. What would you do?
   a. I would quickly go and tell my sister about it. She would be really excited.
   b. I would tell her when I see her. After all, it is not being aired till tomorrow.

Workout

Learn how to breathe properly. Practise this exercise for five minutes daily, and see how fit you feel.

Steps

- The first step would be to breathe through the nose. Many people breathe through the mouth. This is quite unhealthy. Keep your mouth closed and breathe. This will help you to start breathing from the nose automatically.

- Sit up straight and exhale completely.
- Inhale while relaxing the stomach muscles. Feel your body responding.
- Inhale as deeply as you can. You will feel your chest and rib cage expand.
- Hold your breath for a few seconds. Start exhaling as slowly as possible.
- While exhaling, relax your chest and rib cage. At the same time, pull your belly in.
- Close your eyes and feel yourself breathing.

Create

If you want to be healthy, create a diet chart for yourself. Keep in mind the right foods that you should eat to grow in the right way. You can use the words given in the box below.

chicken curry	pav bhaji	sambhar	roti	mixed dal
kachumber salad	parantha	pasta	raita	rajma rice
vegetable fried rice	pulao	fish curry	moong sprouts	fruit
daliya	custard	sandwich	laddoo	vegetable chowmein
kala chana masala	coconut burfi	lemonade	ice cream	doughnut

Remember

- Take the initiative to learn something new every day.
- Be more forthcoming and help people who need help.
- You do not need to be assertive when taking initiative.
- Taking initiative can sometimes be the reason why a project gets completed.

Enjoy

Watch the movie *Jingle all the Way*. Talk about how the father takes the initiative to find his son's favourite toy.

Be smart

Communication is not limited to speaking. Hand signs can also be a way to communicate. Decode the secret message sent using the sign chart given below.

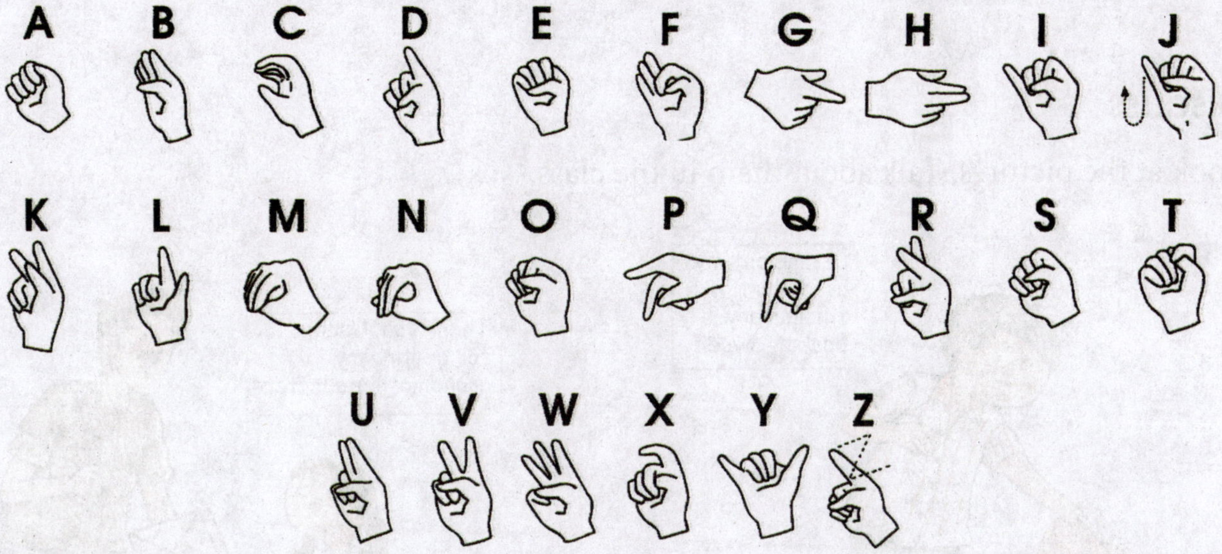

Look at the signs. Identify and write the letters they represent to decode the secret message.

_____ _____ _____ _____

_____ _____ _____ _____ _____

Teaching tips

- Talk to the students about the importance of having ideas and implementing them.
- Give students multiple situations like grandparents' 50th wedding anniversary, Yoga Day, dog's birthday, World Earth Day and other similar situations and ask them what they would do in each. This would enable cross-disciplinary thinking and would also encourage them to think and take the initiative.

2 Birthday Gift

Discuss

Look at the pictures. Talk about them in the class.

Read along

In a faraway town, lived two friends Rani and Geeta. Rani was a wealthy merchant's only daughter. Geeta was the daughter of their gardener. The girls loved each other dearly.

Every day, Geeta would come to call Rani to play. She would say, 'Let us go near the pond today, Rani. We can play on its banks.'

Often, Rani would say, 'Geeta let us play on the swings today.' The two girls would then laugh, giggle and play on the swings in Rani's garden.

It was Rani's birthday. She was really excited. She ran to her friend, Geeta to invite her, 'Tomorrow is my birthday, Geeta. I will have a big party and you have to come.'

'Of course, I will come, dear friend,' replied Geeta, happily.

Back home, Geeta started wondering what gift would make Rani the happiest. She asked her father, 'Father what should I give Rani, as a gift? I want to give her the best present ever.'

At this, her father smiled, 'I have a lot of flowering plants. Choose the best-looking one and gift it to her.'

The next evening, Geeta arrived at Rani's house dressed in her best clothes. She saw that the house was decorated with lights, flower garlands and balloons. Some of their friends had already arrived.

'Happy birthday, Rani!' said Geeta, giving her a pot of beautiful white daisies. 'This is your birthday present, my friend.'

'Is this for me? It is beautiful, Geeta! I love it,' said Rani, taking the pot from Geeta.

'Mother, Father, Tina, Aditya, Sonam, everyone, come here!' Rani called loudly to all her friends. 'Look what Geeta has brought for me,' said Rani. She showed everybody the potted plant happily.

'This is lovely, Geeta,' said Aditya, admiring the flowers.

'A beautiful present indeed, Geeta. Was this your father's idea?' asked Rani's father.

'Yes, Uncle. But, I had also taken care of this plant along with my father. I'm glad that Rani likes it so much,' said Geeta politely.

'In fact, amongst all the presents Rani has received, this is the prettiest,' said Sonam.

That night, Geeta was very happy. Geeta's father was happy too. He said to Geeta's mother, 'Rani's family has always treated us and our work respectfully. It's nice to see that their daughter also respects us.'

Think and Say

You notice that your elder sister talks quite rudely to your house help and other people who work for you. Even if they talk politely, she scolds them. What would you do?

Figure out

A. Tick (✓) the correct option to complete the sentences.

1. Geeta was the daughter of Rani's father's
   a. gardener. ☐
   b. driver. ☐
2. Geeta's father suggested
   a. an expensive gift for Rani. ☐
   b. a flowering pot as a gift for Rani. ☐
3. Geeta picked out the white daisies as a gift for Rani as
   a. she had herself taken care of the daisies. ☐
   b. her father had told her to gift them to Rani. ☐
4. Geeta's gift was special to Rani because
   a. Geeta had herself worked on it. ☐
   b. Geeta was running short of flowers at her party. ☐
5. Geeta's father was happy because
   a. he realized that Rani appreciated their hard work. ☐
   b. he had one plant less to care for. ☐

B. Answer the questions orally.

1. How did Geeta and Rani spend their time?
2. How was the house decorated?
3. Do you think that a pot of beautiful daisies make a nice gift?

Relate

Choose the best option. Draw a smiley ☺ against it.

1. Your domestic help has not come. You see your mother doing the household work. What would you do?
   a. I would help my mother with the household work. ◯
   b. I would continue doing what I was doing. ◯
2. Your gardener asks you to help. What would you do?
   a. I would refuse to help him. ◯
   b. I would help him. ◯

3. You see that the fruit-seller who comes to your house has fallen down. What would you do?
   a. I would check if he was hurt.
   b. I would ignore him and continue to do my own work.

Workout

1. There are different types of jobs that people around you do. For example, the cobbler, the house help, the postman and others. How would your life be if they didn't do these jobs for you? Make a list of ten such jobs that help you and write a paragraph about how they help you.
2. Unscramble the letters to find the names of certain professionals.
   1. tsornuata — _ _ _ _ _ _ _ _ _
   2. pneacrter — _ _ _ _ _ _ _ _ _
   3. ysiciphst — _ _ _ _ _ _ _ _ _
   4. amefirn — _ _ _ _ _ _ _
   5. uffachuer — _ _ _ _ _ _ _ _ _
   6. enmountaier — _ _ _ _ _ _ _ _ _ _ _

Create

Make a waste paper bin out of an empty, discarded carton.

You will need a carton box, coloured paper, glitter, stickets, sketch pens and glue

Steps

1. Cut the coloured paper to cover the carton.
2. Paste the coloured paper to cover all the sides of the carton.
3. Use glitter, stickers and colour pens to decorate the sides of the carton as you like.
4. Your waste paper bin is ready.

Use this bin for only paper and dry waste.

Remember

- No work is small or big.
- Every kind of work has a special place.
- Help your parents with the household work.

Enjoy

Read the story *A Hard Working Cow* by HHTC. You can find it in your library or on the Internet. Discuss it in class.

Be smart

Give two synonyms for each of the given words.

Wealthy __________ __________

Work __________ __________

Big __________ __________

Happy __________ __________

Different __________ __________

Teaching tips

- Talk about how important all work is, even the ones that seem menial.
- Pick out instances in daily life where the smooth flow of one's day would stop if not for certain people's work.
- Tell students how each person's work contributes to the community.
- Organize a community helpers meet where these helpers can come and talk to the students about their work.

Project II: Building Character Strength

There are two types of mindsets: Flexible Mindsets and Flat Mindsets.

Flexible Mindsets: People belonging to flexible mindsets use sentences like

- Let me try it.
- I can do it.
- Let me see, if it is interesting.

Flat Mindsets: People belonging to these mindsets often use sentences like

- I can't do it.
- It's no use.
- I am not interested.

Your personality may also have features of both these types of mindsets. Identify the different areas like trying out new dresses, changing team members, interacting with people of different cultures, where you have a particular kind of a mindset and fill in the grid.

Flexible Mindset	Flat Mindset

Notes